Ghost Trees

*Nature and People
in a London Parish*

Bob Gilbert

Saraband

Published by Saraband,
Digital World Centre,
1 Lowry Plaza,
The Quays, Salford, M50 3UB

ISBN: 9781912235575
ebook: 9781912235285

Printed and bound in Great Britain by Clays Ltd, Elcograf S.p.A.

10 9 8 7 6 5 4 3 2 1

To the people of the parish of Poplar,
and to their rector, Jane.

Contents

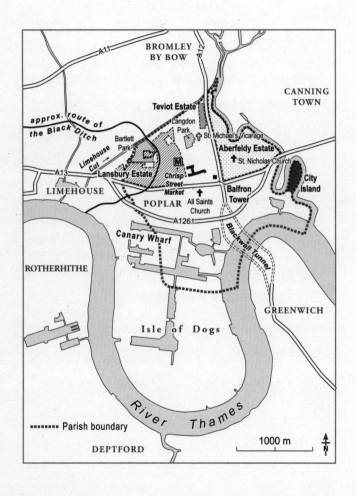

BROMLEY
BY BOW

CANNING
TOWN

approx. route of
the Black Ditch

Teviot Estate

Langdon
Park

Bartlett
Park

St. Michael's Vicarage

Limehouse
Cut

Aberfeldy Estate

St. Nicholas Church

Lansbury Estate

City
Island

LIMEHOUSE

Chrisp
Street
Market

POPLAR

All Saints
Church

Balfron
Tower

A1261

Canary Wharf

Blackwall Tunnel

ROTHERHITHE

GREENWICH

Isle of Dogs

River Thames

Parish boundary

1000 m

N

DEPTFORD

Yet even a 'place' has a kind of fluidity: it passes through space and time … A place will have been grasslands, then conifers, then beech and elm. It will have been half riverbed, it will have been scratched and plowed by ice. And then it will be cultivated, paved, sprayed, dammed, graded, built up. But each is only for a while, and that will be just another set of lines on the palimpsest. The whole earth is a great tablet holding the multiple overlaid new and ancient traces of the swirl of forces. Each place is its own place, forever (eventually) wild.

– Gary Snyder, *The Practice of the Wild*

Introduction

I had never planned to live in Poplar. I had, on a couple of occasions in my younger days, shared its Russian Vapour Baths with some minor local criminals and a taxi driver or two, but those baths were long since defunct and Poplar had become simply a place I passed through on my way elsewhere; to the Blackwall Tunnel perhaps, or out on the road to Southend. But in 2009 I moved with my family from north London to a new home in the East End. My wife had taken the decision to train as an Anglican priest, and the parish church of All Saints' was to be her first posting. I was to accompany her, along with our children, the goldfish and a particularly outraged cat.

The move was not, however, without opportunity. For many years I had, as an amateur urban naturalist, been observing the wildlife of inner-city areas and documenting it in my writing, including a newspaper column that began as a five-week trial and was still running twenty years later. I had become the recorder of plants that grew in the cracks of pavements or that lived out their brief lives at the base of a lamp post. I was the curator of ferns that frequented the wall beneath a broken-down pipe, of birds that nested in gutter or garden bush, of spiders that span their untidy webs around the lights in a dingy underpass. I was friend to the weed and the woodlouse; the warden of moths and slime and mosses.

Perhaps I should give credit to the author Richard Adams, although in a roundabout sort of way, for the enthusiasm with which I had come to address this task.

Browsing, many years ago, in a second-hand bookshop, I had picked up a copy of one of his works. It wasn't one of the more familiar novels, *Watership Down* or *The Plague Dogs* or *Shardik*, but a more personal nature diary based on a year spent on the Isle of Man. The details are vague to me now, but I can remember placing it in the mental category of those idyllic rural reminiscences that make you wonder where your own life went so wrong; the ones where otters frolic on the front lawn of an isolated farmhouse or life's major worry is the red deer causing havoc in the cabbage patch. What still stands out clearly, however, is the passage that I had opened at random; the author is forced to make a brief trip to London and, breaking off from his string of inspiring rural observations, comments, rather sourly, that he sees nothing but a few crocuses blooming in a dismal hotel garden. The envious in me turned to evangelical.

There was, I wanted to exclaim on behalf of city dwellers, so much more than that. I wanted to tell him of the black redstart I had seen feeding in front of a builder's bulldozer, of the pheasant I had found foraging on an urban allotment, and of the skylarks I had heard singing in a landscape of chemical works and pylons. I would, in this imaginary but nonetheless animated conversation, continue with stories of dyer's greenweed on an urban hillside, of the rare Jersey cudweed appearing on a busy docklands path, of the gate-keepers and brimstones and mint moths and Jersey tigers that had appeared in my own backyard. Should he still have been listening, I would have gone on to explain that this was not just about the unusual or the unexpected but the pleasure that could be drawn from observing the everyday: the comings and goings of sparrows and starlings, the exuberance of weeds on a waste site, or the first flowering of coltsfoot on a pile of building-site clay. It is observations like these that came to form the basis of this book; a book that, inspired by the natural history of an inner-city area, came eventually to focus on its trees and how their stories have helped shape both the place and its people.

It is perfectly possible, of course, that, on the basis of this one brief passage, I have completely misrepresented Richard Adams. And, since his death was announced whilst I was writing this book, I will, sadly, never have the opportunity to find out. Nonetheless, it is not uncommon to hear a certain amount of disdain for the city and its environment. I have even heard a well-known writer and environmental activist describe all cities as 'unnatural', as if human beings and their artefacts were not themselves a product of nature.

Much of recent nature writing, too, whilst producing wonderful expressions of wilderness, has turned its back on the urban experience. But there is wildness in the unexpected eruption of nature into the everyday – like the kingfisher I saw this morning on the bank of an urban canal – and it is these small joys that most of us must learn to treasure, and to take them wherever we can find them. The fact is, the city is now where most of us happen to be. Sometime in 2014 the world passed the point where more than half of its population lives in urban areas. In the UK, according to the Office of National Statistics, the figure is as high as 80%. For most of us, the city is our starting point. If we are to restore any connection with nature at all, it is in the cities that we need to begin.

It was not only Poplar that was new to me. Like the move to this part of London, becoming a 'vicar's wife' had never been part of a plan. Like almost everything else in my life, it seemed to have crept up on me whilst I thought I was busy elsewhere. I could not even claim to be an Anglican. I had been brought up in a household that was resolutely and fearfully fundamentalist and which regarded the high church as almost papist, and just as heretical. I had, after some inevitable years in the spiritual wilderness, become a Quaker and it was a long way from the simplicity and silence of Quakerism to the grand theatre of the high Anglican church. And here I was, partnered to a practising parish priest. There would, I assumed, be expectations of the role. They might not be of the tea-and-cucumber-sandwich variety, nor of a place on the flower arrangement rota – those things being rather alien to Poplar – but there would surely be an anticipation that I would be involved in the life of the church and its community. Or worse, that I would have to be a generally pleasant and amenable person.

I sustained myself by remembering that there had been a long and honourable tradition of Anglican clerical naturalists. True, I was not myself a cleric, but I had, I felt, mopped the clerical brow often enough to earn a place in its shadow. Among the earliest of this group was the inspiring figure of William Turner. Born in 1508, he combined his various clerical roles with a study of plants, recording the findings of his many plant-hunting trips with a detail and accuracy that was hitherto unmatched. It was this close observation and meticulous recording that was to become a defining feature of the naturalist clerics. And it was a new departure: an understanding of the natural world that was based not

4

on books or theories or the examination of dead specimens but on the study of living things in their natural settings. It was the beginning of the science of ecology.

A hundred years later it was another ordained priest who was laying the foundations of the science of taxonomy. Born in 1627, John Ray produced important works on botany and zoology, but his greatest achievement was to develop a systematic approach to the classification of living things. The naming of plants and animals had, up to then, been a chaotic and uncoordinated affair, but Ray introduced order with a system based on the observation of the natural differences and similarities in organisms. He was a major influence on Carl Linnaeus, whose binomial system still governs our classification of the natural world today.

Ray's interest in the subject, however, was not just scientific. It was, he felt, an attempt to reflect the wonderful and divine ordering of nature. For Ray, and for those who followed him, the study of the natural world, and the duty to observe and record it, was a logical extension of their faith. He called his approach 'natural theology' and expounded it in his book *The Wisdom of God Manifested in the Works of Nature*. Unlike many of his contemporaries, he saw science and religion as complementary and rejected the criticism that a study of the natural world was a distraction from the work of salvation. In fact, he proposed the complete opposite, suggesting that 'the contemplation of God's creation should be part of everyone's duties on the Sabbath day'. It was an idea that could have enlivened many a puritan Sunday.

John Ray, later labelled the 'father of English natural history', was to inspire many generations of the 'parson naturalists'. Their work brought advances across a wide range of scientific fields, including meteorology and geology, but there is one man, the Reverend Gilbert White, whose work and writing remains by far the most celebrated today. What singles him out is his resolute focus on a very particular place: so closely is he connected with the one village that he now wears its name like an honourable title, and to address him as anything short of 'Gilbert White of Selborne' feels like something of an impertinence. It was in this Hampshire village that he was born, in 1720, in his grandfather's vicarage. He spent most of his life there, serving four times as curate to the parish and dying whilst still in post. For a period of over forty years he kept a personal journal meticulously observing the plants and animals of the surrounding area and recording the annual dates of emergence of over 400 species. Through his questioning familiarity White was able to provide the first accurate descriptions of the harvest mouse and the noctule bat and to identify as separate species three small, brown and almost identical birds: the chiffchaff, willow warbler and wood warbler. He described his many findings in letters to like-minded friends and it was these letters, plus nine especially composed for the purpose, which were put together in his book *The Natural History and Antiquities of Selborne*. First published in 1789, it has been in continuous print ever since. 'It is, I find,' he says in one of his letters, 'in zoology as in botany, all nature is so full, that that district produces the greatest variety that is the most examined.' My 'district', I decided, would be the new parish.

6

The parish of Poplar, located in the borough of Tower Hamlets, sits at the very eastern end of the East End; any further and it would topple over what had until comparatively recently been the historical boundary, into Essex. Here it occupies an angle between the Thames and one of the largest of its tributaries, the Lea. Both in history and in geography, Poplar has been shaped by these rivers, and by the marshes that once framed them. There is water of some sort, in fact, on every side of the parish. Its northern boundary is formed by the surgically straight incision of the Limehouse Cut, reputedly the oldest canal in London, where gulls gather on the ridged roofs of warehouses, coots build nests out of the floating litter, and sand martins fly in and out of drainage holes in the concrete walls.

The Cut joins the River Lea at the complex of Bow Locks and it is this river that forms the eastern boundary. Known along this final stretch as Bow Creek, the river is here coming to the end of its forty-two-mile journey from the Chiltern Hills and winds across the estuarine flatlands in a series of loops so convoluted that it is sometimes difficult to determine on which bank of the river you are standing. At the dwindling peninsular where the two rivers meet, the boundary turns westwards following the Blackwall shore of the Thames, where smart new riverside housing looks out across the water towards the vanity project that was once the Millennium Dome but now, simply, bears a brand name, the O2. Shortly, it reaches the Isle of Dogs, not really an island at all but a once-isolated stretch of land enclosed in a long curve of the river that gives it the shape of the teat on a baby's bottle. Not all of 'the island' is in the parish, however, for halfway down its length the boundary cuts abruptly across it, following a road still known as Marsh Wall. Its busy traffic and modern blocks give little indication that this was once the point where reasonably dry land gave way to the watery ambiguity of the marshland beyond.

The western boundary of the parish is less straight-forward. It forms a wavering line abutting Limehouse, the place once infamous for its sailor-thronged streets, its cheap lodging houses, its press gangs, its opium dens and its whores. Even here, however, the boundary is intertwined with a waterway, coming close to, ducking away from and then briefly running alongside the route of one of London's 'lost' rivers, the insalubriously named Black Ditch.

With water of some sort on all four sides, it is tempting to think of the parish as an island. It had been once, I knew, a landscape of wide and windswept estuarine marshes and, despite its complete transformation over the years, it still bears some lingering echoes of its past in the tiny patches of reed that grow along the railway embankment and in its wide, open skies. We had noticed them as soon as we moved from the tall, terraced canyons of Holloway. Most of the post-war development of Poplar, by contrast, consisted of lower, well-spaced blocks, leaving a great sweep of sky still visible above them. It was possible, on a day of shifting, watery, grey cloud to still feel the imprint of the reed beds and the osiers, of lonely cattle grazing on the open marshes, of the cry of a passing curlew and the silhouette of a hunting short-eared owl. But with the advent of a new generation of high-rise blocks this openness is rapidly disappearing and where once the view had stretched as far as the church of St. Anne's, Limehouse, flying the white ensign on its Hawksmoor tower, now it extends only to the next set of cranes hauling up a new development. The sky, it seems, can be stolen as well as the land.

The riverside setting has given Poplar a very different history from other parts of the East End, with their Jewish tailors and Huguenot weavers and skilled artisans in cramped attic rooms. Here it had all begun around fishing, shellfish and oysters, and perhaps with the trapping of eels that once made their way up the Thames and the Lea in their millions. Later, riverside Poplar became the place from where explorers and adventurers set sail, among them John Smith who, leaving from the Blackwall quay, had founded the first permanent North American colony at Jamestown in Virginia in the early 17th century. This Blackwall stretch of the riverside was, for a time, to become the busiest ship-building area in the country. Later still, Poplar was reshaped again as the heart of the London docklands. The East India Dock, the West India Dock, the Millwall Docks, the Poplar Dock, all of them within the parish, had been scraped out of the soil and become the cacophonous scene of unloading ships and clanging cranes, hoisted bales and heavily-laden barrows, piled crates and swinging sacks, and the sweat and shouts of a myriad dockside workers. It was in these docks and their related trades that, by the mid-1930s, over a third of the population of Poplar was employed. It was through them, too, that many non-native plants were to find their accidental way into the country, and some of them are still found growing in Poplar today. Of all this employment and industry, once of global significance, there remains only a series of sterile and wind-ruffled basins, some fragments of the old dock wall and a single row of the old rum and sugar warehouses, now refurbished as fashionable restaurants.

Present-day Poplar has largely turned its back on the river. Now that it provides neither industry nor employment, nor even a source of food, the parish looks resolutely in the opposite direction. The riverside has, instead, been rediscovered by the rich. Where it used to be a loose rule in London that affluence increased with altitude, now it is the de-industrialised waterside that is the great draw for developers, and the banks of the Thames and the Lea, and even of the Limehouse Cut, are increasingly lined with new, high and balconied blocks for the better off. The river, whose every drop, said dockers' leader John Burns, 'was liquid history', has become a lifestyle accessory and an asset to property prices.

This is a part of the tale of two Poplars. Within the parish is the area shown in official statistics to be the second most deprived in the whole of London. Within it, too, is one of the wealthiest areas in the world. The parish boundaries incorporate a significant part of the Canary Wharf estate, built on the old docklands and now the home of high-rise banks and finance houses, of floor after floor of financial speculation, of money in its various virtual forms and in quantities that are an obscenity. They cast a shadow by day and remain perversely lit by night, with a brilliance that renders the night sky starless and diminishes the dark with a dull orange glow. They form a continuous, anonymous and overweening wall of glass and steel, looking down over the streets and estates of the rest of Poplar. Policed and patrolled by its own private security force, Canary Wharf is separated from the rest of the parish by a six-lane highway, and by the lines and sidings of the Docklands Light Railway.

It is, quite literally, on the other side of the tracks.

The post-war history of Poplar was shaped not only by the closure of the docks and the reinvention of the docklands, but also by the effects of the Blitz and by the impacts of post-war planning. It lacks the mixture of housing styles that characterises other areas of the East End and that has helped to make them more recently fashionable. Rather than terraced housing, it consists almost entirely of three- or four-storey estates: Pennyfields, the Teviot, the Aberfeldy, the Brownfield, the Will Crooks, the Lansbury. They are largely in a yellow stock brick, so pervasive that when I am away from the area I cannot help but recall it as bathed in a pale, yellow light.

This is not, however, the entire picture. There are pre-war blocks in a more sombre red and, more sombre still, some later experiments in concrete brutalism. There are little rows of local shops, a surprising number of barbers, a profusion of ways of buying fried chicken, and a declining number of pubs. There is the old Recreation Ground and a scattering of newer parks, liberated from the need to have any defining feature. There is Poplar High Street, now a high street in nothing but name, and the East India Dock Road, where dilapidated street frontages alternate with the grand old houses of sea captains and spacious seamen's missions, now short-stay hostels or multi-occupied housing. On this main road, too, the imposing grey-brick, art deco swimming baths have now been restored and stand next to the modern station for the Docklands Light Railway. It is named All Saints, after the church just beyond it, which rises in 19th-century Gothic splendour from a large grassed churchyard, dotted with fine trees and surrounded by high black railings.

11

On the opposite side of the same road, and pretty much the focus of the parish, is Chrisp Street Market, which claims, though not convincingly, to be the first covered street market in the country. It has seen far better, and less regulated, days but can still be colourful with its green striped awnings, hanging rows of bare yellow bulbs, racks of clothes, and its stalls spread with soaps or saucepans, fish or phones, or bowls of Bengali vegetables. On its west side, in the shadow of the clock tower, are its three food huts, each surrounded by a clutter of chairs and tables where people sit out to eat in all but the severest weather. The Chinese hut can magic anything out of a wok, the Bengali stand serves, for a few pounds, whole meals of samosas, rice and mixed curries, while at 'Maureen's', the speciality, according to the wording on its awning, is 'pease pudding and faggots'. Between them they are a reasonable representation of Poplar's racial mix.

Like the rest of the East End, Poplar has, for over 300 years, seen successive waves of immigrants. The Jewish population, so characteristic of much of the East End, was less significant here, whereas the Chinese were early arrivals. Their community originated from seamen who, having worked the passage over, had not necessarily been able to find one back again. They formed London's original Chinatown, made lurid in various overwrought literary accounts of characters like Fu Manchu, or in Dickens' opium dens. Here, on the western side of the parish, adjacent to Limehouse, there is still a Canton Street, a Nankin Street, a Ming Street and a Pekin Street, though the community itself is now more widely disseminated and well integrated, perhaps because Chinese men had once been thought of

12

as making particularly good husbands. The contemporary Chinese women of Poplar seem to have a predilection for power walking in Bartlett Park in the early morning, a fact I became aware of only once we had acquired a dog and it fell to me to walk him.

Next to arrive were the Scots and the Irish, most of them as navvies to dig out the docks, many of them staying on to work in them. The Irish had once been so numerous that the streets in which they settled were christened the 'Fenian barracks'. The most recent wave has been the Bengalis and Sylhetis, arriving at the time when cheap labour was still being actively recruited from what was then East Pakistan and is now Bangladesh. Moving in to the East End as a whole, just as earlier immigrant groups were quitting it, they now form its largest ethnic group. In the parish itself they constitute nearly 40% of the population and have opened mosques in whatever buildings were available – converted shops, old warehouses or under the railway arches. I found it an interesting echo of the makeshift mission halls that sprung up in the same sorts of sites, following outbursts of Christian revivalism a generation or two earlier. Walking the streets of the parish, I was also to discover that each one of these waves of immigrants had made its own distinctive contribution to the area's flora.

There are, of course, tensions between the communities, particularly with a white working class that feels it has been 'swamped' by the newer arrivals. There are differences of tradition, language, culture and religion, but it would be as wrong to exaggerate these as it would be to ignore them. The greatest divisions in the community, it seems to me, are as much to do with roads as with race. Arterial roads dissect Poplar like some savage form of surgery, and with no respect for the impact on community. The Aspen Way, created to provide speedy access to the new dockland development, cuts east–west across the parish. At its western end it leads into the Limehouse Tunnel; metre for metre, the most expensive stretch of roadway in the country. Just a few blocks to the north, the East India Dock Road carries the A13, the main road leading eastwards from the City into estuarine Essex and on to Southend. It is, according to Billy Bragg, a sort of Route 66 of the edgelands. Even larger and busier, and running north–south, the A12 sweeps down from Colchester and Chelmsford to form the approaches to east London's main river crossing, the Blackwall Tunnel. Repeatedly widened over the years it has virtually eliminated the community of Bromley.

Between them, these arterial roads create separate islands of population, like the isolated Aberfeldy estate, bound thinly to the rest of the parish through a series of smelly underpasses. Major roads appear more easily in the absence of a middle class, and they highlight the fact that, in recent times, Poplar has been treated more for the benefit of those who pass through it than those who wish to remain there.

This was the area of London to which we had come; to a large, draughty Victorian house with bars on the windows and multi-coloured brickwork. St. Michael's Vicarage was not attached to the main church at all but to one of the smaller, now redundant churches that dotted the rest of parish. Its high clock tower with a conical steeple, worn like

14

a witch's hat, looked out over the area that would be our home, to which Jane would minister and whose wildlife I would record. It was no Walden, and I set out to investigate it with little other expertise than that of experience and a belief in the importance of looking more deeply.

I began the practice of noting down anything that caught my interest or attention: the tall patience dock clustered around a car breaker's yard, the colony of brown-lipped snails surviving on a tiny piece of wasteland, the perfectly formed goldfinch nest revealed in the bare branches of a shopping centre tree. One day, walking with my youngest son, we found a wood mouse cowering at the base of a brick wall; on another we had the rare gift of a peregrine sitting in the plane tree in our garden and eyeing the small birds on the feeders.

Here in the heart of the city, where we have tried so hard to ignore the Earth's natural rhythms, I was to become more aware again of the influence of daily and seasonal cycles. In spring, the horse chestnuts open their leaves far in advance of the other trees whilst the ash holds back to the very last. By April, the lawns are lighting up with daisies, white like a late snowfall, whilst on one estate I find a colony of lady's smock and hope that the mowing gangs will hold off for another week or two. Goldfinches enliven the stiller summer months with flashing flocks that maintain a constant gossipy commentary on existence. For one week a great spotted woodpecker takes up residence in our small garden, before moving on to find a permanent territory elsewhere. In early autumn I find shaggy ink cap mushrooms growing en masse in front of a refurbished housing block, though the family are less than enthusiastic when I bring them home for breakfast. Though the hotter summer months have desiccated the pavement plants, the little gallant soldiers are only now beginning to bloom, in front of a builder's yard and beside the Prince Charlie pub. When winter arrives, the triple bark of a fox, or the shriek of a vixen, join the other night-time noises; and the song of the robin, by night as well as by day, somehow becomes more apparent. And then, approaching spring again, a mistle thrush begins to sing in early February, spilling out its chorus every morning before first light, battling the backdrop of the A12 traffic, the planes taking off from City Airport and the car sound systems turned up full volume.

The inevitable consequence of observation is the questions that it inspires. Why, I found myself asking, had the greenfinches appeared almost daily in one year, then disappeared in the next? How was it that Alexanders, a plant usually associated with the coast, was appearing increasingly inland and even growing as a back-garden weed in Poplar? And why was it, as my notes seemed to indicate, that the great majority of plants that continued to bloom into the winter were white?

At times this increasing familiarity with the natural life of the area led me into odd side alleys of investigation. I took part in a project trapping and measuring elvers as they moved up the River Lea and became fascinated by the relationship between the East End and the eel. Learning of a possible link between housing type and house sparrow numbers, I began to map their population in the parish in order to test the theory that sparrows thrived in areas of greater deprivation. And could I really learn to tell the time by closely observing the sequence in which all the yellow dandelion-like flowers opened across the morning? Or chart the different waves of immigration to the area in the presence of street plants such as Chinese mugwort and the Bengali brown mustard?

It became clear to me that many of the questions I found myself asking were also about past influences on the landscape. I became increasingly involved in a form of ghost hunting, seeking out the resonances of what once had been; the surviving impacts, sometimes shaded or insubstantial, of features from landscapes which had now been lost. I would come across them in the layout of a group of plane trees that marked the location of a pre-Blitz church. I would find them in the organisation of a group of streets that followed old field boundaries or a pattern of marshland ditches. I would walk slight dips in a road that betrayed the route of a lost London river. I was to find them even in my own back garden, where the abundance of rounded pebbles represented my own apportionment of the floodplain gravels, deposited by mile-wide estuaries and once swollen ice-melt rivers.

This idea of natural 'hauntings' is not original. It already exists in ecological studies with the concept of the 'ghost hedge'. Some of our ancient hedgerows were created by planting, but some came about through the very reverse procedure: by removing the trees and plants that had existed all around them. In the practice known as 'assart', the old woodlands were cleared to make way for cultivation, but, as they were felled, strips of the woodland growth would be left intact to provide instant field boundaries. These are the 'ghost hedges', surviving into modern times as shadows of the woodland of which they once formed part. Within them, the woodland species continue to produce seeds and grow on for generations, gradually diminishing as new species arrive and take hold. They become, therefore, something like a half-remembered dream, a ghostly image that is slowly fading over time.

And if ghost hedges, why not ghost trees? I had already included street trees as part of my study. They were, after all, the most obvious feature of the living landscape and, although they were planned and planted, they formed one of the most significant parts of the local ecology. Now I began to see how past generations of trees had also made an important impact on the area: in place names, in local symbols, as survivors from past planting. And also in more nebulous ways: as part of the oral history, the folklore, the very story of the place. This was, after all, a parish that was named after a tree.

It seemed to me, eventually, that I could follow the whole history of the area and its people though its trees. The long centuries of the early marshlands, then the development of farms and orchards to service the London market, had both produced their distinctive generations of trees and both had left their impress on Poplar. Then the expansion of the city, the spread of housing, the development of the docklands, the growth of industrialisation, all of which had eliminated so much of the wild, had brought the deliberate development of street tree planting, sometimes in its early days as a deliberate effort to mimic the rural. Then street planting itself had evolved through several stages, each of which in some way reflected wider social trends and the changing spirit of the times.

That trees could be taken to characterise an area, or to reflect a history of place, should not be surprising. Not only are they both the largest and the longest-lived things in the natural landscape but our relationship with them is profound. They have shaped us in many ways, providing our shelter, our food and our fuel, our meeting places, our place markers and our boundaries. But the relationship has run deeper. It has been psychic as well as social. Trees have persistently fed our mythology and folklore and entered our religious symbolism. In Norse belief it was a tree that linked the heavens with the earth; in Christianity the Bible story both begins and ends with a tree. According to Peter Ackroyd, in his book *Albion*, trees have shaped the English imagination, our English literature and even Englishness itself. According to Wordsworth, they are 'the ghostly language of the ancient earth'. No wonder that for the Chinese, wood was regarded as the fifth element; or that for Jung, trees were important archetypes. In an urban context they are the icons of a natural world with which almost every other connection has been lost.

It increasingly feels as if we are adrift in three directions: cut off from history and a sense of our own story; cut off from nature and a relationship with the species with which we share our space; and cut off from each other and a sense of local community. But in the process of piecing together the story of an area through its trees, I was, I discovered, beginning to reconnect with people, with the past, and with my surroundings. The focus on locality, so well practised by

Gilbert White, was about more than the nature of the area. It was also about continuity, community, relationship and being grounded. It was about a feeling of wholeness.

This, then, is how a move to a different part of London and the attempt to observe its natural history, became a book about 'ghost trees' and simultaneously a lament and a celebration. For the study of a single location, it also became surprisingly full of journeys, both in space and time; whether walking every street in the parish, tracing the course of a lost river, searching other locales for similar examples or watching a single tree through the course of a year. It was to lead to a final, collective journey, a resurrection of the parish 'Beating of the Bounds'. But this was the kind of travelling described by Pádraig Ó Tuama in his book *In the Shelter*. It 'requires us to resist dreaming of where we should be, and look around at where we are'.

Chapter One

Hunting the Poplar Poplar

As the driest March on record gave way to the wettest April, I set myself the task of walking every street in the parish. It was the way, I thought, to know it more thoroughly and to begin to unravel its ecology. Perhaps, too, it would help me enter more fully into the spirit of the place. I wanted to be like the man in Anaktuvuk Pass, met by Barry Lopez in his book *Arctic Dreams*, who, whenever he visited a new place, listened 'to what the land is saying'.

Poplar is large for an urban parish, large enough to have once supported six churches, and the task became a sort of long-distance walk with a difference. It was neither linear nor circular, but maze-like. It had me continually doubling back on myself or following parallel streets and the alleyways that run between them. It had me tracking up and down either side of fume-laden highways or working my way to and fro across the complicated layout of an estate, a layout that remains a mystery even to some of those who live there. And it never took me more than a couple of miles from my home. As I walked I began to take notes, not just on the wild plants and animals of the parish but on the different species of street tree. For there was one that I was actively seeking. I was hunting the Poplar poplar.

London is littered with districts that bear the names of trees; trees that once made them distinctive but which have, for the most part, disappeared. Their names live on as a shadowy reminder of the importance that trees once had in our lives. There is a roll call of oaks in Royal Oak, Honor Oak and Gospel Oak. There was a Vicar's Oak once, too, but that was to become Crystal Palace after Joseph Paxton's glittering creation for the Great Exhibition of 1851 was moved there. There is both a Burnt Oak and a Burnt Ash. There is an Oakleigh and an Elmstead, and a Becontree, named after the tree beneath which the local 'hundred' once held its meetings. There are groups of trees celebrated in Nine Elms and Shirley Oaks and Carshalton Beeches. There is a Copse Hill and a Grove Park, a Forest Hill in the south and a Forest Gate in the north, and any number of 'woods' including Falconwood, Cricklewood, Colliers Wood, Oakwood, Abbey Wood, Norwood, St. John's Wood, Wood Green and Woodford. Their names echo the once great tracts of wildwood, gradually fragmenting under clearance and cultivation and finally disappearing beneath the city's relentless spread.

Poplar was another example. Here was an area of London – by turns a village, a vestry, a parish and a borough – that had, by common consent, been named after the tree that once characterised its marshy acres. Not only did that tree seem to have disappeared but its very identity had become a matter of confusion. In the taxonomy of the local authority, this is the 'Poplar district'. It has its own symbol, displayed on official buildings and on the map boards of estates: it is a looping line like the pocket of a billiard table, depicting the Thames as it curves round the Isle of Dogs; and cradled within this is the shape of a single tree. It is not, however, the native tree, not the proper black poplar at all, but a Lombardy poplar, a much later Italian import with an upright and pencil-thin silhouette. A graphic artist, somewhere, has looked up 'poplar' and chosen the shape that is most visually distinctive. The local housing association, which took over much of the housing stock in the early 2000s, has echoed the mistake. It uses a symbol of three Lombardy poplars, casting their shadows to the left, as though to suggest that the sun is always rising. Poplar has not only lost the tree, it has forgotten which tree it was.

It is not just locally that the black poplar has disappeared. Here is a tree that was once among the most commanding in the English countryside. Yet, by the late 20th century, it was regarded as our rarest native species. If there are such things as ghost trees, no species would be more justified in conducting a haunting. In prehistoric times it had been the typical tree of lowland rivers and densely wooded valleys washed with winter floods. These were amongst the earliest areas to succumb to cultivation, but the poplar survived in remaining wetland habitats; a tree of the marshlands, of river banks, of drainage ditches and wet meadows. According to Oliver Rackham in *Woodlands*, it is 'the last shadow of the floodplains wildwood' and 'more than any other tree, reminiscent of the splendour of the mediaeval countryside'. As recently as 200 years ago it remained a familiar component of the rural landscape, older trees providing local landmarks and boundary markers, newer ones planted for their usefulness around homesteads and farms.

Its significance is clearly demonstrated by its appearance in landscape paintings of the time, most notably in the work of John Constable. 'The Hay Wain', painted in 1821, was once voted 'England's favourite painting', though it was the French, in fact, who first appreciated its virtues. It now hangs in the National Gallery in London and part way through my walk I broke off to pay it a visit. It is rather a surprise, after all its many miniature reproductions, to confront its six-foot magnificence face to face. A little dog stands on the near side of a river which a young waggoner and his cart are just beginning to ford. Beyond the river, and occupying the great bulk of the picture, the scene divides into two. The black poplars stand on the left, their billowing leafy branches seeming not just to cast a shade but to gather a darkness towards them. They radiate storminess, not just in their colour but also in their shape, a storminess that is echoed in the gathering of dark cumulus clouds above. In their shadow, and tucked tight to the river, is the cottage still named after Willy Lott, the tenant farmer who lived there and is said to have never left home for more than four days in his life. It is to the right of the picture, however, that the eye is drawn. Here, by contrast, is a pleasant, level, sunlit plain where barely visible farm labourers are cutting the hay.

There is something of a mystery about this painting that gives a clue not just to the status of the poplar at the time but to its looming fate. Art historians have pointed out that though the picture portrays a bucolic English scene, it was painted when the countryside was seething with discontent. Low wages, high rents and the impact of the new threshing machines were leading to unemployment and a worsening of rural poverty. Nowhere was this more pronounced than in the East Anglian counties where the painting is set. It was here that a new commercial agriculture had been pioneered with disastrous consequences for rural labour, and which had led to regular outbreaks of violence and unrest. It was a situation of which Constable would have been well aware, for he refers in his letters to the glow of burning hayricks that he was seeing almost nightly. Year by year the situation was to worsen until in 1830 the same flames were igniting the whole of the English countryside. This was a time when the burning of ricks and barns and the smashing of threshing machines was commonplace, when unemployed rural workers marched from village to village, and when landowners and parsons received threatening letters signed in the name of the mysterious and menacing 'Captain Swing'. Those caught, or framed, for these offences were to suffer transportation, or even execution, yet in Constable's picture we witness only the idyll of the tranquil cart and the hand-cut hay, while bright sunshine still lingers on the plain.

Perhaps, however, there is a tension in the picture that does represent something of the tension of the times. In the striking dissonance between the two halves of the background, there seems to be a contrast between a nearer, darker and foreboding present, and a distant, disappearing and idealised past. It is, after all, towards this past that the cart is heading, whilst the reapers are already reduced in size to almost nothing.

Constable's picture does not just have historical significance. It also presents a botanically accurate portrayal of the poplar. Whilst most of the trunks are upright, one of them has developed the distinctive lean that is characteristic of black poplar growth and which often begins around middle age. In what seems like an arboreal version of the Greek myth, they stretch out over the water to catch a glimpse of their own reflection. But there is nothing narcissistic about *Populus nigra betulifolia*. It is a tree that looks, metaphorically speaking, as though it can't be bothered to brush its hair. Described by one earlier writer as 'grotesque', it is a distinctly unruly tree with a vigorous surge of competing branches. Densely twiggy when young, it forms, in older age, a heavy spread of boughs, breaking from the low trunk to ascend and arch, and sometimes to sweep downwards again. It can reach, in its unpollarded growth, a height of over a hundred feet, the record being a specimen of 125 feet in Shropshire. And nowhere is its ruggedness so marked as on the trunk. Not smooth like the beech, or plated like the plane, it produces an untidy mass of burrs and bosses, swelling up and bursting out at random. Between them the bark is dark and deeply fissured, reminiscent of an old countryman's worn and weather-beaten face. It is, altogether, a horny-handed, artisanal sort of tree, but one that displays an undisciplined exuberance at odds with the rest of a modern and manicured countryside.

What is not apparent from its appearance is whether a tree is male or female. The poplar is one of a select group of trees that are dioecious – a word derived from the Greek and meaning, literally, 'two houses'. As in the holly, male and female flowers are separate and grow on completely different trees. From early spring they produce catkins in such quantity that, in bud, they suffuse the tree with a gingery glow. Opening in April, those on the male trees are red, short and fat. Fallen to the ground, they resemble nothing so much as the grubs of some oversized fly. Children gave them the name of 'devil's fingers' and spread the belief that touching them brings bad luck. The female catkins, by contrast, are green and graceful, hanging on extended strings like rows of beads or tiny necklaces. Each of these rows contains around fifty flowers that produce a prodigious quantity of seed. Released in midsummer as a fluffy white down, it drifts on a lazy breeze, filling the air, like a gentle, out-of-season snowfall. For city dwellers, it is most closely replicated on those balmy days when whole streets are filled with the white parachutes of willow, or, later, with those of the rosebay willowherb.

I was encountering days like those as my parish walks continued late into May, days when seeds would catch in my throat or bring on a fit of coughing while I sat at a market-place table. From some invisible and uncertain source, they floated through streets, were borne through backyards and filtered across open spaces in a hopeful but largely doomed diaspora.

The agricultural revolution that had ended Constable's idyll also spelt the beginning of the end for the black poplar with its favoured damp meadows and marshes disappearing under the demands of intensive cultivation. But the coming of the Industrial Revolution was to lead to an unlikely resurgence. In the shadow of the mills that shot up across north-west England it was planted as one of the few trees able to withstand the smoke, the soot and the atrocious new levels of atmospheric pollution. For the mill workers, the seasonal mass of its drifting seeds gave rise to another connection, for they resembled the blizzard of cotton threads that surrounded the looms and filled the air in the factories. This was 'fluff' of an altogether crueller kind, described by Bessy in Elizabeth Gaskell's 1855 novel, *North and South*:

> *Little bits, as fly off fro' the cotton when they're carding it, and fill the air till it looks all fine white dust. They say it winds round the lungs, and tightens them up. Anyhow, there's many a one as works in a carding-room, that falls into a waste, coughing and spitting blood, because they're just poisoned by the fluff ... I shall ne'er get the whirr out of my ears and the fluff out o' my throat in this world. That's all.*

It was not long before the mill workers had renamed the poplar the 'cotton tree', or 'cottonwood', a name that was later carried on another diaspora by hopeful emigrants to America. While the American species of poplar still bear the name of 'cottonwoods', it survives here as a place name across the 'cotton counties' of England. Driving from Yorkshire to watch a football match in Wigan, I noticed one almost as soon as we had crossed the Lancashire border: a Cotton Tree Street in the small town of Colne. Just a little time spent with Google and some gazetteers was to yield many more: there were Cotton Tree Streets in Manchester, Stockport and Oldham; a Cottonwood Road in Liverpool; a Cottonwood Drive in Sale; a Cottonwood Lane, again in Colne; and a Cottonwood Grove in Stoke. In Bury,

Droylesden, Middleton, and in the small village of Wine-wall, it had given its name to the local pub.

Between them these names map the area where cotton once drove the economy and dominated working life. To this day, one of the greatest concentrations of remaining black poplar is in Manchester, so much so that the tree has here become known as the 'Manchester poplar', in the same way that London has bestowed its name on the plane. Here, then, was a tree that had links with both the decline of traditional rural labour and the travails of the new industrial working classes. It was more and more, I felt, an appropriate symbol for Poplar.

As late spring slips imperceptibly into early summer, the Poplar poplar remains elusive. The valerian blooms in bright Mediterranean shades along the canal where the old stone walls collect and reflect the heat, and then the swifts arrive. Though I have looked for them daily, their appearance here is uncertain, our Poplar housing not being suitable for their nests. Nonetheless, I know the summer has truly arrived when I see them; high, black dots circling below cirrus clouds. Now the trees put on their fullest canopies: those that have recently been pollarded, with the unfortunate appearance of newly clipped poodles; the others luxuriating in foliage at the peak of their summer power. The shifting and shivering of their leaves in a breeze now adds to the city's soundscape.

It used to be said that country people could tell the species of a tree by the sound it made. In the spirit of truly 'listening', I tried it out on my walks – though, it has to be said, with only limited success. My idea was to approach it in the same way that I had taught myself birdsong: by developing a personal mental picture for each different sound. The birches in the Recreation Ground, with the fine foliage on their pendulous branches, produced a particularly sibilant tone, whilst the plane trees on my local streets sounded to me like waves breaking on a shingle beach. They summoned childhood memories; of long south coast summer days spent sitting or swimming, picnicking or playing on the pebble beaches of Sandgate. In their rustling I could hear not only a wave breaking but even the distinctive whoosh of its receding backwash through the pebbles.

I had listened to poplars once on Hampstead Heath. They stirred into action, when almost every tree about them remained motionless, and produced a sound like running water. Not the slower streams or almost stagnant ditches by which they most often grow but the younger sounds of a fresh mountain brook, of water rushing and tumbling in exuberance between and over rocks. Others, of course, might hear the tree differently. Writing in 1890, the Surrey schoolmaster George Sturt gives his own description. 'I noticed,' he says, 'in the poplar tree above me two sorts of sound; the leaves pattering and rustling against one another, each with its own separate chatter; and then as accompaniment and continuous ground-tone, the wind itself breathing audibly and caressingly between leaves and round twigs and limbs.'

I remembered, too, a story from the Bible. I was familiar with the Bible from childhood – as perhaps everyone ought to be, if only for its use of language and its great store of archetypes – and remembered a strange account concerning David. It appears in the Second Book of Samuel where, after years of guerrilla warfare, he has just become king, reuniting Judah and Israel, the two long-separated parts of the country. His old enemies, the Philistines, decide to mobilise against him and to make a pre-emptive strike by driving a wedge into the heart of the new state. On hearing of this David leaves his recently established capital at Jerusalem and heads for his 'stronghold'; probably the cave system at Adullam. Below him, in the valley of Rephaim, the Philistines draw up their forces. David is uncertain what to do next and turns to God for advice. He is told not to undertake a frontal assault but to wheel round to the Philistine rear. Here he is to wait with his men by a grove until he hears 'the sound of marching feet' in the treetops. Taking this as the signal to launch his attack, his movement masked by the sound of the leaves, David sweeps down on the Philistine position, routing their armies and driving them back beyond their borders in retreat. In the Authorised Version these trees are given the unlikely translation of 'mulberries', but in the later versions they are more correctly rendered as 'balsams' or 'aspens'. Both are species of poplar and the 'marching feet' that David is to listen for is the rustling of their restless leaves. It becomes for him the sound of the armies of God, marching out ahead of him to do battle; the reassurance that God is with him.

Behind this story, behind the continual noisy flutter of the poplar leaves, lies a botanical explanation. Not only are the leaves small for such a large tree but they are attached to the twig by elongated leaf stems that are flattened horizontally, at right angles to the blade of the leaf. Together these features give the tree its most endearing characteristic. It is tremulous. Its leaves exist in a state of almost permanent agitation. In even the slightest breeze they spring to life, fidgeting and rustling, whilst those around it remain largely unaffected. It has earned it the country name of the 'shiver tree'.

It seemed curious to me that members of the poplar family should share this distinctive feature and I began to wonder whether the development had an evolutionary significance. In his book *The Lost World of the Kalahari* (Hogarth Press, 1958), Laurens van der Post describes how, in his search for the last of the free-living Bushmen, he travels not only deep into the Kalahari Desert but also into the watery wildness of the Okavango Delta. There he describes approaching a dense group of trees standing 'with sombre determination' on one of the many low, frequently flooded islands. 'Like so many trees in love with water,' he writes, 'great and straight as were their stems, their leaves tended to be frail, tender and pointed.' What applies to the distant Botswana wetlands seems equally true of our British waterside trees. The willows, those characteristic riverside trees, have, for the most part, long, narrow and gracefully drooping leaves. And their close relative, the black poplar, has leaves that are small and triangular, tapering to a fine point, and undeniably delicate in their attachment to the twig.

The main function of leaves is food production. Together they form a factory, powered by photosynthesis, and the greater the total leaf surface, the greater the energy available to the tree. But there is a risk attached to this, for increasing the surface area of the leaves also increases the amount of resistance they offer to the wind, and the chances, therefore, of being damaged or toppled in a storm. Perhaps, then, some of the ways in which trees have evolved are attempts to balance this equation; to maximise surface area in a way that offers least resistance. The development of divided leaves – palmate or, even better, pinnate with separate leaflets arranged along a central stalk – will surely reduce wind resistance, as evidenced by all those plastic bags stuck in urban trees which eventually take on a shredded appearance. And perhaps the 'tremulous' leaves of the poplar fulfil a similar function: enabling movement with the wind rather than presenting a barrier to it. If this is so, the 'frail, tender and pointed' leaves of waterside trees observed by Laurens van der Post, may stand alongside the trembling leaves of the poplar as particular evolutionary adaptations by trees that specialise in growing in soft and boggy, and less supportive, waterside land.

The black poplar has another adaptation to its waterside life, and one that has come to determine most of its uses. In order to cope with the waterlogged soils in which it grows, as much as 34% of its wood, by volume, is made up of water-conducting vessels. The timber is, in consequence, very heavy on felling but dries out to become a wood of surprising lightness, creamy white in colour and slightly woolly in texture. The lightness, however, is combined with toughness. It is able to absorb shock, it is bendable, it does not splinter, and it is resistant to both fire and heat. It is also durable, and it has been estimated that if kept dry, its timbers can survive for more than 700 years. As an old rhyme from Herefordshire has it, 'Cut me green and keep me dry, And I will oak or elm defy.'

It is these characteristics that have shaped the traditional uses of the tree; in floorboards and in kitchen ware, in brake blocks, bellows and pumps. As a further part of its relationship with the industrial north-west of England, it was used in Lancashire in the making of clogs, as it was also in the Netherlands. Its resistance to damage from flying stones also ensured its use in the beds of barrows and carts. Thus, in Constable's picture, the hay wain is passing beneath the trees from whose wood it is made.

Where it should not be used is in stocking the household fire, for 'Poplar gives a bitter smoke; Fills your eyes and makes you choke'. This reluctance to burn has, however, some advantages. Poplar was the wood to use where resistance to fire was most required: in the flooring around a fireplace, or in buildings particularly prone to conflagration, such as barns, smithies, hop kilns and mills. Perhaps the earlier inhabitants of Poplar had made such use of their local trees, for mills had once been a major feature of the area. Windmills lined the defensive sea walls of the Isle of Dogs, so visible in these flatlands that they gave their name to the district of Millwall. Along the length of the Lea was another type of mill, in their dozens. These were tidal mills with reversible wheels, working one way as the tide pushed up river, and the other as it rolled back down again. Their floors, and sometimes their walls too, would have been cut from poplar wood.

All these mills are now gone; except for two. They survive at the site known confusingly as Three Mills, just beyond the northern tip of the parish. Their red-brick walls rise high over the river, strengthened with rows of black iron studs and punctuated with neat lines of white-framed windows. They are serious-looking, with business to attend to, but they are not severe. That would be difficult to achieve, next to the conical oast houses with their jaunty white caps, where the herring gulls perch to survey the river beneath. They are the last of their kind on the river, a surviving link with the one-time local use of poplar.

It was not the last such link that I was to encounter. With its resistance to fire, it seems almost contradictory that making matches was probably the best known and commonest use for poplar wood, but it stems from the lightness of the wood and its ability to absorb paraffin. When Mr. Bryant and Mr. May joined forces to sell matches in 1843 they began what would grow to be the largest match-making business in the country. Given the company's later history it is a real, and largely overlooked, irony that both these men were Quakers, active in the cause of social reform and in the fight against 'phossy jaw', the disfiguring disease caused by the phosphorus with which the matches were coated. Their plan had been to design a model factory, making only safety matches, a new invention which did not, unlike the 'strike anywhere' matches, use the deadly white form of phosphorus. It came to nothing. The public refused to pay the higher prices and the factory was driven to resume production of the aptly named 'lucifers'. Then as now, it seems, the market does not have a conscience.

By 1861 the company was large enough to buy a number of existing factories across a three-acre site in Bow, at the northern end of what was then the borough of Poplar. It was the biggest match factory in Britain and, for a time at least, the largest factory of any sort in London. But it had also moved far from the 'model' factory its founders had dreamt of. By 1888 its workers were employed for fourteen hours a day in poor conditions and on low rates of pay. On top of this, and the high chance of contracting the still prevalent phossy jaw, the company was levelling a punitive system of fines on the workforce, many of whom were teenage girls. The stage was set for the strike that was to give this Poplar factory a place in national social history. Led by the women workers, with the assistance of the indomitable Annie Besant, it was to result in the establishment of the first ever trades union for women, as well as some of the earliest welfare institutions for industrial workers, including the provision of an on-site dentist to counter phossy jaw.

The Bryant and May match factory was still active and important in the area as the 20th century dawned. Eileen Baillie, daughter of the Reverend George Reginald Preston, was an earlier resident of our vicarage and wrote *The Shabby Paradise*, a memoir of her life here between 1901 and 1910. She describes how you could always tell which way the wind was blowing, with 'the cardinal points of the compass identifying themselves faithfully by a particular smell: west, horseflesh (for dog biscuits) ... north-east, fish manure; and due east, the pungent stench of a paint-works, with gas thrown in for good measure.' From the north, it was always 'sulphur fumes, for matches'. Since St. Michael's Vicarage is more than a mile, as the wind blows, from the match factory, the smell could obviously carry.

In 1911, shortly after the period covered by Baillie's account, Bryant and May built a new factory on the same site. It was visited by Arthur Mee in 1937, as he was preparing the 'London' volume of his *The King's England* series. The books, one for each English county, are hugely endearing. I loved them as a child and explored the churches of Kent carrying a copy in a hand that was often stained red from its binding. I continued to collect them as an adult and have fifteen of them sitting on my shelves. But they also paint a patriotic and highly sentimental picture of the kingdom, in keeping with which there is no mention here of the matchgirls' strike. Instead Mee describes the 'colossal factory … one of the most impressive buildings of Bow', inside of which he finds a 'unique museum of fire-making appliances, the best and most complete collection in the world'. Through the windows he catches a glimpse of 'huge stacks of tree-trunks for the matches of today', some of 'the thousands of tons of timber' used every year. By this time Bryant and May was not just buying in timber but had set up its own forestry venture, acquiring first an aspen planta-tion in Argyllshire and then a number of estates for growing poplar in East Anglia, Bedfordshire and Herefordshire. Having denuded itself of poplar trees a couple of centuries earlier, the borough of Poplar was now seeing the annual importation of thousands of tons of the wood from different types of poplar and from other parts of the country.

This later massive factory building still stands, though since the 1980s it has become another of those inner-city gated developments. The building that once provided employment for the local community has now locked its gates against it. Converted into expensive apartments it has been retitled the 'Bow Quarter', since every contemporary urban development, it seems, must now be either a 'village' or a 'quadrant' or a 'quarter'. The entrance block on Fair-field Road is pitched somewhere in style between a baronial pile and a fairy tale castle, but there is no denying the austere magnificence of the main factory building. Best seen from across the complex of railway lines that back onto it, it is not dissimilar to some of the great northern mills: a huge red-brick range with five floors of windows intersected by the strong vertical lines of brick buttresses. Rising above these are two towers with the more jaunty air of Italian campaniles. It is a further irony in the history of a site that once housed a museum of 'fire-making appliances' that these towers were later used for the siting of ground-to-air missiles, part of the anti-terrorism defences for the 2012 Olympic Games.

Poplar wood has played its own part in the history of warfare. Both the ancient Greeks and the Etruscans used shields fashioned from poplar and this use continued into at least the Middle Ages. By that time the wood was also being used for arrows. As they were an expensive and well-crafted commodity, an advancing army would restock itself by collecting the arrows it had already fired. This made it all the more important to use a wood that would absorb shock rather than snapping on impact – just as it was critical to use a wood in shields that would not split on receipt of a blow.

Quite coincidentally while I was writing this, I came across a reference to the use of poplar arrows in one of Chaucer's poems. In the early sections of his long poem, 'The Parliament of Fowls', composed between 1382 and

1383, the poet dreams that he is guided by a character called Africanus on a visit to the 'Garden of Love'. There, amidst many other natural wonders, he encounters trees

> *... whose foliage would for ever last*
> *Each kind as fresh and green as emerald*
> *In its own way a pleasure to behold.*

Not only are they beautiful, but useful too:

> *The builder's oak tree and the hardy ash;*
> *The elm for stakes and coffins for the dead;*
> *Box for pipe-making; holly for whips to lash;*
> *The fir for masts; for grief the cypress dread;*
> *The yew for bows; poplar for shafts smooth-made;*
> *The peaceful olive; and the drinker's vine;*
> *The victor's palm; the laurel, augury's sign.*

Here, the arrows of poplar are juxtaposed not with shields but with the bows of yew, the references to warfare leading on to items that are peaceful and, finally, celebratory.

Some of these early poplar arrows still survive. In 1535, 235 ships of the French fleet, carrying some 35,000 men, set out to take the Isle of Wight, preparatory to invading the English mainland. Among the ships that sailed out to meet them was Henry VIII's favourite, the *Mary Rose*. She did not get far. Racing out along the Solent at the head of the English response, she fired a broadside then tacked rapidly to bring the cannon on her opposite side into play. Caught by a sudden gust of wind she heeled over and sank with alarming rapidity. Quite why this happened is still a subject of intense debate but the consensus seems to be that she was top-heavy and highly unstable following a recent refit that had increased the number of cannon she was carrying. Whatever the reason, the effect was catastrophic, and so quickly did she go down that fewer than thirty-five of her crew of 400 escaped. A side effect of such a rapid sinking was that she took all her contents, largely intact, down with her. When the *Mary Rose* was raised in 1982 these provided an unparalleled insight into the Tudor world; a detailed inventory of everyday life, seafaring and warfare. Some 19,000 objects were recovered and among them some 2,300 iron-tipped arrows, most of which were made from poplar. According to local legend, they were cut from a tree still growing in the town of Portsmouth. Good as a story, perhaps, but unlikely.

It made a fascinating footnote to this tale to discover that the *Mary Rose* had spent some time in the parish. It was another of the strange connections that I was increasingly encountering. In 1514, after two years in action, the ship had come to Blackwall, in the Thames-side south east of Poplar, for repair. Set in a sheltered bend of the river before it turns southwards to round the Isle of Dogs, Blackwall was to later become the largest shipbuilding site on the Thames, but at this stage there were neither permanent docks nor slipways. Consequently, it took thirty men four days 'dykynge and castyng' to prepare a berth for her. And here she was to stay for six years, placed in reserve and manned by a skeleton crew till she was called back into action in 1520. Her first task was to accompany Henry VIII on his passage across the Channel to visit the French king, Francis I. Just two years later she would be doing battle against him.

As I worked my way street by street southwards, it was early autumn by the time I had actually reached Blackwall. Of the area's long romance with the sea there was now little trace. Gone were the huge shipyards and the quays from which Elizabethan explorer Sir Martin Frobisher had set out in search of the Northwest Passage, or John Smith to found Virginia, and gone, too, were the pubs to which, a few centuries later, Londoners had travelled in their trainloads to partake of whitebait suppers. So lost is all this that the original river frontage now lies several hundred feet inland and the area, once among the busiest and, sometimes, the rowdiest, in London, is squeezed into an unsplendid isolation, a sterile space between a trunk road and the Thames.

It was the cormorants alone that seemed to invest it with some sort of seafaring significance. Here was a bird with which those earlier sailors would have been familiar, haunting the rocky coastlines, hunch-shouldered, almost a constituent part of the cliffs. But just as this quayside had abandoned adventure for a sort of Bellway Home's domesticity, so had these cormorants swapped their black, wave-dashed rocks for an inland river and the rusting railings of a disused jetty. They still maintained that air of perpetual watchfulness, of supremely disinterested observers taking it all in, summing it up, and seeing beyond, but their ancient sinister reputation now seemed a little overwrought. The birds that Milton had used as a simile for Satan in *Paradise Lost* now just looked as if they had time on their hands.

Under their gaze I poked around along the Blackwall riverside. Along the top of the river wall, especially where it met the frame of older supporting timbers, small patches of plant were establishing themselves; fern grass and water bent, shepherd's purse and pellitory-of-the-wall, willowherb and ivy-leaved toadflax. The cracks between paving slabs were filled with liverworts, those tiny, overlooked pre-flowering plants that creep damply in shady corners producing their strange, umbrella-like sexual structures. So densely clustered were these that, down on my hands and knees, I seemed to be hovering above the packed parasols of a sun-soaked stretch of tourist beach.

Walking up from there to a higher paved platform, I came across the aspens. With three quarters of my walk completed I had yet to find a single black poplar, but here, at least, was one of its closest relatives. It is the most delicate-looking of the family: a small, open and lightly branched tree with crinkled and bluntly toothed leaves. It seems most at home on northern streamsides and rocky valley bottoms, not on city streets, so it felt incongruous to find them in the formality of carefully spaced tree pits laid out in neat rows on a platform above the river; a constriction to which several of them had responded by dying. I had, nonetheless, a sneaking regard for the arrangement. It had something rather courtly about it; an air, if you could sufficiently separate yourself from your surroundings, of the formal Elizabethan garden. No doubt the planners had intended the site to echo the name of the nearby Aspen Way, an otherwise horrendous trunk road funnelling the Essex-bound traffic over the Lea. Along its sides, in an otherwise inchoate planting scheme, a few more had been planted, the rushing tide of traffic a replacement for the rushing of mountain streams.

With the exception of the aspen, the names of our other poplars have a clear, if somewhat monochrome, theme. They are either black, white or grey. As I pounded the streets and counted trees, it had been the white poplar that was turning up most often. Known for many years as the 'abele', it gets its current name from the beautiful white felting on its shoots and the underside of its leaves. It may or may not be a native species, but if it was introduced it happened so long ago as to be almost irrelevant, having been imported by settlers moving across from the continent after the last Ice Age. It is most often found in coastal areas and is not particularly recommended for cultivation, but I had found around twenty of them, on roadside strips, beside the river or planted in a churchyard. The number, however, is only approximate. They are so prone to producing suckers that it is sometimes impossible to decide where one tree ends and another begins.

Unlike these others, the grey poplar is a hybrid species. Logic would suggest that it is a cross between the black poplar and the white, but logic would, in this case, be wrong. It is, in fact, a naturally occurring hybrid of the white poplar and the aspen. The grey poplar probably arrived alongside the white poplar and the two trees are not always easy to distinguish as their leaves have a similar felty underside. The leaves of the grey, however, are much less deeply cut, and closer to the aspen's in shape. The smooth grey bark is marked with darker spangles and in February it bears catkins with a purplish hue. Like most hybrids, it is much more vigorous than either of its parents, often growing to twice their size. It also suckers freely but, given the space and freedom from pollarding, can grow to a fine specimen tree.

It was one of these that was to become a favourite of mine. Perhaps this was to do with its setting. On the eastern edge of the parish, between the River Lea and the Blackwall Tunnel's thunderous approach road, lies an area of the sort that has now come to be known as 'edgelands'. Here, a single road describes an erratic circuit through an anarchic jumble of scrapyards and dilapidated workshops. Behind vari-coloured sheets of corrugated iron or high, spiked, metal railings, cars can be glimpsed in every stage of decomposition. There are two wood yards here, not the organised sort with neatly stacked shelves of planed planks for the builder or DIY weekender, but chaotic yards with fascinating jumbles of uncut trunks, boughs and bark-clad logs, spilling, together with half-cut carvings, out across the indistinct and puddled pavement. The cleaning carts rarely call round here and the street is strewn with dumped and wind-blown debris, supporting, somehow, its own population of straggling street plants. It is an area with a rare energy of its own, one of dynamic and defiant individualism and of under-the-counter deals, but it is the sort of area that is disappearing. The larger nearby edgelands of Stratford Marsh and Hackney Wick have already been swallowed up by the vast Olympic site, and it can only be a matter of time before the developers find this one, too.

It was here, however, that I found a large grey poplar. Set on a strip of jumbled growth fringing the main road, its branches spreading energetically, both upwards and outwards. A few yards away sat a burnt-out caravan and the conflagration had scorched the growth beneath its outermost arms. The tree had the place pretty much to itself, for no one lived here and no one walked this isolated area. It towered above the surrounding trees and I found myself surprised that I had never noticed it before. It could be seen from a considerable distance on both sides of the main road, and even when driving along the A12 its shimmering, greyish shape could be seen picked out in the summer months, standing well proud of all surrounding growth. It might not be a black poplar, but it was a tree to look up to.

There was another poplar that I was to come across locally, this one an imported American planting. The Western balsam poplar is remarkable for its smell, a powerful fragrance emitting from its resinous buds that is so strong it can be detected from as much as a hundred metres away. It is at its best in spring when the buds are first opening, but it is also redolent of warm summer evenings, when it hangs on the air with a drowsy sweetness. It seems to have something of the Orient about it, of ornate oil lamps and carpeted halls in an Ottoman palace, but underlying this there is something rather medical, a hint of childhood chest rubs and burning muscle balms. Such is the connection between smell and memory that I can clearly remember the first time I encountered it, as I walked one evening up a country lane in Essex. I came across it twice in Poplar; once on the Robin Hood estate, a controversial piece of 20th-century brutalist architecture now scheduled for demolition; and again off the East India Dock Road, in an area that had once been part of Chinatown.

Locating trees by their scent would be an even more unlikely proceeding than identifying them by the sound of their leaves. Nonetheless, there were a few that I became familiar with and it was good, when I could, to be employing another sense in my explorations. There was the occasional cypress with a smell that mixed lawn mowings with pine resin; there was, on a hot day, the heady fragrance of the eucalyptus; and there was the sweet summer scent of the lime blossom. There were also the poplars, for though the balsam poplar has the strongest smell, it is present, too, in some of the other species. There was a group of hybrid black poplars in a far corner of Bartlett Park that I especially enjoyed. I would walk to them with the family dog (I had wanted another cat but was the unfortunate victim of democracy) and while he sniffed the trails of squirrels and the traces of other dogs' urine, I would hold out for the heady scent that could be discerned as you approached the trees, a soft sweetness to the air emerging from the resin on their glistening brown buds.

This resin can be extracted from the buds in boiling water and has long been put to healing uses. Its constituents include populin, a name derived from the poplar, and salicin, a name derived from the *Salix* genus, or willow. Salicyclic acid is the main ingredient of aspirin, and an infusion of willow has been used since antiquity for pain relief and as an anti-inflammatory. The poplar resin shares some of the same properties.

Popilion, the name given to an ointment made from black poplar buds, can be traced back to Middle English. It appears in the 14th century as part of a complex religious allegory. In 1395, Philippe de Mézèries, a French soldier and author, wrote an open letter to Richard II bemoaning the divisions that had beset Christianity. He describes them as an 'open wound', the poison from which is affecting all the faithful. Up to now, he says, it has been treated only with popilion, 'the discourses of flatterers', whereas what is really called for is 'the ointment of the apostles'.

A recipe from the 15th century is more down to earth. It describes how poplar buds should be pounded to make a paste, then mixed with a variety of other plants, including henbane, house leek, plantain, endive, violets and water-cress. In his massive *Herball* of 1597 – the most widely circulated botanical book of the 17th century – John Gerard describes an *Unguentum Populeon*, which he recommends for bruises, inflammation and gout. Three hundred years later, in her 1931 book *A Modern Herbal*, the estimable Mrs. Maud Grieve was still recommending a tincture of poplar resin mixed with lard or oil. Perhaps it was a mixture of this sort that formed the basis of the black poplar oint-ment especially favoured by boxers and prizefighters for the treatment of their bruises and swellings. For this use it almost certainly played a role in Poplar.

It is hard to convey the significance that boxing once assumed in the life of the Poplar community. It was in the people's blood, or, more accurately, it was in their bodies; the bodies of the stevedores and the corn porters and the coal heavers and all those who, day after day, spent their time lifting and shifting heavy loads around the docks and yards. It was there in the rowdy brawls outside the count-less pubs, and there in the more disciplined atmosphere of boxing clubs in church and municipal halls. It was a pastime espoused by whole families and passed down from grand-father to father to son. It provided the entertainment and the excitement; and, for the few, it was the route out of the mean streets, the poverty and the overcrowding, into a fabulous world of celebrity and wealth.

Boxing figures strongly in the many published memoirs of Poplar people. 'We had thousands of professional boxers born round here,' says a Mr. Morgan in 1974, 'because everyone was broke.' There were clubs in Hay Currie Street, Culloden Street, Knapp Road and North Street. There were professional bouts in St. Michael's Hall or at the Tramway Depot in Levens Road, where 'there were more fights outside than in, to get into the hall.' At the Premierland, it would cost you sixpence to watch four good fights, at the Wonderland a shilling would buy you 'all the finest boxers you want to see'. There were families like the Fishers or the Softleys, where all the sons followed boxing careers. 'I've even done a bit myself,' says a Mr. Shed, who'd 'had a good hiding, given a good hiding'. Over in the docks, the 'many good fighters' included Joe Lucy, lightweight champion of Great Britain, who would be 'working on shipping all day and then going fifteen rounds at night.'

Of the many well-known boxers produced by the parish, none was as celebrated in his day as Teddy Baldock, the man who took on its very name and became the 'Poplar Wonder'. Born in 1907, he was the son of a fairground boxer and the grandson of a bare-knuckle fighter. He began fighting at almost the same time as he started school, training first at the St. Michael's Boys Club, the hall attached to St. Michael's Church, and later, in a loft above a banana drying shed in nearby Dewsbury Street. At the age of fourteen he fought his first paid bout in Barking. It was the start of a five-year run of forty-one unbeaten fights. By nineteen he was World Bantamweight

Champion, the youngest man ever to achieve the title.

No London fighter had a larger following. When he took on the Frenchman Anton Merlo, in 1925, crowds lined the streets of Poplar awaiting his return from the Royal Albert Hall and special late editions of the papers were printed to announce the result. In 1927 fifty-two charabancs of his supporters followed him to the Royal Albert Hall for a title fight against Archie Bell. When he won it, the organist burst into a spontaneous rendition of 'For He's a Jolly Good Fellow'. Baldock returned to Poplar to a civic reception and the award of Freedom of the Borough. Following his wedding, in 1931, the crowds on the streets were so dense that the traffic was stopped for more than half an hour, with many climbing lampposts to catch a glimpse of the newly-wed couple.

But neither his marriage nor his career was to last. By twenty-four he was burned out and, despite only five defeats in his eighty fights, he was suffering from a swollen left hand, broken ribs and increasing eye trouble. When, in 1971, he died at the age of sixty-three, he was penniless, homeless and alone. He had spent his last years sleeping rough on the streets or in dismal lodging houses. He owned nothing but a shabby suit and was too ashamed to let his daughter see him. None of the papers that had produced those special editions noted his parting.

Here, then, is a tree that is exciting to look at, soothing to listen to and pleasant to smell; a tree whose every part has a use; a massive tree, a landmark tree, a meeting place and a boundary marker. Yet this same tree was to suffer an almost catastrophic decline. Even while Constable was painting poplars beside the River Stour, it is probable that their heyday was already coming to an end. It is suitably symbolic that while the very trees that Constable depicted have long since been lost, Willy Lott's cottage, which once stood beneath them, survives. But it is in poetry rather than in painting that we find the closest record of the loss of the poplar. Poetry is, after all, better placed than painting to deal with the absence of things.

It begins with William Cowper, one of the real precursors of the Romantic Movement. A gentle man, he was a keen observer of the natural world and of what it told us about the human state; able to draw inspiration from the tiniest detail of the everyday. He lived through the years of intense change at the start of the Industrial Revolution, change to which the Romantic Movement was largely a reaction, and the turbulence that he saw around him was reflected in his own inner condition. He suffered from an intense 'melancholia', a depression and despair centring on a sense of worthlessness and a conviction of his own damnation. It was to lead to three suicide attempts and nearly three years spent in an asylum. 'Hatred and vengeance,' he wrote, 'are my eternal portion,' but his sense of despair reaches its most intense expression in his poem 'The Outcast'. A man washed overboard struggles in the churning waves, wrestling with abandonment and with fear before finally succumbing to drowning. 'But I,' concludes the poet, 'beneath a rougher sea, / Am whelmed in deeper gulfs than he.'

For seeing the natural world as it was, rather than as it was construed to be, Cowper was credited with changing the direction of nature poetry. He became a fervent Christian, but I suspect that it was his love of nature as much as his religious conviction that was to give him the periods of calm that he craved; time spent tending his cucumbers or writing biographies of his favourite trees. It was moments like these that best equipped him to survive his bouts of madness.

Much of his personality is expressed in his 1784 poem 'The Poplar Fields'. It is a close observation of trees and a comment on the changing nature of the countryside, one that also expresses a sense of loss and which produces an observation on the fleeting nature of human happiness. Returning after an absence of twelve years, he finds that the poplar trees beneath which he once played are gone:

> *The Poplars are fell'd, farewell to the shade*
> *And the whispering sound of the cool colonnade,*
> *The winds play no longer, and sing in the leaves,*
> *Nor Ouse in his bosom their image receives.*

Here is another description of the distinctive sound of the poplar, and of its habit of leaning out across the river to catch its reflection in the flow. But the grove is gone, the blackbirds that once sung there are fled, and the poet will be long dead before any new trees are grown. Human life is short, and its pleasures are even shorter.

At a different time, and in a different way, Gerard Manley Hopkins was equally tortured, both as a man and a poet. It is in his work, almost a hundred years later, that we find the next famous poetic reference to poplars; and it is also about their felling. 'Binsey Poplars', written in 1879, laments the loss of another riverside grouping, this time beside the

River Thames near Oxford. Within the text he refers to them as aspens but this is generally taken as poetic licence to enable the alliteration with 'airy':

> *My aspens dear, whose airy cages quelled,*
> *Quelled or quenched in leaves the leaping sun,*
> *All felled, felled, are all felled;*
> *Of a fresh and following folded rank*
>   *Not spared, not one...*

From this act of destruction he goes on to produce one of the most poignant accounts of man's relentless war against nature:

> *O if we but knew what we do*
>   *When we delve or hew –*
> *Hack and rack the growing green!*
>   *...*
> *Where we, even when we mean*
>   *To mend her, we end her.*

Hopkins spent the first eight years of his life in Stratford, immediately north of Poplar along the River Lea, and on that sole basis I feel justified in laying claim to him. The Stratford he knew, however, is long gone. Not only the trees but the riverside marshes have disappeared and, in recent years, even the river itself has been dammed. A more complete example of hacking and racking and ending not mending, it is difficult to imagine.

❀

The first references to the name of the parish, as Popeler, Popelar or Popler, date back to 1327. Though probably derived from the general prevalence of poplar trees that grew here, some have argued that the name comes from a particular tree, or group of trees, that grew on an area of higher ground to the north of the Isle of Dogs. To home-coming sailors, making their way upriver to London, these would have been a welcome sight, as well as an important navigational aid as they approached the tight bend that carries the Thames in its great curve around the 'island'. Whichever explanation is correct – and it could be that both apply – confirmation of the presence of poplars comes from the very same source that provided the recipe for *Unguentum Populeon*. They are to be found, says Gerard, in his *Herball*, 'in a lowe meadow turning up at a lane at the further end of a village called Blackwell.'

They were still common in the parish some 130 years later, for they are mentioned by John Strype in his 1720 work, *A Survey of the Cities of London and Westminster*. He clearly believed them to be the origin of the area's name: 'There be yet remaining in that part of the hamlet (of Poplar) bordering upon Limehouse, many old bodies of large Poplars, standing as testimonials of the truth of that etymology.'

Between 1832 and 1840, a Mr. W. Smith prepared a memorandum naming parts of the parish where poplar trees still grew. He handed it to his friend, the editor of the *East End News*, who later confessed to having lost it. But he remembered some of what it had said in an article he wrote for his own paper some years later: "Two or three splendid specimens flourished in the front garden of some ancient wooden cottages in High-street, Poplar. Others stood along the hawthorn hedge formerly lining that portion of East India Dock Road when the area from the northern portion of the dock wall to the bank of the River Lea was an open expanse of marshland."

Just like Strype he goes on to describe another concentration of many fine trees along the Limehouse borders, which disappeared, he says, some forty years earlier. By the middle of the 19th century, then, the last poplars were vanishing from Poplar.

What is it that accounts for the tree's dramatic decline? It can really be summed up in two words: 'habitat' and 'hybrids'. First, there is the story of a nationwide wetland drainage, originally for agriculture and then for development, the poplar disappearing along with the habitats that sustained it. Then, by the mid–18th century, a second factor was coming into play. The native poplar, as a planted tree, was giving way to a range of newly developed horticultural forms. The hybrid black Italian poplar was the first to arrive, produced in 1755. By the early 18th century there was a veritable race to breed the 'perfect' poplar. These new varieties arose from the crossing of different species, and then from the crossing of the new varieties themselves. They were given names like Serotina, Marilandica or Gelrica. There was a Berlin poplar, a Eugenei and a Robusta. There was also a Regenerata, which grew up with the railways. It was the tree of choice on railway embankments, along main lines into cities and around coal yards and sidings, eventually earning itself the nickname of the 'railway poplar'.

These new hybrids were more vigorous than the parents from which they had been created. They lived longer, grew faster, had a more regular shape and lacked the boles and burs that characterised the native tree. Some of the new varieties were exclusively male and therefore lacked the 'messy' masses of down produced by the female tree. They were manufactured and manageable upstarts, purpose-bred products, which displaced the native tree, first in forestry and, soon, in amenity planting, too. Where poplars were still being planted, they were no longer *Populus nigra betulifolia*, our eccentric and individualistic, original wetland tree.

It is the hybrid black Italian poplar that we find most commonly in towns today and I encountered twenty-two of them on my walk. There was the group in Bartlett Park, of course; large, forthright, no-nonsense sort of trees, and if they did carry a scent, it was like eau de cologne on a boxer. If they lacked the individuality of the native species, they made up for it in self-confidence. There were more at the opposite end of the parish, where the 'Blue Bridge' carried the road over the entrance channel to the Millwall Docks. Nearby, another group of these large, upstanding trees lined the main island road running parallel to the river. They were the closest I would come to glimpsing the poplars as they might once have been; lining the creeks and channels, rising over the drainage ditches, and warming the hearts of the sailors at the end of their journey home.

By the end of the 20th century the black poplar was not just almost gone but also largely forgotten. The fact that it did not disappear completely from public consciousness was largely the work of one man, Edgar Milne-Redhead, the hero of their rehabilitation. In 1973, he began surveying the country's black poplars, the first time such a task had been attempted and one that he was to continue for another fifteen years. It was a survey in which, as a young and distinctly amateur naturalist, I played a very small part. I never met the man himself but he corresponded with me on those old-fashioned blank white postcards that seem now like a slow version of the telegram, or an even slower equivalent of the email. I was asked to check a report he had received, of a black poplar growing alongside the Regent's Canal in east London. I found the tree but was disappointed to have to respond that it was a Lombardy poplar and not the native species at all. Even a negative record, he told me in response, was useful. I doubted it, but it made me feel better.

Across those years, Milne-Redhead recorded just over a thousand trees. The same number was arrived at when Peter Roe organised the *Daily Telegraph*'s 'Black Poplar Hunt' in 1994. Both these surveys, however, left out the two largest concentrations of black poplar in the country, the urban population around Manchester and a rural one in the Vale of Aylesbury. When these were included the tally rose to nearer 7,000. For the moment this number continues to grow, not because there are more trees but because there are more people looking for them. The black poplar now has its own dedicated band of enthusiasts, with more organised counts and more expertise in distinguishing the various hybrids, a difficulty which, in the past, probably concealed the true number of native trees.

Even this increased number remains, of course, a fragment of the population that once lined our lowlands, and the situation for the tree remains serious. With few new native black poplars now being planted, the remaining stock is ageing and, since the poplar is a fairly short-lived tree, this could, in twenty to thirty years' time, lead to a situation where many of them are dying simultaneously.

And then there's the matter of sex. With the female tree requiring a damper and more nutrient-rich soil, it was probably always the case that males were more abundant, but this has been exacerbated by the planters' preference for the 'less messy' male tree. The sexual disequilibrium is striking: of that earlier estimate of 7,000 trees, only 600 were said to be females. The poplar does not actually need both genders to regenerate. It can do it easily, and asexually, from cuttings – or 'truncheons' as they were once known. In the wild this is useful since it allows broken branches being swept downstream the chance to root should they alight on a suitable patch of bare mud. But when used extensively in cultivation it can have other effects. Trees grown from cuttings are clones, exact genetic replicas of the parent, with no variation in the gene pool. They are, in effect, the same tree, with the same weaknesses and susceptibilities, growing simultaneously in different places. The obvious and immediate danger to arise from this is that of decreased disease resistance – or the more rapid spread of diseases once they do arise. The reality of this threat is currently being demonstrated by the Manchester poplar. The several thousand trees of the northern and eastern suburbs are derived from just one clone. Since 2000, about half of them have died or been felled as a result of the spread of poplar scab.

The details of this depressing back-story did not bode well for my chances of finding a local black poplar. But poplars, I knew, could be found when you least expected them. Working in north London a decade earlier, and with responsibility for the borough of Islington's tree stock, I had been contacted by a professional botanist who had realised that two of the presumed hybrid poplars on our streets were actually the genuine article. The Natural History Museum had confirmed the identification and thus it was we learned that two of our inner-city trees, passed by hundreds of people daily, had been harbouring a hidden identity.

This ability of black poplars to 'pop up' unexpectedly was confirmed by the business with the bishop. In a fine display of synchronicity, it happened at the end of a day I had spent entirely in researching the story of the poplar. Returning home, I was reminded by my wife that we had an evening date with the Bishop of Stepney. In the confusing but historically fascinating construct that is the Anglican church, Stepney is the name of the whole of the episcopal area covering east London and therefore including our parish. A new bishop had recently been appointed and had organised a series of evenings to meet the clergy and their partners at his home in Mile End. It was to have been a garden party but the rain had driven both the jazz musicians and the guests indoors. When the drizzle eased, and perhaps to escape an over-exposure to the clergy, I took my glass of wine into the garden. A solitary noctule bat was ignoring the rain and swooping to and fro around the upper branches of a large ash tree occupying pride of place at the end of the lawn. The East End is not best known for its bats and this would have been reward enough for my outside sally. But walking to one side I found myself looking at a tall, pollarded poplar, its trunk carrying the characteristic mass of bosses and boles of the native tree. The bishop, it seemed, had his own personal black poplar. And this, I thought, was the way to see them; not pounding the urban pavements of Poplar but standing with a glass of red wine in a garden at dusk, the faint sound of jazz music drifting through the open kitchen door. Perhaps the church was backing my search.

Despite what I took to be a bishop's blessing, September passed into October and I had yet to find a black poplar on my own patch. It was raining again and the wettest summer on record was on its way to becoming the wettest ever year. And I had by now encountered a further hazard in the form of curious, and sometimes agitated, local residents whose anxiety was aroused by my habit of closely examining a patch of ground, or staring at a tree, outside their front door. Invariably I was thought to be 'from the council', a certain indication that one is up to something nefarious. But once I had explained myself, or at least made an attempt to do so, the response was always friendly – and generally led to an offer of further information. Certainly, I avoided the fate of J.D. Summers-Smith who, whilst researching his 1963 book on house sparrows, had been questioned by the police as to why he was staring at people's homes with binoculars. Such are the risks the urban naturalist must run.

But still, there were no black poplars and spurred on by my vision of the riverside poplars, I decided to get a glimpse of the one place where they still grew in a semi-wild abundance. Thus it was that I set off with one of my sons on a brief trip to the Vale of Aylesbury, omitting to tell him the full purpose of our visit, on the grounds that I could foretell all his objections in advance.

The Aylesbury area may be more connected in the popular mind with ducks, but it also holds the largest concentration of black poplars in the country, and it is, after all, the same wet conditions that support both the ducks and the poplars. They were, I had read, focused in an area surrounding the village of Long Marston. Many of them were pollards that had contributed significantly to the local economy, their lopped branches providing cattle fodder and material for matchsticks, wattle, bean poles and fruit baskets. They had been cut for hedging poles, the upright supports used in traditional hedge laying, and this, it was thought, accounted for their appearance at regular intervals along the hedgerows – the 'poles' having sprung back into life and grown to become trees themselves.

The wood had also been used in hurdles to confine the sheep at night, when they were brought down from the Chiltern downland, and it was on the edge of this downland that we camped. Arriving after dark in unseasonal cold and freezing rain, we awoke to a beautifully clear day, the brilliant blue sky highlighted by tiny cirrus clouds the shape of seagull feathers. Behind us, across the rounded chalky fields, the low mist was still wrapping itself around the bulk of Ivinghoe Beacon, which, attached to its long, low outlier of the Chiltern downs, resembled the head of a dozing dragon. Before us, the Vale was spread out like a map. There were more pockets of mist here and there about a pattern of small fields, some grazed, some with the remnants of a cabbage crop, and all fringed with hedgerows or lines of trees: a 'landscape plotted and pieced', as Hopkins would have it. Cutting across this scene, piercing it as well as piecing, were power lines, the railway and the Grand Union

Canal, with a line of brightly painted narrow boats moored along its length. From across the far side of the Vale, the distant turrets of Mentmore Towers stared back at us, until we were distracted by the sudden eruption of an agitated flock of house martins, rising above the corrugated black farm buildings as a sparrowhawk dived among them.

The campsite manager was fascinated by our expedition. His family, he told me, had occupied the farmhouse for three generations, having bought it when the landowning local lord had sold off portions of the estate to pay off his father's death duties. He had his own theory about the black poplars. The Vale, he said, had originally been used to raise cattle, and was farmed with a system of ridges and furrows; the furrows to take the flooding, and the ridges to rise above it and provide the cattle with dry land to feed on. During the agricultural revolution, he told me, there had been a move to greater arable use and it was then, as part of new drainage systems, that the black poplars had been deliberately introduced 'to help soak up the water'.

We started our walk from the village pub in Long Marston – our meal there being my son's reward for accompanying me. In fact, we could already see black poplars from the pub window, making this the second time recently I had seen poplars with a glass of something in my hand. The trees, when we started our walk, were everywhere and they displayed the unruliness appropriate for any self-respecting black poplar: vigorous and ill-disciplined and bearing the scars of a dissolute middle age. Some were decently draped in ivy. Some had boughs pointing bolt upright as if in shock. Others had branches sweeping down before curving back up again in a sort of indecision. They lined ditches tangled with willowherb and water parsnip, and dwelt on field fringes where they glinted silver in the sun. Many were pollarded and on one tree the new growth rose from a completely hollow trunk and appeared to be in imminent danger of toppling into the ditch over which, in an ill-balanced sort of way, it was leaning. Many stumps were already dead, evidence of a simultaneous planting, but there was also the encouragement of new plantings, encased in the ugly but inevitable rabbit guards.

In one field a large tree had completely split in two about fifteen feet from its base. The top half of the old tree lay lengthwise on the ground whilst new growth sprouted from the fractured trunk beside it. Sometimes the trees could be identified from their fidgetiness alone, for even in the slightest breeze, they were more active than anything around them. And sometimes they could be detected by colour, their leaves a greyer-green than surrounding species, though some were already turning an autumnal apple-yellow.

We walked across fields where the grass had been turned stiff with slurry. Jackdaws settled in distant copses and four red kites sailed, at ease, overhead. We came to the little church of St. Mary – more of a tower with a bit of church attached than the other way around – and found it locked, as are a disturbing number of rural churches. Unable to gain access we spent the rest of the walk concocting stories about the secrets it might be hiding, returning along the Grand Union Canal towpath, where two little owls were calling and a man was incongruously tuning bagpipes.

Back in Poplar, the closest I was coming to finding a black poplar was in the form of a dead stick. It was in the grounds of St. Matthias, which stands at one end of Poplar Recreation Ground with a strange little spire that makes it look as if it had been transported direct from an Alpine village. It was not one of the parish churches but had served as a chapel for the East India Company, which had had a presence in Poplar ever since building its first dock here in 1610. In fact, it has long since ceased to be a church of any sort, being now a community centre, 'Neighbours in Poplar', led by a redoubtable and ever-campaigning character that everyone knows as Sister Christine. The evidence of the company lives on in a coat of arms set high in the ceiling as well as in the wooden columns that line the nave and are said to have come from the masts of company ships.

Behind the church, in what was once its graveyard, I stumbled across the stick. It had been hopefully thrust into the soil, just in front of a living white poplar, and hanging from it was a handwritten cardboard sign announcing that it was indeed the much sought-after species. But the stick was indisputably dead. Walking back around the church I came across one of the helpers and asked her about it. It had been planted, she said, to celebrate the 100th birthday of Tony, one of their lunch club members who had lived in Poplar all his life. And yes, she was well aware of the difference between a black poplar and a Lombardy poplar, even if the council wasn't. I hope that Tony is still with us, even if the cutting isn't. And I hope, too, that one day, perhaps on his next birthday, they will try again.

Which left me only with the Lombardy poplars that seemed to have taken the place of the black poplar, deposing it as a local symbol. It is only fair to point out that they appear in 'The Hay Wain', too. You have to look very closely to see them – close enough to provoke an uneasy stirring in the nearest curator – but peer beyond that idyllic sun-dappled meadow and you can just make out a line of four of them, in the distance. They figure much more prominently in Constable's paintings of Salisbury Cathedral, where they seem to echo the shape of the cathedral spire, and sometimes even to overshadow it.

It should also be said that the Lombardy poplar is not one of those confusing hybrids. It is, in fact, the same species as the native poplar but a cultivated variety given the name Italica. It was developed for its distinctive shape, initially somewhere in Asia, but it came to us via Lombardy, around the middle of the 18th century. Some accounts say it was first planted here by the Duke of Argyll, while others name a Lord Rochford, who also introduced the red-legged partridge to the country. Either case would make it undoubtedly aristocratic in origin, a fact attested to by the straightness of its demeanour. For a Mr. T. White of West Retford, it earned a Royal Society of Arts gold medal in the 1770s, for his planting of 10,400 of what were then known as Po poplars, after the Italian river valley in which they grew. It is possible that had this name survived, their popularity might not.

As the growing London conurbation engulfed the local area, the people of Poplar would have been far more familiar with the lean and slightly funereal form of the Lombardy poplar than with the shape of the original tree. I had found thirteen of them in the parish, hugely visible symbols in parks and green places that rose as sentinels above the surrounding trees and defined the spaces in which they stood. It may have been an impostor but it had taken on a local meaning. The Poplar Board of Guardians, a far more enlightened group than their counterparts over most of the rest of the country, took a radical approach to their duty of running the local workhouses and administering the poor relief. One of their many innovations was to set up their own training school for 700 poor Poplar children on a 100-acre site in Essex. Established in 1906, it even had its own school magazine. In it I was to find a poem, by one R. Jones, entitled, 'The Poplar Tree'. It is, from the start, both a moral and a patriotic ditty:

> *Oh! The Poplar Tree stands straight and true*
> *Like a sentinel on duty*
> *And every twig slants upward too*
> *For every twig's on duty*
> *That's a hint for me*
> *And a nod for you*
> *For I'm a twig*
> *And so are you*
> *So sing with me to the Poplar Tree*
> *That stands up straight on duty.*

The succeeding verses are punctuated by a chorus:

> *One and all, one and all*
> *Twig and trunk and root and all*
> *Together, together,*
> *In every weather,*
> *Storm and trouble and toil and moil,*
> *The Poplar Tree stands sturdily*
> *With its roots sunk deep in English soil.*

What it lacks in poetry, it makes up for in enthusiasm and I would have been happy to have met R. Jones. But for all the 'English' virtues it proclaims, this is undoubtedly a description of that 'Italian' tree, the 'straight and true' Lombardy poplar, making its eternal upright salute to the sky. Here, at the beginning of the 20th century, it is the Lombardy poplar that is already being used to characterise the borough – as well as to set an example to all the borough's children. It had replaced the black poplar even in the imagination.

It was approaching winter as I completed the walk, around one corner of Canary Wharf and along the Limehouse borders. I had followed every street, passed down every passage, threaded every estate. And I had, I hoped, been listening. Browning bunches of 'keys' hung from the ash trees, and seed balls like baubles dangled from the planes, but the leaves seemed reluctant to leave this year, having to be torn from the twigs by a sequence of late autumn storms. I had, in my meandering course, found grey poplars, white poplars and aspen; American poplars, Italian poplars and Lombardy poplars. But the poplar that had given the parish its name was gone, and with it was gone a landscape and a way of life. There were no native black poplars in Poplar.

Somehow, however, the long-gone tree had left its imprint, and the thought of this faint haunting encouraged me. I had found its echoes and impressions in place names, in the timber of tidal mills, in the stories of the old match factory, in the boxers' ointment, in the folk memory and in the marking of a resident's 100th birthday. It would, I had already decided, be one day making a comeback.

Chapter Two

Myth and the Mulberry

Beside the vicarage, beneath the spreading planes, I garden glass. I can never understand why there is so much of it but every spade I turn reveals a shard or three. The chickens are even better at unearthing it and though their run has been on the same spot for a year or two, they daily turn up more. For a while I threw it in the recycling bin but more recently I began to collect the fragments in a bowl, feeling that some artistic purpose would eventually reveal itself. The bowl is beside me as I write, its attraction increasing with accumulation as I throw in splinters of all shapes and varying sizes, the plain white glass enlivened by shards of green or brown or stained-glass blue.

David Hockney once produced a print called 'Digging up Glass'. It seemed so appropriate when I heard about it that I determined I must get a copy, even if it meant pawning the children. A tiny work, just four and a half inches by five, it is one of a series illustrating tales from the Brothers Grimm. In this case it accompanies the strange account of a character called Old Rinkrank:

> *Here stand I, poor Rinkrank*
> *On my seventeen long shanks*
> *On my weary, worn-out foot,*
> *Open the door, Mother Mansrot.*

But he is not poor, and neither does she open the door, for Mother Mansrot is a long-lost princess, kidnapped by Old Rinkrank and imprisoned by him beneath a glass mountain. She manages to escape (by the strange expedient of trapping his beard in a window) and is reunited with her father, the king, who digs up the glass mountain and finds, buried deep beneath it, a treasure of silver and gold. Hockney, however, eschews the drama, simply showing us a spade and a foot, and some sprinkling shards of glass. Except for the fashionable nature of the boot, it could be me in the garden. And I have the picture now; it hangs in my study, and I have still retained the children.

As well as glass, I garden stones. They too appear in limitless quantity, rising from deep beneath the surface like fish coming up from the bottom of a lake for air. Here, close to both the Thames and the Lea, we live on the river terrace gravels and the stones are round or oval pebbles, moved and smoothed by centuries of running water. They are, most of them, composed of flint and among them are more jagged fragments, sharp-edged and shattered to reveal black or fudge-brown faces. These are the exotic denizens of an even deeper zone, formed as nodules in the chalk, fractured from them and working their long way upwards.

I found, in the borough archives, lists of the boreholes that had been driven beneath the gasworks or beside the docks, and which detail the layers that form the land beneath us.

Lying over much of the area, a surface layer was formed by the fine alluvial deposits, brought down by the spreading rivers and their seasonal floods. Below these was the heavier load from when the rivers were larger still, the gravels that formed a bed about a metre and a half thick. And beneath this the drills had continued through more than eleven metres of clay. This, however, represents the London clays at their thinnest: from the Thames, they deepen as they climb to north and south, achieving a thickness of more than ninety-one metres beneath Hampstead and the other London heights. They provide the characteristic soil of much of London. Blue or orange in colour, hard-baked in summer and turning in winter to a slippery and unworkable sludge, they are the London gardener's curse. Below this are more layers of sands and pebbles and shells, and then, some forty-seven metres down, the chalk. It forms the bottom of London's geological bowl, spreading outwards and sweeping upwards to form the North Downs and the Chilterns on either side of the city. It was from this deep layer that the flints had travelled, patiently pushing upwards through the dark compaction of rock and soil to eventually reach my garden and the light of an east London day.

Because of them, gardening has become, for me, a means of connection. Surrounded as I am by concrete, this small oasis of soil, this pore in the city's otherwise impenetrable skin, turns up remnants from inconceivably distant times when strange life-forms swam in shallow tropical seas. And deeply pressed down on though they were, they had refused to remain there, making their way, millimetre by slow millimetre, up to the surface. They are not just stones, they are metaphors, poems in the process of being realised, forcing their way from the dark unconscious and into the everyday mind.

This awareness of geological strata, of time arranging itself in layers, began also to influence the way I saw the trees. Their history had also formed distinct periods, influenced this time by human action but each with its own characteristics and with species shaped to the conditions of the times. The black poplars were my bedrock. Apart from the pre-human eras of tree ferns and tropical palms, these were the original wildwood of the waterside, the tree of the local river valleys and the fringing marshes. But the period of the poplars had passed. The drainage of the marshes, the spread of cultivation and the growth of the city was being accompanied by a new generation of trees; not wild, or semi-wild, like the poplars, these were planted, pruned and picked from. In Poplar, at least, it was the turn of the fruit trees.

As the 18th century opened, London was in the throes of a massive expansion. As it pushed outwards, the city's rim, according to the Reverend Henry Hunter, became 'a ring of fire and pungent smoke' arising from the clay pits, tile works, brick kilns, slaughterhouses and smouldering mountains of rubbish. Around this, the countryside, for some five or ten miles beyond, was pressed into food production for the increasing population.

What exactly happened where was a function of London's geology. The heavy London clays supported a grassland that was excellent for grazing, and here the city's horses and its dairy cattle were put out to feed. Here, too, the thousands of sheep and cattle, herded on foot from as far afield as the Scottish borders, were fattened before taking their final walk into the London meat markets. But diets were changing and there was now an increased demand for fresh fruit and vegetables. For this, the lighter and more fertile alluvial soils that, in some places, coated the clays, were ideal. One of these places, especially in its northern half, was Poplar. It was about to become one of the market gardens of London.

It is in this part of the parish that our vicarage stands, in an area that was once known as South Bromley, though it has nothing to do with the better-known Bromley that straddles the London/Kent borders. It once had both a station and a church named after it, but it is a name that has now almost completely disappeared except, anachronistically, in the pages of the *London A–Z*. Not one in a hundred local people would recognise it. As was once said of the London suburb of Greenford, not even the people who live there know where it is.

Walking these urban streets today it is difficult to envisage that as recently as the 1850s, at the same time as the last black poplars were disappearing, the area was covered with small farms and vegetable gardens. Here, where St. Leonard's Road runs alongside the Teviot estate, in the concrete shadow of the Balfron Tower, was once 'Farmer Steven's land', holding a 'good herd of cows', whose milk, along with fresh vegetables, could be purchased at the farm house. Nearby was a market garden known as Salter's Farm and another known as Palmer's Fields, through which a pathway ran by the side of a ditch and down to the River Lea. Mr. Palmer, it was said, was a 'pork butcher and large pig breeder' – though whether it was Mr. Palmer or the pigs that were large is not clear. Another garden, surrounded by a ten-foot wall, stood on the site that is now our vicarage. Through it wound a pathway, 'with three posts at the entrance', leading to Farmer Radford's House, 'a large building with beautiful palisading and iron gates', and beyond it four gardeners' cottages and a large wooden storehouse. Here, the garden produce was kept, as well as the wagons that would transport it to the London markets.

I found these descriptions in Tower Hamlets' estimable local history library, in a collection called the *East London Papers*. Among them, from a William Fairbairn, came this poignant and poetic reminiscence of the area. 'Dear charming, beautiful Bromley!' he wrote, 'I can see it all now with its trees, its blackbirds and thrushes, its fields, its lovely gardens with their beautiful scents, its strawberries, which I used to gather and eat *ad libitum*! A sweet country place to which our town friends came for refreshment.' It is an account to be read and reread whilst standing at the stump end of the old churchyard, between the 'High Street' and the post-war estates, listening to the roar of the Blackwall Tunnel approach road.

Much of this extent of farms and gardens was devoted to orchards. That became clear from the maps I consulted in the same library. The London map of 1746 shows six of them here, whilst another, dated 1799, includes an additional plantation divided into twenty-four separate sections. Meanwhile the members of the Mathematical Society, meeting at the Ben Johnson's Head in Spitalfields, had resolved to conduct a survey of the grounds of 'Bromley Hall' and, by 1762, had mapped four orchards, including a cherry orchard, on this property alone. Of all these orchards, of the brilliant displays of spring flowering apple and cherry, of the bushels of fruit being carted to the London markets, virtually nothing now remains.

There is one part of the parish, however, where a name continues their memory. Down in its south-eastern corner, where the Lea finally, and tortuously, reaches the Thames, the parish tapers away into a strange double peninsula, the shape of a hitch-hiker's extended hand and thumb. Always an isolated area, it was little known even to the rest of Poplar, and remains so today, cut off by the combination of ancient rivers and modern roads. Now in the process of a massive redevelopment, it was once the site of an orchard and the thoroughfare along it still bears the name of Orchard Place.

There was an 'Orchard House', too, a large moated property built in the 16th century. By the end of the 17th, it had become a well-known tavern with its own river stairs, and it was to remain a 'tippling house' until falling vacant in the 1860s. By then, however, this rural peninsula was on its way to becoming one of the poorest and most neglected areas of London. The orchards were grubbed up and the area packed with housing, with at least five new pubs springing up to serve them. These two small, river-bound points of land were further isolated with the building of the East India Docks to the west. They contained a closely knit – and closely related – community, living in tight brick terraces that backed directly onto the Thames, and were sometimes awash with it. 'Hardly human. Incarnate mushrooms,' a Father Lawless had described them in the 1890s, with a distinct lack of Christian charity; 'God must have made a mistake in creating them.' Packed into this small area were shipyards, a glass factory and, to counter the influence of the pubs, a chapel. Of the 160 children on the roll of the local school in 1930, 100 of them shared the same surname: Lammins. In that same year the *East End News* provided another lurid description: 'On winter nights [the children] say to their mothers "Can we have a candle?" "Why?" ask the mothers. "To look at the rats" they reply.' Such were the people, according to press accounts at least, of Orchard Place.

My first visit to this part of the parish had been only partially successful. The developers had bought up the whole area and on the Good Luck Hope, the northern of the two peninsulas, the development of 'City Island' was already under way. The tongue of land between loops of the Lea had been stripped of housing, warehousing and its old vegetable oil factory, and was closed to public access as the pile drivers arrived to pound it into a new era. And so I returned when the site was nearing completion, walking from the tip of the 'tongue', where a new footbridge now linked it across the river to Canning Town, down to its southern, Thames-side edge. The new, high blocks were each of a different shape and size and colour, and all set at different angles. The effect was as if a giant box of children's building bricks had been emptied haphazardly onto the site.

At their centre was a garden, planted in the now fashionable faux-wild style. On the plans this had been 'Orchard Square', but the developers had changed their minds on any such cultural resonance and renamed it Botanic Place. I was investigating the tree planting of the garden (some ginkgos and tulip trees, a Scots pine, an exotic species of oak) and regretting the absence of apples, when I was approached by a uniformed security guard asking me what I was doing. Such is the nature of the new privately owned public space. In fact, he was a personable man and we fell into conversation about the nature of the development. I had once been told, when visiting the 'Sales Suite', that the colour of each block represented an aspect of the area's history. He had a vague idea that this was something to do with the goods that had once been traded through the nearby docks and we speculated for some time on what those particular associations might be. The dark orange of Java House, it was a reasonable supposition, represented coffee, whilst the blue of Hercules House, he had heard, was the sea. The white of another block, I guessed, might stand for sugar, but after that, with the brown, the tan, the black and the grey, we ran out of ideas; or possibly of interest. If this was history, I thought to myself, it was of an abstruse, and abstracted, kind.

The history of the area was clearly something he had his own views on, telling me that it had once been populated with 'inbreds'. But now this development was, he said, attracting a better sort of people and would, in his view, become the 'Mayfair of the East End'. He was clearly a company man through and through. Later I checked the average price of a house in Mayfair and found that it now stood at £2,498,043. Clearly there would be no room for the inbreds.

I had progressed only a few more yards after this conversation when I came across another uniformed worker. He was carrying a canister and spraying the edges of the lawns and paths and I thought, at first, that he was applying some sort of herbicide. When I asked him about it, he informed me that it was actually a fox deterrent. I asked him why the foxes needed deterring. He shrugged his shoulders and replied, 'They poo everywhere, don't they?' After months of walking the streets of Poplar I have to say that the presence of large amounts of fox poo littering the highways and byways was something that had completely passed me by. The irony of this treatment was that the hoardings that surrounded the uncompleted parts of the site proudly boasted their environmental credentials. For several hundred yards these hoardings bore a continuous life-size frieze of a beautiful birch wood, a sort of IKEA version of nature that was entirely clean and wholesome and lacking the problem of fox poo. Nature, to paraphrase that old cliché about communism, is all very well in theory, it just doesn't work out in practice.

It was refreshing to reach the still undeveloped southern peninsula, for the moment still called Orchard Place, where history, natural history and community had yet to be simultaneously eliminated. Its unsprayed pavements and its unregulated spaces supported flowering sow thistles and yellow Oxford ragwort, cushions of grimmia moss and the little flowers of gallant soldiers with their gap-toothed smile. Sallow shrubs grew over warehouse walls and bushes of buddleia flowered riotously, unaware that their days, like those of the Lammins' were numbered.

As for the apples and cherries, they are back in Poplar but of a completely different kind; ornamental species planted for their flowers or their bitter but brightly coloured fruit. They grow on streets and estates, in small front gardens, in churchyards, in playgrounds and parks. There is even one, presumably bird-sown, growing ten feet from the ground on a pediment on the old St. Michael's Church.

You can mark the year by them. They start their flowering early with the thin blossoming of the wispy winter cherry, struggling to make an impression against cold winds and the iron-grey sky and somehow succeeding in emphasising the bleakness of the season. But in April and May comes the great explosion of pink and white blossom; on the cherry-plum and the almond, on the weeping cherry and the upright 'spire' on the confusing multitude of Japanese forms. But the season is too soon over and then the blossom falls in masses, forming drifts across the pavements like a heavy and unseasonal snow. For the rest of the year it is their bark that remains the main attraction, burnished and red, shining as if the street sweepers had an additional duty of polishing it as they passed. The foliage, by contrast, can be rather drab, especially in our strange enthusiasm for purple-leaved varieties such as the frequently planted Pissard Plum. It stands in ordered ranks on our municipal open spaces, a tree dismissed by Alan Mitchell in his *Trees of Britain and Northern Europe*, as 'a muddy brown twiggy mess'.

There are ornamental apples too, the crab apple species, though they are not as numerous as the cherries. Among them I had found the red-fruited John Downie, the bright yellow Golden Hornet, the Japanese and the Siberian crab, the pendulous Magdeburg and the narrow-crowned Pillar apple. Of the edible apples that once stood in ranks in the local orchards, I found only two. One of these stood next to St. Nicholas' Church, the small church that serves the community of the Aberfeldy estate and one of the two surviving parish churches. Here, the tree stands pressed up against the church window on one side and, on the other, leaning out over the scruffy and often uncut lawn that is all there is of a churchyard, the bare ground beneath it covered with violets in the spring. It is a rather untidy tree but it bears a mass of white blossom that ripens into outsize fruit. Did the first vicar, or the architect, or the gardener, who planted it, know just how appropriate a choice this was? For the apple was once one of the most sacred trees in England. In his *Notes from Walnut Tree Farm*, Roger Deakin asks, 'Why don't vicars plant orchards in their churchyards? … The apple is such a symbol of continuing life, of eternity, of completeness and goodness. Surely it is the perfect church-yard tree?' The clergy of Suffolk may have disappointed him but here in Poplar we have, in a small way, stepped up to the mark.

The apple has been in cultivation in England since Neolithic times and probably already then had cultic associations. According to Robert Graves in *The White Goddess*, the Celtic Druids regarded it as the symbol of consummation. It was one of the 'seven sacred trees of the grove' and so significant that the penalty for illicitly felling it was death – a penalty reserved for this tree and the hazel alone. Across much of Europe it was a symbol for immor-tality: cut an apple across the middle and the arrangement of the pips around the core reveals a five-pointed star, the ancient symbol for eternal life. The apple runs as a theme through English folklore, occurring even in our great Arthurian legend. Avalon, the place where Excalibur was forged and where our 'once and future king' was to journey after receiving the mortal wound from Mordred, is a transliteration of the word 'Attalon'. It was, literally, 'the island of apple trees' to which Arthur travelled to make his recovery and where, asleep or awake, he awaits his recall at his country's darkest hour.

With this back-story, the role of the 'apple' in the story of Adam and Eve takes on a new significance. The apple appears just three times in the Old Testament, not including a further three references to the 'apple of one's eye', an expression which, despite its entry into common parlance, arises from a mistranslation of the Hebrew word for pupil. Perhaps the most affecting reference is in the erotic 'Song of Solomon', where sweet fruits take on an almost sexual significance:

> *Sustain me with raisins*
> *refresh me with apples;*
> *for I am faint with love.*

Where the apple does not appear, however, is in the fateful events in the Garden of Eden. It is with the fruit of the 'tree of knowledge of good and evil' that Eve is tempted by the serpent. Nonetheless, in story and art, it has become the apple. I cannot help but see in this the influence of its long and magical association upon the workings of the English imagination.

Now and again, like the rising flints, this influence reasserts itself. The apple is often thought of in connection with Halloween and with games such as apple bobbing played at this time of year. Even in my rigidly fundamentalist childhood we plunged our faces into bowls of cold water whilst struggling to grab an impossibly slippery apple in our teeth. I continued to play the game with my own children, until they determined themselves too mature for such pursuits. Whilst thinking we were playing at innocent childhood games, we were, it seems, revisiting the ancient rites; invoking the sacred tree on this most magical night of the year.

The main celebration of the apple was not, however, at Halloween but at Christmas and, in particular, Twelfth Night. This was the time for the annual practice of 'wassailing' the apple tree. The company would gather with their lanterns in the orchard, singing to the trees, drinking their health and pouring hot cider over their roots:

> *Old apple tree we wassail thee, and hoping thou wilt bear*
> *For the Lord doth know, where we shall be, till apples come*
> *next year.*

Cider-soaked toast would then be placed in the branches for the guardian birds and, to scare away the evil spirits, the ceremony would end with the raising of a great howl and, in later centuries, with the firing of guns into the air.

Perhaps people once gathered like this in the orchards of Poplar and South Bromley, singing and toasting and celebrating the trees. It seemed to me high time that the spirit, at least, was reinvoked. But I decided against wassailing. The howling at night, and the discharging of firearms, might be misinterpreted on our local streets. I settled instead for scrumping. Setting out, one Saturday morning, with my two youngest sons and a couple of step ladders, we climbed and shook the local crab apples, collecting the fruit in plastic bags and baskets. It would look less suspicious, I reasoned, if done in broad daylight, and though a police car did go screaming past, it seemed to have more serious offences in mind. We struggled home with our load and chopped and boiled and strained and bottled to a recipe for crab apple jelly. 'A Poplar Parish product,' we described it on the labels, and coloured them with felt tips for good measure. I hadn't really been sure that the recipe would work with our ornamental crabs, but the result was pleasant enough, making a fine and rosy pink accompaniment for meat and cheese. I hope the various friends who received it for Christmas felt as positively about it.

This was my first act of resistance to the obliteration of the local apple and it fired me up for more. Gathering apples from the St. Nicholas' Church garden tree, I brought them home to make cider. The simple fact that I lacked a press meant that I settled instead for an apple wine. The crop was chopped and simmered and strained and put into a bucket for its first fierce fermentation. Then I poured it into demijohns, in order to undergo the rest of the slow process that would, miraculously, turn a cloudy fruit water into wine. I was encouraged by the fact that a 2nd-century Roman court physician had prescribed apple wine as a cure for almost every ailment and that our subsequent drinking could thereby be excused as an entirely medicinal process. My enthusiasm must have waned over the long months it took for the wine to be ready and I completely forgot that I was in the process of subverting the modern state. The demijohns gathered dust in a corner of the kitchen and soon became so much a part of the domestic landscape as to be invisible.

It was when a visiting friend pointed them out to me that I was finally fired into action. Gareth happened to be en route to a funeral but I hoped that in enlisting his assistance I might be providing some sort of occupational therapy.

Together we cleaned my disturbingly large collection of empty wine bottles, Gareth even inventing a new way of drying them with the imaginative help of a hair dryer. The wine looked a little cloudy as we siphoned it from the demijohns into the newly coiffured bottles, so we decided to think of it as a rosé. Then we sat down for the tasting.

Given the length of time I had left the liquid sitting on the 'must', it was more pleasant than I had anticipated. 'Vibrant, warm and rich,' wrote Gareth in his tasting notes on the back of an envelope. 'With a hint of stewed apples,' I added on mine. These were simple offerings, however, and the more we sampled, the more expansive our comments became. After a couple more glasses Gareth got hints of deckchairs on a country house lawn on a sunny summer afternoon. I, meanwhile, with that slight mustiness in mind, had already gone through the metaphorical French windows and was rummaging about some leather-bound books in the library. But by now it was possibly more than a 'tasting' and my wife returning home, like the person from Porlock, broke the spell. 'It tastes,' she told us, 'like home-made scrumpy. Only worse.'

Walking on Peckham Rye at the age of ten, William Blake had his first encounter with angels. He had seen them in a mulberry tree, their 'bright angelic wings bespangling every bough with stars'. Reading Eileen Baillie's book about our vicarage, I had come across an intriguing sugges-tion that mulberries might once have grown not just in Peckham but in Poplar, too. There has been a traditional association between mulberries and the East End and, with this in mind, I set out to investigate the possibility of a more local connection. I did not get a glimpse of angels, though I would very much have liked one, but I did learn that almost every aspect of the mulberry is surrounded with myth.

We do not know, to begin with, how it actually got here. Some accounts attribute its arrival to the Romans, but the Romans are credited with the introduction of a suspiciously substantial portion of our flora and fauna. Other accounts give a later date. The oldest surviving tree in this country was planted in the reign of Elizabeth I, who had her own mulberry garden at her palace in Greenwich. Despite this, others anachronistically attribute its arrival to her successor, James I.

Some of the myth-making around the mulberry is the fault of the tree itself, or at least, of its appearance. The common, or black, mulberry, *Morus nigra*, is an attractive small tree with a low broad dome. Its variable leaves, sometimes heart-shaped, sometimes three-lobed, are always noticeably toothed around the edges and rough and hairy to the touch. The fruit is helpfully distinctive: green in the summer, turning to orange and eventually to a deep blackish-red, like a large and pendulous blackberry. Even when the fruits are no longer on the tree you can detect their previous presence by the purple staining on the ground around them. Their impact on surrounding pavements has occasionally led some antiseptic councils to call for their removal.

It is a relatively fast-growing and short-lived tree, with a life expectancy said to average about 300 years, but it takes on, whilst still quite young, various aspects of an arthritic old age. The bark, dark orange in colour, develops stringy fissures, bosses and sprouting burs and the whole tree will sometimes lean to one side, even becoming completely recumbent, as though too tired to hold itself upright any longer. And here is the cause of the confusion; masquerading as venerable elders, these middle-aged trees become surrounded with stories of supposed antiquity. Just as every old house in England was once slept in by Elizabeth I, or provided a hunting lodge for Henry VIII, so every mulberry must have some interesting or aristocratic ancestral connection. A tree in the Archdeacon's garden at Canterbury is claimed as the place where the knights who murdered Thomas Becket wiped their blades as they fled the cathedral; a fact that would make it a remarkable 850 years old. And here is Henry Irving, speaking confidently about the mulberry in his 1910 book on *How to Know the Trees*:

> *Its associations are aristocratic. The presence of a mulberry on the lawn, so it is said, is itself a patent of nobility. The tree is usually in grounds that are, or have been, attached to 'stately homes'. Specimens survive from far away times, venerable with age and reminiscent of courtly dignity. Some of those, as at Syon House, date back to pre-Reformation times, marking the site of some ancient monastic institution long since put to other uses. Many that still survive were planted in the reign of James I.*

Here is James I cropping up again. He provides the most oft-repeated story about the mulberry. You will hear it on tree walks and read it in reputable books and I have even been known to repeat it myself. It goes something like this: jealous of the wealth of the continental silk industry, James was desperate to establish a British equivalent. To do so he encouraged the import of mulberry trees, the tree on whose leaf the silkworm feeds, overlooking the fact that there are two species of mulberry. As well as the black mulberry there is, in cultivation on the continent, a white mulberry, *Morus alba*, also deriving its name from the colour of its fruit. James, according to the story, had not realised that the silkworm will feed only on the leaves of the white mulberry. Thus, in his haste, or his ignorance, or perhaps as a result of a deliberate deception by the French, he introduced the wrong tree, initiating an expensive and futile project that was doomed by his foolishness to failure. The only problem with this otherwise engaging tale is that it almost certainly isn't true.

I am not well known for rehabilitating the royal reputation, especially one as autocratic as James, but it was the very frequency with which I heard this tale that led me to begin to suspect it. Besides, it does not fit with what we know of James as a man. He was grossly vulgar. He suffered from paranoia. He was profligate and autocratic and he repeatedly made unwise choices for preferment, based on the intense crushes he developed for various members of his male circle. But he was far from stupid. Learned, enquiring and intellectual, he was, according to many accounts, the most intelligent king we ever had. It was the combination of these two sides of his character, his intelligence and his foibles, that led to him being described as 'the wisest fool in Christendom'. Here, therefore, was another reason that the story of the mistaken mulberry might merit at least a little more investigation.

It was the returning Crusaders who were credited with introducing silk production to Western Europe. It first took root in the wealthy Italian city-states and spread from there into France, under the sponsorship of Louis XII. By the middle of the 16th century, Lyon had become the capital of the European silk trade, with that one city eventually supporting more than 14,000 looms. It was some of these French weavers who were to form the basis of an English industry. The long sequence of bitter civil wars between Protestant and Catholic factions in France had led, in 1572, to the notorious St. Bartholomew's Day massacre when up to 30,000 Protestants were slaughtered in Paris and other major cities, including the silk-weaving centre of Lyon. Though it would be more than another hundred years before the great diaspora of the Huguenots, as the French Protestants were rather obliquely known, many of them were already leaving the country and settling elsewhere – and taking their skills with them.

The real difficulty with the establishment of an English industry was the uncertainty of the supply of raw silk. Imported as it was from continental Europe, it remained vulnerable to both political interference and to price fluctuations, a fact that was highlighted in 1600 when the Italian mulberry crop failed. It was only three years after this that James VI of Scotland ascended to the English throne, where he took on the title of James I. He determined to make the establishment of a local silk industry a priority by encouraging the planting of mulberry trees and the local rearing of silkworms. In 1607 he granted a licence to a William

Stallenge to produce a manual on the subject, a sort of early
'Teach Yourself' book. The *Instructions for the Planting and
Increase of Mulberry Trees and the Breeding of Silkworms and the
Making of Silk* came out as a two-page pamphlet; the title,
therefore, being not much shorter than the contents.

At the same time Stallenge was licensed to import
mulberry seeds and to plant them 'anywhere in the
country'. Further orders were issued to the Lord-Lieu-
tenants of the Counties, and to Justices of the Peace, to
encourage the planting of mulberry trees in their areas and
to set an example by growing them themselves. Towards
this end, 10,000 mulberry plants were ordered and efforts
made to distribute them in every county. Take-up varied
across the country and it was, of course, the aristocracy
who were primarily involved; major landowners seeking
to curry favour with the new regime, or peers of the realm
preparing for a possible royal visit. It seems highly likely that
in this nationwide distribution of mulberries to the landed
gentry we have the origin of the aristocratic association still
attached to the mulberry today.

The associations have long outlived the trees. As far as
we know, only one of these Jacobean mulberries survives;
a many-stemmed and wide-spreading specimen in front of
Charlton House in south-east London. It is now one of the
official 'Great Trees of London'. Though the vast majority
of these mulberries are lost, their legacy survives in the fact
that one of the main cultivars of the mulberry now on the
market is known as the 'King James'.

James was indeed personally involved in the planting
project, paying Stallenge a further sum to establish a
mulberry garden on a site close to his palace in Westminster.

Though the plantation was established in 1609, investors in the project had still received no dividend by 1613. This is hardly surprising since it would inevitably take some years before the newly planted trees could produce a reasonable supply of leaves. Nonetheless an impatient public had already begun to turn against the scheme. Though it struggled on for a few more years, it could not long survive the death of the king, its patron, in 1625. Just a few years later it was abandoned and the plantation turned into a pleasure ground known as the Mulberry Gardens. These too were to eventually disappear beneath the development of another and newer royal residence: Buckingham Palace. It is another form of continuity that the modern palace gardens now house the National Collection of Mulberries.

The failure of the Westminster plantation was matched by the failure of the scheme nationally. Much of this was due to the difficulty of competing with a long-established and well experienced continental industry, and with the much lower labour costs in France. Neither does there seem to have been a proper appreciation of the length of time it would take for a profitable industry to become established and therefore of what sort of long-term investment would be needed. The market wanted quick returns and the fact that a mulberry tree must reach at least six feet before it can provide a sustainable crop seems to have gone unnoticed, even in Stallenge's *Instructions*. Meanwhile the unprofitable trees were tying up land that could be making money from faster and more customary crops.

Perhaps William Stallenge was never a good choice of advocate for the scheme. He had enjoyed a successful career as a merchant, even being used during some of his foreign trading trips to collect information for the government; to spy, in effect. He had served for a time as the MP for his native town of Plymouth and had also worked there for Francis Drake, who described him as 'both honest and discreet'. But there is no evidence that he had any experience in horticulture, or in sericulture, or was otherwise equipped to promote the mulberry project. Even his pamphlet, it turns out, was not his own work, but the translation of an existing French publication.

The attempt to establish an English silk industry had failed. But how much can this be put down to James choosing the 'wrong' tree? It is not, in fact, true, as the story has it, that silkworms will feed only on the leaves of the white mulberry. They will feed on both mulberries and on a variety of other plants as well. Crucially, both of the mulberries produce the coagulating milky juice that gives strength to the fine filaments of silk spun by the silk moth caterpillar. There is evidence that the entire Italian silk industry was founded on the black mulberry and that it was used there till around 1434, when the white mulberry was introduced from the eastern Mediterranean. James himself had some success with the black mulberry and it is recorded that nine pounds of silk were spun from the cocoons of his own worms – silk that was then used to make a dress for the Queen.

The real question seems to have been not to do with which leaves the silkworm would feed on but which of them produced the best silk. Though most of the continent was using the white mulberry by the 16th century, the subject was clearly still open to debate and was to remain so for some time to come. Over 150 years later the learned pages of *The Transactions of the Society Instituted at London for the Encouragement of Arts, Manufacture and Commerce* were still carrying a correspondence on the relative merits of the two mulberries and reporting the results of trials in which the worms were fed on black or white mulberry or on lettuce. Both trees had their proponents, as did the lettuce, but the consensus that gradually emerged was that silk produced from worms fed on the black mulberry was of a lower quality. Being of an uneven thickness, it was more liable to break when wound and, whilst suitable for spinning the coarser thread used by the early silk knitters, it was increasingly less so for the finer clothes that were later to come into fashion.

At the time that James was promoting the planting of mulberry trees this was still a matter for debate, but there is a further factor which seems to have been largely ignored, and which would have influenced James. It is the matter of the English climate. The white mulberry is a far more tender tree than the black and barely hardy in this country. Sensitive to frost, wind and cold, it remains rare in Britain to this day and confined to a few sheltered southern sites. Even more to the point, Britain was at this time in the grip of the colder climatic conditions known as the 'little ice age'. It was an era of bitter winters with the Thames freezing thickly, not just in London but right out into the North Sea. Indeed, it was only a year after James began work on his mulberry plantation that the first of the famous Frost Fairs was held on the frozen river. It is almost certain, therefore, that had he introduced the white mulberry it would not have survived even that first winter. It was the introduction of the white mulberry that would have been a mistake. The choice of the black, less fine in its product perhaps, but more hardy, was entirely appropriate for the time. James I ran a dissolute and scandal-ridden court. He was in constant dispute with parliament, he was obsessed with witchcraft, and he died a toothless drunk. But on the charge of masterminding a great mulberry mix-up, I find him acquitted.

But does it actually matter; the gullibility or otherwise of a Stuart monarch, the true story of the mulberry and how it got here, or, indeed, this whole line of historic enquiry? What had begun as an intriguing but possibly peripheral investigation had, by now, become a more substantial piece of detective work and I was wondering if I might not be wandering too far from my purpose. I found these intersections of social and natural history fascinating, however; adding dimensions to the story of who and what we are. Just as we have increasingly lost a sense of our relationship to other species, and to the wider environment to which we belong, so too, it seems to me, we have become increasingly unaware of our place in the flow of time. As my Orchard Place experience had demonstrated, the two are linked, and can be simultaneously lost. Without our stories we can become abstractions in a virtual world, floating in an eternal present that is not so much 'here and now' as 'now and nowhere'. As a saying from the Sioux nation puts it, 'A people without history is like wind on buffalo grass.'

Perhaps then, to dig into history as well as into natural history, was an act of recovery, of putting back together pieces of the stories that form and frame us and the places where we live. Besides, the history of the English mulberry was just a forerunner to the question of when and where, and whether, it had ever had a place in Poplar.

The long history of struggle between the Protestant and Catholic factions in France had come to a resolution of sorts in 1685 when Louis XIV passed the Edict of Fontainbleu, making Protestantism illegal. Up to a million Huguenots fled the country, some to neighbouring Protestant lands, some as far afield as the Cape Colony or the English colonies in North America. In England itself they were welcomed and offered financial support to help them settle. They did so in several different parts of the country. It was to here in east London that the silk weavers came, many of them settling in the area around Spitalfields. Their typical wooden-shuttered houses survive here in tall terraces that form dark canyons of the narrow streets and it is the general belief locally that they planted mulberry trees in their gardens to support them in their trade.

Writing his history of the Huguenots in 1867, Samuel Smiles states that 'there are still some of their mulberry trees to be seen in the gardens near Spital Square'. For this, and other sites, supporting evidence was hard to find but 'mulberry' names continue to dot the East End. There is a Mulberry Street, a Mulberry Place, a Mulberry School and a Mulberry House. Previously there was also a Mulberry Court, two Mulberry Tree pubs and a Mulberry Gardens.

And then there was Eileen Baillie's book, which suggested there had been a Mulberry Street in Poplar as well. Her account remained the best clue I had so far come across that mulberries once grew here. 'In the 18th century,' she wrote, 'my mother's family had owned a large mulberry garden – demanded by the silkworm industry – almost on the spot where we then lived; and Mulberry Street and Dewberry Street commemorated their existence within a stone's throw of the vicarage.' The maps of that period, principally John Rocque's map of 1754, seemed to support her suggestion, showing 'plantations' on the site of the house. The fact that they are labelled as such, rather than as 'orchard' or 'cherry orchard', I thought, might be significant; but I had a problem with her street names.

Of the Mulberry Street said to stand just a stone's throw from the vicarage, I could find no evidence. The name did not appear in the rates books of the period and the nearest similar name, a Mulberry Tree Row, was more than three-quarters of a mile away. It would have made a very significant throw. There was, and still is, a Dewberry Street. It runs just yards from the vicarage, lined with post-war, low-rise, yellow-brick blocks on one side, and opening onto the municipal flatness of Jolly's Green on the other. As far as I was concerned, however, a dewberry was a blackberry and not a mulberry at all.

Even the oldest of dictionaries that the municipal archives could offer seemed to confirm this view. The *Oxford English Dictionary* was even more specific, a dewberry being 'a low growing, procumbent species of blackberry, its black fruit having a bluish bloom'. I was curious, however, that when the *OED* went on to cite the earliest written uses of the word, two of the references mentioned mulberry and dewberry in the same literary breath. The first of these came from one of those early self-help health manuals that were to provide a radical alternative to the high fees charged by the physicians of the time. According to Moufet and Benet's *Health's*

Improver, written in 1655, 'when mulberries cannot be gotten' – for the various remedies for which they are recommended – 'blackberries or dewberries may supply their room.'

The second reference took me further. It came from Shakespeare. In the third Act of *A Midsummer Night's Dream*, the Queen of the Fairies is woken from her enchanted sleep by the singing of Bottom, who is now mockingly adorned with an ass' head. With Oberon's love potion secreted in her eyes, Titania falls deliriously in love with this strange apparition:

> *I pray thee, gentle mortal, sing again:*
> *Mine ear is much enamoured of thy note:*
> *So is mine eye enthralled to thy shape;*
> *And thy fair virtue's force perforce doth move me*
> *On the first view to say, to swear I love thee.*

In a beautiful speech, full of natural detail, she instructs her attendant fairies, Peaseblossom, Cobweb, Moth and Mustardseed, to wait upon him:

> *Be kind and courteous to this gentleman;*
> *Hop in his walks and gambol in his eyes;*
> *Feed him with apricocks and dewberries,*
> *With purple grapes, green figs, and mulberries;*
> *The honey-bags steal from the humble-bees,*
> *And for night-tapers crop their waxen thighs,*
> *And light them at the fiery glow-worms' eyes,*
> *To have my love to bed, and to arise;*
> *And pluck the wings from painted butterflies*
> *To fan the moonbeams from his sleeping eyes.*

Nod to him, elves, and do him courtesies.

There was a copy of the play on our shelves and, since my wife had once been a student of English, it contained a learned commentary. In these accompanying notes was another link. 'Dewberries,' I was informed, are, 'normally blackberries but the context has been thought to require a cultivated fruit, like the others.' Among the other suggestions put forward was one by James Halliwell, a Shakespearian commentator from the 1850s, who thought it might refer to the 'dwarf mulberry', 'still called … dewberry by the Warwickshire peasantry, and plentiful in lanes near Stratford'. Whether Shakespeare had meant 'mulberry' by 'dewberry' or not, the 'Warwickshire peasantry' that he had once moved amongst had seemingly conflated the two names and here was at least a hint that my own Dewberry Street might be a reference to the presence of mulberries.

By one of those strange chances that seem to attend a detailed attention to any particular subject, we had family tickets, long since booked, for a performance of the play the very next day and thus it was that on a distinctly unsummery Saturday afternoon, we made our way to the West End and the Noël Coward Theatre. Since this was a notably starry performance, including Sheridan Smith, as a rather lascivious Titania, and David Walliams, as a distinctly camp but bisexual Bottom, we had taken the whole family. The fairies were played as 1970s' hippies, though more like hippies from an Austin Powers movie than any I had met in my own very personal experience of the era. The set was suitably shadowy for its night-time forest setting, and dominated by a huge full moon, and I was looking forward to hearing the mulberry words 'live' and in their appropriate context. In an attempt to make this a participative experience, I had primed the boys – 'bribed' might be a better word – to listen out and alert me when they appeared. They did so, less ostentatiously than I had begun to fear, and I went home the exorbitant price of two West End bubble teas the poorer. My wife had rather smugly gone one better and picked up a second reference towards the end of the play, but having once been an English student that is only to be expected and she didn't get a prize.

Whilst the peasantry walking those Warwickshire lanes near Stratford were using 'dewberry' and 'mulberry' synonymously, those in other parts of the country were, it turned out, similarly conflating the 'blackberry' and the 'mulberry'. In his magnificent book *The Englishman's Flora*, Geoffrey Grigson lists mulberry as a local name for the blackberry in both Norfolk and Suffolk, and this is supported by G.E. Evans in 'Aspects of Oral Tradition', an article in the journal *Folk Life* (Volume 7, Issue 1, 1969). According to this, some East Anglian countrymen still used the word mulberry for a blackberry, particularly one with a large berry. In earlier times this seems to have been common, with the practice of gathering blackberries referred to as 'going a-mulberrying'. Only 'people of substance' could afford a mulberry tree and ordinary people therefore made ironical reference to the blackberry as the 'poor man's mulberry'. It is this botanical equivalent of the English class system that seems to unite these usages, from the 1655 reference in *Health's Improver* through to East Anglia in the present day. The mulberry, not just expensive but with all its aristocratic associations, is the rich man's tree. The blackberry, the free wild bramble of the hedgerow, is the poor man's substitute. And the dewberry, bearing the largest berry of all the bramble bushes, is the blackberry species that most resembles the mulberry.

If 'going a-mulberrying' was gathering blackberries, what might the reason be for going 'round and round the mulberry bush'? The first written reference to the children's song 'Here we go round the mulberry bush' comes as late as the mid-19th century, though its origins are probably much earlier. Of the several available explanations for the rhyme, the one that is now most widely cited is that it relates to prisoners at Wakefield Prison. In an account that is repeated even on the prison's own website, there was a mulberry tree growing at the centre of the prison yard and it was the prisoners, walking round and round it in their daily exercise hour, who first invented and intoned the song.

I find this story unconvincing in a number of ways and it is, I would suggest, another myth of the mulberry. Whilst it fits the modern fad that every innocent nursery rhyme must conceal a story of death, disease or destitution, the fact remains that the mulberry grows as a tree and not a bush, and it requires a rather unlikely imaginative leap to convert the dismal daily trudging of convicts into this gay childhood tune, even if it was meant in irony. More likely, and more steeped in that irony, would be that the prisoners had mockingly adopted a song that was already in existence. The rhyme is first recorded in *Popular Rhymes and Nursery Rhymes*, compiled by the appropriately named James Orchard Halliwell-Phillips in 1849 (the same 'Halliwell', coincidentally, who had annotated

Shakespeare with the note about the Stratford peasantry). He goes on to mention another, and possibly earlier, version of the song with the lyric, 'Here we go round the bramble bush'. In other words, the blackberry.

Perambulating the bramble, rather than the mulberry, would certainly make more sense. A common country cure for a variety of ailments, was to walk around a bramble bush a certain number of times at a certain time of day. Three times a week would cure rickets in Wales; three mornings at sunrise would deal with boils in Dorset; nine times round the bush would banish blackheads in Cornwall; and a complicated formula involving a stem rooted at both ends would sort out whooping cough in Staffordshire.

Pre-dating the Wakefield Prison usage, therefore, is the suggestion of an ancient and widespread curative rhyme, in the suitably repetitive form of a spell. The word bramble is replaced in some local dialect versions by mulberry and, perhaps on publication of the song, it is this version that gradually gains currency. It is worth noting that the true mulberry was itself widely used, not for its own powers but as a syrup for flavouring or colouring other cures, and therefore appeared in a wide variety of medicines. Here again, the free wild blackberry, with its many curative powers, becomes the 'poor man's mulberry'.

Despite my initial scepticism, the name of Dewberry Street might well be evidence of the existence of a local mulberry plantation. If this is the case, it is likely that whatever the original purpose of the plantation, its eventual use would have been not the supply of leaves for the silkworm trade but that of fruit for the London markets, for throughout this period mulberries remained highly prized and consistently sold for a good price in the capital. Conclusive or not, it becomes possible to imagine a time when groves of leaning, red-barked mulberries stood on the site of our yellow-brick estates and our flat, dull and litter-flecked park; and when crates of mulberries joined those of apples and cherries on the carts conveying our local produce into London.

Names can, however, prove deceptive and sometimes the most obvious association can be the wrong one. I found this for myself when investigating the origin of Mulberry Place in the south-east corner of the parish, but it was to lead to a story that was, in its own way, just as fascinating.

Mulberry Place sits on the infilled site of the old East India Dock. It is one of those large developments that sit uneasily between the public and the private realms and aren't really at home in either. Disturbing, alien and uncomfortable, it is a grid of straight, short streets with faux canals set between postmodern blocks of concrete, glass and steel. Even the lake, installed on a small part of the old basin, adds emphasis to the general greyness rather than assisting in its relief. It is home to one of the least hospitable town halls in London as well as to the blacked out high-security block through which most of our European emails are routed. It is surrounded on two sides by the old brick walls of the dock and though they were built to be forbidding, time and familiarity has softened them and, in contrast with the rest of the development, they have become its most human feature. It was within these dock walls that the word 'mulberry' once took on quite a different connotation.

When the tide of the Second World War finally began to turn, and the Allies to plan their massive assault on the European mainland, one of the biggest problems they faced was logistical. How, after the initial landings, could they supply and reinforce the largest and most complex military operation ever undertaken – with food and fuel, arms and ammunition, transport and heavy machinery, with tanks, field guns and all the many other needs of a massive, moving army? The obvious answer was to secure a French or Belgian deep-water port, but these were frighteningly well fortified and an earlier raid on Dieppe had proved disastrous and costly.

It was then that a number of engineers, including Major W.J. Hodge, a peacetime officer from the Port of London Authority and now serving at the War Office, came up with another idea. If the Allies couldn't capture a port then they should build one of their own: a harbour, not on shore but floating just off it. It was a madcap scheme of just the sort that would appeal to Churchill and, armed with a film of a floating pier, he attended a conference in Ottawa in the autumn of 1943 where he managed to convince Roosevelt of its merits. He gave orders for the go-ahead in characteristic fashion: 'Don't argue the matter. The difficulties will argue for themselves.'

Put simply, the scheme was to erect an off-shore floating platform anchored to the sea bottom but rising and falling with the tides on a system of pylons. The ships would be unloaded there and their cargoes reach the shore along a long, floating roadway of linked and anchored sections. But to be a harbour in the proper sense it needed protection;

some bulwark against the North Sea, its bitter winds and high waves, and its many tempestuous storms. Initially, a flotilla of old ships, code-named 'gooseberries', were to be sailed down from a gathering point in Scotland and scuttled to form a protective line. Following this, a large number of massive and specially constructed watertight chambers, or caissons, would be sunk on the sea bottom and built up to form a 'harbour' wall. Though each of these components had its own designation, the overall concept was code-named 'Mulberry'.

There were, in fact, two of these mulberry harbours. Mulberry A would be assembled by the Americans off the Omaha beach-head, Mulberry B by the British off the coast at Arromanches. The huge, complex and highly secret task of constructing all the constituent parts was carried out at sites across southern England. It had been envisaged that the caissons would be built in dry docks but insufficient of these were available. Thus it was that in the heart of Poplar, the East India Docks were drained for the first time since their construction.

It was uncertain, at the time, whether the old walls, unexposed since Victorian times, would collapse, but they held and the emptied basin was rapidly lined with bomb rubble. To ensure sufficient capacity, additional sites had to be opened at the Rotherhithe Docks and in hastily dug basins along the Thames estuary. These were separated from the river by earthen banks which would need to be breached at the appropriate time. But the East India Docks remained the heart of the operation.

Here, in full view of thousands but successfully kept secret as to intent, 200 caissons were constructed with a total weight of over a million tons; enough to stretch for eight and a quarter miles. To undertake this work, a team of 16,000 dockers and other workers had been assembled and housed in specially created camps where, according to contemporary accounts, 'beer was easier to get than drinking water'. But despite (or perhaps because of) this, work went on uninterrupted for twenty-four hours a day during a period of unremitting air attacks, heavy bombardment and enemy surveillance. So important was the work that Churchill himself visited the East India Dock in February 1944. He was followed, not long after, by General, later Field Marshal, Montgomery, who addressed the assembled workers. 'My theme was the same as to the railway men,' he later wrote, 'that there is a job to do and together we will do it.' And not only did they do it, but they did it rapidly, the first six miles of caissons being completed in just six months.

The caissons were given their own code name: Phoenix. They were designed to be built of steel but since this was in short supply and prioritised for other war work, concrete was used instead. They were hollow inside so that they could be flooded and sunk to the sea floor or pumped and refloated, as required. As if the high-speed construction work was not difficult enough, it was followed by the task of getting the caissons into position at exactly the right moment during the landings. At the appropriate time, the dock was refilled and the caissons manoeuvred into the river. Tugs then towed them down the Thames to join others that had been temporarily sunk for concealment at sites off the British coast. Equipped with temporary crew quarters and fitted with Bofors guns for defence against air attack, the whole flotilla was towed, some for over a hundred miles, across the Channel to designated positions off the French coast. Here, with fighting still raging on the beaches, with bombardment from the shore and attacks from the air, the work of assembly went on. At the same time troops from the US 'Ghost Army' simulated the installation of a fake Mulberry harbour at another site, using lights at night to draw gunfire away from the real 'Mulberries'.

There was an interesting contrast in the way the British and the American teams went about the task of assembling their respective harbours. The Americans were by far the speedier and were proud to have their harbour completed and in operation some time ahead of the British team. But to achieve this they cut corners, using fewer anchors and links than the slower and more thorough British engineers. The real test was to come just a few weeks later when, on June 19th, the worst storm in living memory hit the French coast. It raged for days, throughout which time a team remained on the caissons, trying to minimise damage or repair it as it happened. Several were to lose their lives in this struggle but when the storm finally subsided the British harbour, despite sustaining damage, was still in use. Mulberry A however had been destroyed beyond redemption. Salvaging its useable parts for Mulberry B, the surviving harbour continued to supply the war effort. Popularly known as 'Port Winston', it continued in active service for eight months, despite having been designed to last for only three. Manned throughout by uniformed London dockers it had, by the end of its working life, landed over 2.5 million men, 500,000 vehicles and four million tons of supplies.

It was the mulberry harbour, probably the greatest triumph of British military engineering, and not the mulberry tree, that gave its name to Mulberry Place. But could the code name have been chosen because of a known connection of the locality with the cultivation of mulberries? Sadly not. The prosaic truth is that wartime code names had no specific significance. They were simply chosen as the next unused item from an official list.

There were no mulberry trees in Mulberry Place; and little else of natural history interest, it seemed. I had explored it thoroughly on my parish perambulations and, with the possible exception of the lake, where I had once seen a common tern diving amongst a shoal of young carp, its collection of saplings and its close-cut lawns, jammed between the office blocks and the old dock wall, seemed a totally sterile setting. I was to return to the site, however, with John Swindells, of the London Natural History Society, and to learn that there was yet another layer of looking.

Examining those seemingly uninteresting lawns more closely, we were to find unexpected treasures; plants that were living their whole lives in miniature. Shaven close to the ground there were species of vetch and oxalis. There were tiny plants of field madder, with neatly-formed flowers a shade of delicate purple-pink. There were buck's-horn plantains, more characteristic of a seaside setting, their tined leaves held flush to the ground. And, most surprisingly, there was a plant of fool's water-cress, a large creeping plant normally but here, though cut down to centimetres, still bearing a tiny umbrella of flowers like a bonsai version of itself.

It was John's suggestion that this diversity of plants was

due to the use of contract grass cutters, spreading seed from site to site on their machinery. For me, however, it fuelled the thought that real wildness is less and less to be found in the once wide-open spaces but down here in the dirt and the detail. It is out in the back garden lawn, it is said, that you can still find species of nematode unknown to science. Or take one spoonful of its soil and you will be holding bacteria enough to outnumber every human being on the planet. It is only at this level, perhaps, that we still have abundance.

Having found no surviving mulberries, either here at Mulberry Place, or anywhere else in the parish, I decided to search them out in other parts of the East End. I cycled to sites described in the various accounts I had been reading without success. There were no longer mulberries in Spital Square, nor the one that had been 'a unique feature', standing outside the schoolmaster's house at St. James's, Ratcliffe, for many years. Nor was there any remaining evidence of a pair of trees that had once stood in Arbour Square Gardens, and where a retired naval officer had given lessons on silk-spinning to local children. It was only a chance conversation with a fellow clerical spouse that eventually led me to the church of St. Paul's in Shadwell.

The church was built beside the old Ratcliffe Highway in 1657 and so many seamen were buried there that it became known as the 'Church of the Sea Captains'. The tree was not in the churchyard itself but in the shady and pleasantly secretive garden of the rectory next door. According to the church website, it had been planted there by Huguenot immigrants, but I took this with a pinch of sea-salt.

It was a garden set about with high, ivy-clad walls against which thick growths of cotoneaster, hawthorn and holly heightened the sense of enclosure. More trees overshadowed a thin lawn of perennially struggling grass and here and there, about the shrubs, were ornamental pots, half-hidden benches, a small stone child squatting under a cherry tree, and an old white dinghy. Garden weeds grew through its rotted base and more ivy was draped like tattered sails across its spars. The mulberry was set in the middle of the lawn, leaning at an angle of forty-five degrees. Perhaps I had become rather over-influenced by the nautical associations of Shadwell for I saw it as one of those sea captains standing on the deck of his ship and leaning bravely into a storm.

The trunk was covered with burs and bulbous knots and swellings, beginning from the very base and looking like outsize warts and boils. Around them were silvery snail trails and faint spider webbing, across a bark that was darkened with age but still sported the distinctive orange patches. A couple of long splits, I was told, provided a home for a wood mouse but it did not emerge for me. Elder and pellitory-of-the-wall were springing up around the base, and tight, dark bunches of tapering, heart-shaped leaves sprouted from even the lowest part of the leaning tree. From halfway up, heavier branching boughs swept upwards and forked into a fretwork of short, fat twigs, the leaning tree being here supported by a wooden A-frame. Resembling a crutch, it gave the captain a rather piratic air.

I was to find another tree by the simple expedient of having an appointment at the London Chest Hospital in Bethnal Green. This had once been the site of Bonner Hall, home of the notorious Protestant-burning bishop, and I found it in the grounds, squeezed between a haphazard assemblage of hospital buildings, outbuildings and prefabricated extensions; the ugly and unplanned accretions that all ageing hospitals seem to collect.

Like every other mulberry it had great claims made on its behalf, and a plaque informed me both that it had been planted by James I and that this was the tree beneath which Bishop Edmund Bonner had hatched his pyrotechnic plots. It therefore credited him with the unlikely achievement of sitting beneath a tree some fifty years before it had been planted. I mentioned this to the gardener, who had come to stand beside me as I examined it, but immediately wished that I hadn't, for he was rightly proud and protective of his mulberry and already concerned about how it would manage when the hospital moved in a few months' time. From him I learned much more; most notably, how it had survived a Second World War bomb that destroyed the nearby hospital chapel. One side of the tree had caught fire and this part of its trunk, reduced to a few precariously balanced spars, still bore visible marks of charring. The other half of the tree had hung on and was still producing an annual crop of fruit. I hope that it will survive the relocation of the entire hospital, and the subsequent redevelopment of the site, and am glad that it has a champion in the gardener.

There was a footnote to the story of the Poplar fruit trees. Searching those old maps for signs of orchards and plantations, I had noticed small compartments marked out along the riverside as 'oziers' or 'ozier grounds'. The ozier, or osier as we would know it today, is *Salix viminalis*, a species of willow that grows in dense stands on damp ground, throwing up tall, straight stems to six metres or more. In keeping with its waterside habit, its elegant leaves are linear; long and pointed with their margins inrolled, a dull green above but an attractive silvery grey below, from their dense covering of short, silky hairs. They were cultivated for generations for the making of lobster pots and eel traps but also for the manufacture of baskets, crates and trugs. At one time as much as seven to eight thousand acres of the Thames valley was devoted to these 'withy beds' and to the growth of osiers.

Part of the value of the plant is its productivity. Cut back to ground level in the winter, the osier can grow as much as forty-five centimetres in a week, or two and a half metres in a season. Their strong but flexible shoots were known as poles and would be cut in the early spring then stood in shallow water until the buds were about to burst, which would signal the final harvesting. The poles might then be simply peeled to produce 'white' rods, or alternatively, boiled before peeling so that they would be stained by their tannins and produce a 'brown' variety. For the traditional trug, larger poles would be used; cleft into thin strips, they would be steamed so that they could be bent to the desired shape and then fitted with a rim made from a harder wood, such as sweet chestnut.

The proximity of the osier grounds to the market gardens was no coincidence. They supported an industry producing the baskets in which our apples and cherries and mulberries, and perhaps even those strawberries that once grew here '*ad libitum*', were conveyed to the London markets. It was an industry that was both local and sustainable and based on a naturally occurring growth; and, unlike the mulberries and the poplars, there were still osiers in the parish today. I had come across them on the course of my parish walk and went back to see them again now; not many, and not the original beds to be sure, but a few stands planted, and then neglected, at sites here and there along the Lea.

There had been stands of osier on the riverside, I realised, when black poplars lined the marshlands; and when the wild poplars became a cropped and managed tree, so did they. A cultivated landscape had replaced the wild one – the poplars making way for apple and cherry and mulberry – but the osiers had survived, now bent to a new purpose and serving the needs of the new commercial gardens. Then the gardens had gone and with them the last of the trees that had a produce and an economic purpose. In their place were to be the docks and the gasworks and the factories and the rows of terraced housing. But the osiers hung on, or had returned, planted, in isolated patches along the Lea and, no doubt, with no awareness of their local significance. But they were here. They were my buried flints rising somehow back to the surface.

Chapter Three

The Recuperative Power of Planes

Late winter has prematurely given way to spring and I garden in the new, bright sunshine. I am spacing out the over-wintered leeks, clearing the last of the unswept leaves and preparing a vegetable bed for planting. My companions, the chickens, fuss and scrape around me as I work, resolved to undo whatever it is that I am currently doing.

A wren visits briefly. It stops so close to me that I can briefly make out the beautiful barred pattern on the edge of its wing. Male pigeons puff themselves importantly and strut their stiff way in pursuit of the females, who hurry away from them with equal determination. A blackbird takes on the role usually ascribed to the robin, watching me closely while I dig and eventually diving in to seize an upturned earthworm, which it pecks in two before devouring. I have been indoors and ill for far too long, and throughout that period it seemed to rain incessantly; a long succession of wet, dim and dreary days. But now I am out and feeling better and the sun is shining. It is a clear indication that the pathetic fallacy is not a fallacy at all.

I am as ambivalent as many Londoners about my city, loving it but longing, much of the time, to be out of it; living somewhere overhung with trees, or with a sight of the sea or with the shape of hills to look at. And this is my compromise; this untidy patch of garden with its chickens and its struggling vegetables, this defiant gash in the city's concrete skin. It is a wound that I tend with broccoli and potatoes, with broad beans (dying of brown spot), with the constant comings and goings of birds to the feeders, with a tiny pond that fills with leaves, with the plane trees that they fall from. These planes hang over me as I work. They line one side of the garden and reach out almost halfway across it. They are defiantly and cheerfully urban, their bark orange and grey with patches of a brighter sandy yellow. Their branches and twigs form a fine tracery through which the sunlight filters and, through their sieve, the city sounds are sifted.

They have not always been loved. Eileen Baillie describes what must be exactly the same trees dripping 'poisonously' onto the garden, a garden that contained little 'but sour earth and a smell of cats'. But for me they are less of a poison and more of a tonic. They give the garden its shape and its form, and, with their height, they add a new habitat and dimension. They are my urban woodland.

Further up the street, on the other side of the great bulk of St. Michael's Church, a darker grouping of limes occupies a small grassy area outside the estate. In the other direction, just behind the corner shop, there is a handsome and shapely horse chestnut. These are the trees of the city's expansion, of the time when farm gave way to factory and when grids of streets replaced the orchards. With them came a new generation of planting, and the first that was purely ornamental in purpose. They are the oldest of the trees that are still with us in Poplar.

The plane, the lime and the horse chestnut were the most significant among the trees chosen by the Victorians to accompany their massive urban expansion. Selected for their size, their resilience and their rapid growth, they were none of them native but species that had been introduced from abroad, or produced by hybridisation, or both. These relative newcomers to the country lacked that deep and sometimes atavistic significance that comes with generations of close association; the myths and the meanings, the local usage, the wealth of herbal and healing lore. Despite this, they brought with them echoes of other traditions and, as the largest and most familiar living elements in an increasingly denaturised landscape, they were to develop their own new associations. In ways that were sometimes half-hidden, or only half-acknowledged, these three trees became connected with childhood memory, with the personality of the Londoner, and with love.

George Cruickshank is now best remembered for his illustrations for the novels of Charles Dickens, but in 1829 he produced a cartoon entitled, 'London Going out of Town, or The March of Bricks and Mortar'. It shows an advancing army of poorly constructed and already shabby terraces, all of them called 'New Street'. Marching with them are platoons of soldiers concocted from bits of builders' paraphernalia; hods, pipes, ladders, spades and picks. A brick-spewing kiln represents the artillery while, in the background, factories belch a black smoke that almost conceals the dome of St. Paul's, prefiguring the famous wartime photograph. The subject of this blitz, however, is not the city but the countryside around it. It is on this that the forces of urbanisation are advancing, whilst haystacks and cattle flee, and trees bend in terror at the oncoming tide. 'Our fences, I fear,' says a disembodied rural voice, 'will be found to be no defence against these barbarians who threaten to encase and destroy us in all manner of ways.'

It was a fate shared by the fields and the farms and the fruit trees of Poplar. 'The Great Wen', as the radical journalist William Cobbett had described it in 1820, was exploding outwards, growing from a population of one million in 1800 to reach nearly seven million by the end of the century. By then it would stretch its all-embracing arms from Streatham in the south to Hornsey in the north; from Woolwich in the east to Ealing in the west. The market gardens of Brentford, on one side of London, would suffer the same fate as those of Bromley on the other.

In the Poplar area this expansive impulse was given a huge additional impetus by the arrival of the docks. The West India Docks came first, built in 1802 with accompanying stone warehouses so large that they could contain much of the nation's supply of rum and sugar, a position that enabled their owners to easily manipulate the national market. The East India Docks followed soon after, built in 1806 to handle trade from 'the Orient'; tea, silk, spice and porcelain. Dirtier, and more down to earth, was the Poplar Dock added in 1852 to handle the coastal coal trade. Finally, in 1868 and further down the Isle of Dogs, came the

Millwall Docks, dealing specifically in grain. Together, they were to bring not just trade but a further massive expansion of the local population.

Overall, the pattern of development was exactly as depicted in the Cruickshank cartoon. First the land would be cleared for brickfields and kilns, then the developers would mark it off into sites to be sold on to the speculative builders. Unlike many northern towns, where areas of identical terrace were erected by the largest industrialists to accompany their factories and mills, here was a competitive free-for-all, a scramble by a multitude of small, and often short-lived, building firms to put up as much as they could as quickly as they could and as cheaply as possible.

Beneath this onslaught, rural Poplar was to disappear within a surprisingly short time. On its western side, the East India Dock Road, the route from the City, was driven though a landscape of fields and market gardens. Initially lined with the elegant houses of shipbuilders and sea captains these were, by 1810, giving way to a maze of meaner streets, fourteen of them deriving their names from the daughters of the demolished manor house that had only recently stood there. The new development site had not only its own brick kiln but also a 'Bricklayers Arms', an increasingly common pub name that was to encapsulate the Victorian building boom. Meanwhile, on the eastern side of the parish, the excavations from the East India Dock were being used to infill the marshes, the Bromley Marsh or 'East Marsh'; the low-lying Lea-side land that would soon be supporting housing both for the dockers and for the factory workers of Poplar and Canning Town. To the north of Poplar, the unhedged and uncultivated open land of Bow Common, thick with furze and with the broom that had given Bromley its name, and populated with just a small clutch of country cottages, was to disappear under streets and factories.

Supporting just 7,700 people in 1811, the village of Poplar was, within fifty years, to reach a population of 43,500. Within its confines, people were now living back to back with the bone-yards and the guano company, the match factory and the gasworks, the cat meat shop and the dog biscuit makers, the chemical works and the canneries, the docks and the distilleries. The densely packed and over-crowded housing descended rapidly into 'rookeries' and slums. It had become, along with the rest of the East End, 'outcast London', 'the inferno', 'the city of dreadful night', and its people, 'the people of the abyss'.

The land 'encased' continued, however, to dream of the countryside that had only recently covered it, and the people, removed by just a generation or two from their rural past, continued to carry the memory of its cultivation. Despite the grimness of the surroundings, summer would bring, according to Eileen Baillie, 'a fine display of window-boxes; for the East Ender of those days rated horticulture as a pastime on only a slightly lower level than that of keeping pets ... He was a great "fancier" and employed his leisure a great deal more productively with his whippets, rabbits and pigeons as though the last vestiges of his country inherit-ance still struggled for expression. Their back gardens were,' she continues, 'a wonderful example of concentrated culti-vation in the face of difficulties' with flowers, vegetables and 'a tiny square of sooty grass'.

The allotments provided another of these echoes of a lost rural past. Those on the Isle of Dogs were locally famous for their fruit and vegetables whilst Bromley supported a further 150 plots, each beautifully kept and equipped with a hut. In these the whole family would sometimes spend the weekend, earning the area the name of 'Allotment Town'. Will Crooks, the son of Poplar who became its mayor and, later, one of the very first Labour MPs in the country, is said to have had a favourite party piece that encapsulated this urban enthusiasm for cultivation:

> *Red cabbages and pickles, I do grow*
> *Potatoes round and round*
> *Savoy greens and scarlet beans*
> *Fine apples a penny a pound.*

In one of his war verses, the poet Wilfrid Gibson includes some very similar lines, listing the vegetables he is to sow in his plot. Here, however, it is far from being an entertainment. The words are muttered over and over in the back of a field ambulance by a war-maddened soldier with both his legs shot away. Gibson's First World War poetry is unusual in being concerned with the lot of the ordinary working man and in the years immediately preceding the war he had been employed as a social worker in the East End. Perhaps it was here that he had come across this sort of allotment incantation.

Though the more tightly packed terraced streets contained few trees, they appear, with a degree of insistent surprise, in a poem by C.C. Martindale, a long-serving

Catholic priest in the parish. In 'What's o'clock in Poplar?' he describes a young man listening to the night-time sounds outside his bedroom window. The breeze through the 'twisted twigs' seems to whisper to him that even in Poplar there are trees; vine and fig in particular, though they bear little fruit in such bitter ground.

As with the mulberries, the planting of vines and figs in the East End was said to date back to the early Huguenot immigrants, trying to create, in their tiny East End gardens, a reminder of Tours and Lyon and the sunny, southern French homelands from which they had fled. It was a tradition that was to hang on in the proudly cultivated backyards of the working-class terraces of Poplar, right into the early 20th century. As a priest, Martindale would also have known of the Biblical usage of the fig and the grape as a metaphor for peace, fruitfulness and prosperity. The promised land of the Israelites is a 'land of vines and fig trees'; the tranquillity of King Solomon's rule is a time when people lived in peace 'all of them under their vines and fig trees'. The trellises of vine and the fig trees in the backyards of Poplar represented both a nostalgic yearning for the past and the hope for a better future; a future of peace and prosperity that few were ever to experience.

Vines and figs aside, the close-packed streets of 19th-century rookeries were largely treeless. In the better off parts of the parish, however, the Victorians were demonstrating their passion for tree planting, using them in an almost architectural manner to line the larger thoroughfares, to complement municipal and public buildings and to elevate the more ambitious developments. The lime, the plane and the horse chestnut are trees that make a statement. In the same way as the grand civic buildings, they represented Victorian self-confidence; the spirit of expansion, of endeavour and of civic pride.

The common street lime, *Tilia x europaea,* makes a monumental tree. It grows up to forty-six metres in height and has the additional advantage of being long-lived. In almost every other respect, however, it seems totally unsuited for the purpose to which it has been put. Walking the local streets, I found their shallow, spreading roots lifting the pavements and breaking up the paths in parks. I negotiated my way around the profusion of suckers they produce at the base of the trunk, and up its lower length, disfiguring the shape of the tree and hindering the progress of pushchairs and pedestrians along the street. I watched their coarse leaves across the seasons and noted how they collected grime and ended the summer coated in a dark, sooty mess; and how they were infested with aphids and with scale insects that dropped the trees' thick, sticky honeydew onto the streets beneath. And in autumn, when the maples and the cherries and the narrow-leaved ash were putting on their seasonal colour, I found the lime leaves just anaemic.

So what, I asked myself, came to explain its popularity; and just why had it been planted so often? The answer, I found, had a lot to do with the sentimental side of the Victorian character, and with the lime tree's association with love.

The defects of the lime tree – 'defects' in an urban setting, that is – are balanced by its one great virtue: its flowers. They are rather odd in structure, each one a constellation of tiny yellow-green blossoms with fine, projecting stamens hanging from a flimsy green blade. The tree books will tell you that they flower in July, but here they are already coating the trees by mid-May. Fine though they are, it is not their appearance that is their most important feature but their heady, honeyed scent. One of the most fragrant of our trees, a lime in full bloom can be alive with the thrumming of feeding insects. There are stories of bees becoming so intoxicated by the flowers that they fall unconscious to the ground. It may be apocryphal but I love the thought of it; drunken bees lying feet-up beneath the trees, lost in the swoon of such sweet nectar. Perhaps it was this fragrance, this sense of inebriation, this profusion of life attendant upon the flowers, that gave the tree its association with love and with fertility.

It was a fertility goddess, Freya, to whom the lime tree was dedicated among the early Germanic tribes. They met beneath its boughs and named a dance after it; the *tanzlinde*. Later it was adopted by the courtly love poets of mediaeval Germany and northern France, perhaps the best known of whom was Walther von der Vogelweide. He lived some time between 1170 and 1230 and his work includes the poem '*Unter der linde*';

> Under the lime tree
> On the heather,
> Where we had shared a place of rest,
> Still you may find there,
> Lovely together,
> Flowers crushed and grass down-pressed.
> Beside the forest in the vale,
> Tandaradei,

Sweetly sang the nightingale.

Of course, they have been doing far more than just resting. The woman has come to meet her lover on the green and he, in turn, greets her enthusiastically:

Had he kisses? A thousand some…
See how red my mouth's become.

He has already prepared a bed for her in the bower, strewn with every kind of flower. And what did he do there?

May none but he
Ever be sure of that – and I,
And one extremely tiny bird,
Tandaradei,
    Who will, I think, not say a word.

When the Germanic tribes – the Angles, the Saxons and the Jutes – invaded Britain, they had brought with them the associations of a tree that was central to their culture. They had also brought its name, the *linde*, which became the 'linden' and, eventually, the 'lime'. By the Middle Ages it had been implanted into English folklore and was seen as a distinctly female tree. English poetic symbolism also followed its German precursors and the lime became a trysting place for lovers, who lay beneath it on a bed of crushed and sweetly-scented flowers.

It was probably from Germany, too, that we borrowed the practice of planting the lime tree in ornamental avenues. The idea of the avenue goes back much further; to the

Bronze Age and the beaker-making people who began linking their religious sites to their burial sites with long ceremonial avenues, such as those that criss-cross the area around Stonehenge. It is tempting to see in the later avenues of grand houses and palaces, and later of major city streets, an echo of these early treeless ceremonial avenues, combining them, perhaps, with the notion of the sacred grove.

However, it is in Berlin that we find what is still the oldest and most famous example of the urban avenue of limes. The Unter den Linden was planted in 1647 to connect the Elector's Palace with the city gates. By the 19th century it had become the best known and the grandest street in the city. Many of the trees were nonetheless cut down in 1934 to make way for the Berlin S-Bahn, and more were felled for firewood during the last, desperate days of the Second World War. The Unter den Linden is today a fashionable shopping street, and the limes that line it are replants from the 1950s.

Influenced, perhaps, by these German originals, grand arrangements of tall limes became a feature of the landscaped grounds of English stately homes and country houses, and even of royal palaces like Hampton Court. In such places they still line avenues, fringe great lawns, form long vistas or frame a distant view.

The practice of 'pleaching' further varied their uses. The lime tree is particularly suited to pleaching, a form of cultivation adopted from France in which shoots from adjacent trees are tied or grafted into each other and encouraged to grow along a supporting framework. In this way they can be shaped into screens or arbours, tunnels or arches. They became almost essential features in the popular pleasure grounds of the 18th and 19th centuries. Here the crowds came to stroll in the gardens, to see the illuminations, to listen to music, to watch dancers or a balloon ascend, and to walk arm in arm beneath an avenue of interlacing limes. It was an almost certain way to ensure the enduring affection of your intended.

It was these centuries-old associations that the Victorians inherited. They may not have invented the avenue of limes, but they extended it, urbanised it and suburbanised it until it became a regular element of town planting. From the tree's long association with love, and from its presence in the pleasure grounds, it conferred upon the urban development a discreet hint of romance and, from its courtly past and presence in the country houses, a hint of affluence and of aristocracy. Here was a line of descent from the Bronze Age ceremonial avenue, through the Germanic fertility goddess and mediaeval courtly poetry, to Victorian sentimentality and the urban planting of limes. But it was sentiment mixed with an equal measure of shrewdness; for the competing developers were using it to make their speculative new estates more valuable and to attract sales. The limes bestowed both cachet and cash value. They spoke of lucre, as well as of love.

The common lime of our streets does not occur as a natural, wild tree. It is a cultivated hybrid created from two of our native species, the broad-leaved and the small-leaved limes. Though much reduced today, their distribution thin and patchy, they once covered much of our countryside. The small-leaved lime was once one of the dominant trees of lowland Britain, until its early clearance for agriculture. Across the huge stretches of a now lost woodland, the very features that make the lime unsuitable for street planting would have served as its strengths. The shallow roots allowed it to colonise a wider range of soils and settings; the ready sprouting to recover rapidly from heavy grazing by deer or the other herbivores that ranged the early forest. Even the sticky honeydew had its function, for as it fell to the forest floor, it attracted nitrogen-fixing bacteria that added to soil fertility. There is an interesting chicken-and-egg question that arises from this: did the lime trees grow in these areas because of the fertile soils, or was it the limes themselves that created the soil fertility?

The answer remains uncertain but the initial great loss of our lowland limes was much later followed by a growth in their use in amenity planting. As befits one of our commonest street trees, there were limes in at least fifteen locations in Poplar and I was on familiar terms with many of them. They grew on almost every side of the twenty-seven-storey Balfron Tower but did little to disguise its concrete brutality; they did, however, provide an unlikely wooded strip where wrens sang, robins nested and long-tailed tits fed in winter parties.

In the Recreation Ground, they suited the Victorian earnestness of the site, whilst elsewhere they lined the larger streets or huddled in conversational groups on the greens. They were some of the oldest trees in the parish but outside of the flowering season I found them the opposite of romantic. They were rather gloomy trees whose already dark bark blackened on a wet day as if it had absorbed the two centuries of soot that poured from surrounding chimneys. The nearby planes came to look almost jaunty in comparison. It was strange to think that these dark trees produced the light, white wood so highly prized for carving. It can be seen at its best in the work of Grin-ling Gibbons which adorns many of the City of London churches just a mile or two away. Here on pulpit, font and reredos it becomes almost unbelievably airy; flowers, fruit, fir cones, foliage, pea pods, hops, ears of corn and bunches of grapes so finely carved that they are said to tremble when the church organ thunders or when the singing of hymns swells around them.

This once favoured tree is little planted now. Its place has been taken by new forms and varieties that lack the limitations of the common lime. There are many of these too in Poplar, especially on the post-war estates where relatively large trees can still be used. Early in my walks I came across one, a cultivar of the small-leaved lime just as it was in fullest flower. It was in Dewberry Street, not far from the house, but I had clearly overlooked it until the blossom appeared. Its dark grey trunk, free of sprouting twiggy bunches, was enlivened with patches of paler wood and freckled with flecks of orange. Its crown was shapely, its upsweeping branches forming into a dense cone. But it was the flowering that took my breath away, especially in the contrast between the delicate primrose yellow of the blossom and the darkness of the heart-shaped leaves. Unlike those on other limes, its flowers were not hanging down-wards but standing upright or pushing out at jaunty angles and standing clear from the surrounding foliage. They were like pale stars emerging against a darkening evening sky.

The horse chestnut is less common in Poplar than the lime and I encountered it in only seven locations; but it was a handsome and well-shaped tree wherever it was growing. Here and there I also came across the red horse chestnut, a tree which I find far less appealing. This is an opinion which has caused some dissension on walks with friends. While they defend it, I find it insipid. It is short and twiggy and its leaves, compared with the long elegant palms of the white horse chestnut, resemble fat fingers on an over-chubby hand. The flowers are a disappointment, too. Dullish and dark red, they stand out poorly against the even darker leaves, while those of the white horse chestnut glow like proudly upright candelabra.

The red horse chestnut is a hybrid that was first raised in Germany; the white horse chestnut a Balkan species, introduced to Western Europe in 1576. No native tree can beat it for its associations with an English childhood. Its cut twigs must once have adorned every school nature table in the country; fascinating for their fat, sticky buds, for their horseshoe-shaped leaf scars and for their early and dramatic leaves. They appear from the buds as stiff, downward-clutching hawk's claws but soon open into the magnificently spreading palms. More than anything else, however, this childhood association is with the fruit of the tree: the conker.

The earliest versions of the game of conkers were played not with these round glossy nuts, but with the shells of snails or winkles, which were bashed or squeezed together until one of them cracked. According to some authorities, it is from this version of the game that the name arises, conkers being derived from 'little conches'. Others, however, suggest that the name is an abbreviation of 'conquerors', one of the names – alongside 'conkers', 'konkers' and 'oblionkers' – that was used when the game became popular in the late 19th and early 20th centuries. By that time, the game was being played with the fruit of the white horse chestnut, those of the red species producing a weaker variety known dismissively as 'water conkers'. The best and strongest conkers are said to come from the top of the tree, a fact that led to frequent complaints about the damage to trees, and to surrounding property, caused by children throwing sticks, stones and each other's trainers in an effort to dislodge them. Inevitably some local authorities responded by suggesting their complete removal.

Local councils need have less anxiety today, for the playing of conkers has become a more organised obsession. While events such as the World Conker Championship, held each year in Northamptonshire, have grown in size, the sight of children playing conkers in school playgrounds across the country has almost completely vanished. Gone with it is the multiplication of regional rules, the vocabulary of 'oners' and 'twoers' and 'tenners', of 'cheesecutters' and 'last-yearers', the cries of 'fuggy smack', 'strings' and 'stampsies', and the sharing of secrets of preservation, pickling, or baking in the oven. The access to ritualised violence is now, of course, much more readily available in computer games.

I have tried to keep the tradition alive in our house, gathering the nuts with the children, piercing them through with a skewer and threading the strings. The interest rarely survives beyond one or two games, but we continue to collect them in large numbers. We find them strewn across the pavement on our regular route to church, so shiny and shapely that it is impossible not to pick them up. They are one of the finest products of the urban harvest, still damp when taken from the prickly outer casing, a rich deep brown in colour with the gloss and the grain of some highly polished and exotic wood. We fill our pockets with them, tip them out into bowls and leave them around in the kitchen until eventually they cease to shine and a thin white mould creeps over them. Even then I have to dispose of them in secret.

A hundred years ago, and for a relatively short time, conkers were collected by children for a very different reason. The story has a particular connection with our parish but also with events on the world stage. And its ramifications still have a massive impact on international politics today.

By the beginning of the First World War, the main propellant used in both rifles and artillery was cordite. Earlier substances had produced a plume of smoke that both interfered with aim and betrayed the location of the gun being fired. The advantage of cordite was that it was virtually smokeless. One of its essential ingredients is acetone, which was traditionally produced from the destructive distillation of wood. Much of the supply came from the European charcoal burners, but following the outbreak of war, both this and alternative American supplies became increasingly disrupted. There was little possibility of using local supplies; the process then used for extracting acetone from wood was very wasteful with 100 kilograms of wood producing only one kilogram of acetone. It would have taken the deforestation of the British countryside to meet the wartime need and by 1915 the generals were becoming seriously alarmed at the possibility of running out of fire-power.

It was at this stage that David Lloyd George, the newly established Minister for Munitions, was introduced to Chaim Weizmann, a lecturer in chemistry at Manchester University. Weizmann had developed a method using bacteria to ferment starch, a process which gave rise to a mixture of ethanol, acetone and butyl alcohol. Initially it seemed to have no practical function and was dismissed by his professor with the words 'butyl alcohol, futile alcohol'. Now, however, its time had come.

The government sought first for a place to carry out the distillation process. Winston Churchill, who as First Lord of the Admiralty was also involved in the discussions, remarked that while he would be worried about any disruption to the flow of whisky, that of gin was a different matter. And so in 1916 the Ministry signed a contract with gin-makers J. & W. Nicholson for the distillation of acetone from starch, with Weizmann appointed to act as the company's chief scientific adviser.

Nicholson's was a family company originating, as did so many gin companies, in Clerkenwell, along the valley of the River Fleet. In the course of its history the company had lent Marylebone Cricket Club (the MCC) enough money to buy Lord's cricket ground and was rewarded when the MCC changed its official colours to those of the company; the red and yellow that it has retained to this day. By 1872 Nicholson's had acquired a second site for the distillation of 'Lamplighter' gin. This was at Three Mills, the site of the old tidal mills at the northernmost tip of Poplar, a strip of land surrounded by the channels of the River Lea. It was here that the vital distillation of acetone was to happen.

When the new process was implemented it was based initially on extracting starch from grain. But grain, too, was soon in short supply and required primarily for the feeding of a hungry populace. It was then that Weizmann turned to the horse chestnut. Not only could conkers provide the necessary supplies of starch but they could do so cheaply, and much more efficiently than wood. In the autumn of 1917, the national collection of conkers began. Just as in the Second World War, with the collection of rose hips for Vitamin C, it was largely the work of children; of school groups, or scouts and guide troops, sent out to do the gathering and to deliver the results to local collection centres for onward transport to a supposedly secret destination.

Here in Poplar, on the factory's doorstep, the secret seems to have been less well guarded. Families would supplement their meagre income by sending their children out to collect the conkers and deliver them to Nicholson's. It was an almost unique example of a street tree providing more than an ornamental purpose – and it contributed to the war effort as well as to the local economy.

Towards the end of the war there was a discussion as to what reward Weizmann might himself receive in recognition of his efforts. He is said to have replied to Lloyd George, who was by now Prime Minister, that he wanted no personal honour and spoke instead of his 'aspirations as to the repatriation of the Jews to the sacred land they had made famous'. It is possible that Lloyd George's openness to this idea might have come from his own nonconformist upbringing and the belief that the re-establishment of the

Jews in their own homeland would herald the 'second coming'. Whether this was an influence or not, he introduced Weizmann to his Foreign Secretary, Arthur Balfour. In November 1917, the Balfour Declaration committed Britain to the 'establishment in Palestine of a national home for the Jewish people'. The conker had helped kick-start a process that would lead, in 1948, to the foundation of the modern state of Israel. Its first president was the chemist, Chaim Weizmann.

There is a horse chestnut near my house in which a mistle thrush sings. Not the repeated phrases of the song thrush but its own varied melody, hard to separate from a blackbird sometimes, but different in tone and punctuated with thoughtful pauses. It does not sing casually, but determinedly, starting every year in February, and long before first light.

I had become a connoisseur of birdsong in Poplar and sought it out and sampled it like a wine-taster sought out wine. There was a blackcap which sang throughout the spring in the All Saints' churchyard, a rapid sweet chorus like a blackbird on speed. There were goldfinches that chattered incessantly in the garden, and robins that sang with a trickling melancholy, even in the heart of winter. There were dunnocks, more easily heard than seen, that daringly exposed themselves on bush-tops to sing over and over their single line. There were sand martins that twittered over the canal and the drumming of a great spotted woodpecker that I once heard in the Recreation Ground.

I had even got up at dawn to seek out these songs and

more, but I did not need to do it for the mistle thrush. From its perch in the still bare chestnut, it brought its song to me. Urban birds have to work hard against the city's incessant backdrop of noise, and studies have shown that they sing louder than rural birds, and still have less range. As each morning progressed my mistle thrush would pit itself against the hum of traffic on the Blackwall Tunnel approach road, the roar of planes taking off from City Airport, the sound of car radios played too loudly and the diesel coughing of the buses at the stop outside my window. But still it would sing, and continue to sing, through March and well into April. True, it comes at an unreasonably early hour, but I stir, half-awake, and enjoy it. And I wait anxiously each winter for its return. Against the sounds of the city, it seems a singular act of defiance.

Of the Victorian trilogy of street trees, it is the plane that is most numerous in Poplar, as it is across London as a whole. It is a tree that has become inextricably linked with the character of the Londoner. Readily reaching up to forty metres, it is the tallest broad-leaved species in Britain and, when not pollarded by council contractors to ugly and leafless swollen stubs, it has a fine spreading structure of upward-sweeping boughs that divide eventually into a final curtain of trailing twigs. It is not unruly like the black poplar, nor twiggily untidy like the lime, nor ethereally wispy like the birch; it is a tree unquestioningly sure of itself and of its vigour. It is the supreme architectural tree.

The other features of the plane are also attractive. It is

bright in profile, its bark a smooth, silvery grey, with a hint of orange as it ages. It is further enlivened by the peeling patches that reveal fresh, clean areas of pale yellow bark below, one of its most recognisable features. The leaves add to its lightness. Divided into semi-palmate pointed lobes and edged with a few long curving teeth, they are a bright glossy green that can take on a yellowish, buttery tinge in the summer sun. The seeds are contained in dangling balls that continue to hang on the tree over the winter; it is, as John Betjeman described it, the 'bauble-hanging plane'.

It is perhaps surprising that the true identity of such a familiar tree remains a mystery. It has long been the accepted wisdom that our local plane is a hybrid between two other species; the Oriental plane and the American plane. The accounts of its genesis are varied, some saying that it arose in the 17th-century Lambeth garden of the great plant collector John Tradescant the Younger, whilst others assert that it arose in the Oxford Botanical Garden at a similar time. But neither is likely as the American plane is intolerant of the damp English climate and rarely survives here long enough to flower. A third version suggests that it first arose in France or Spain in the 1650s and was introduced to England ten years later, where the first of its plantings, at Ely and Barnes, are said to survive to this day.

There is, however, a more recent, and growing, body of opinion that our local plane is not a hybrid at all. Two of the best London botanists of recent times, Ted Lousley and John Burton, have both disputed it, evidencing the fact that, unlike most hybrids, it has sufficiently demonstrated its fertility, regenerating freely in central London (though not, interestingly, outside of it). Perhaps, then, it is a species in its own right; or perhaps not a true species at all but a variety of the Oriental plane, a tree from which it is almost indistinguishable.

Whatever its origin it became, soon after its arrival, the iconic London tree. Planted first in Lincoln's Inn Fields and Berkeley Square, its use was soon to spread to the other squares of London, and then to spill out onto its streets. By the end of the 19th century it was said that over half the trees in London were planes. It had become, in fact, the 'London plane'.

There are other countries that might have cause to quarrel with this English appropriation of the plane tree. What is probably the most beautiful, and certainly the most famous, avenue of planes is in France, lining the Canal du Midi. Created by the Sun King, Louis XIV, it winds its way from Toulouse to the Mediterranean Sea, lined with 42,000 over-arching plane trees. Shading the length of the canal against the Mediterranean heat, they form what a 2011 article in the *Guardian* infamously described as a remarkable 'canapé of trees'. This World Heritage Site is now under threat, many of its 200-year-old trees dying, or being cut down, following infection by the fungal disease *Ceratocystis platani*. It is another example of American invasion, having been introduced, it is said, by GIs in the Second World War in wooden ammunition boxes made from the American sycamore.

Its use in France is not restricted to the canals and a much later ruler, the Emperor Napoleon Bonaparte, ordered that planes be planted along the roadsides to provide shade for marching troops. It is perhaps hard in the cooler English climate to recall the absolute significance of shade in the middle of a relentless, clear-skied Mediterranean day. Its importance to a marching army is underlined by a story first told by the Greek historian Herodotus in the 5th century BC. It is a source that may well have influenced Napoleon in his choice of the plane tree. It concerns the great Persian commander Xerxes on his long march across Asia in order to invade Greece. Passing through the town of Kallatebos, close to the Meander river crossing, he saw by the roadside a magnificent plane tree. He was so moved by its beauty and by its shade that he fell in love with it, presenting it with golden ornaments and arranging for one of his men to remain behind as its permanent protector.

Being Greek rather than Persian, Herodotus may well have been biased in his telling of the story, though in subsequent accounts the actions of Xerxes continue to be mocked as much as admired. In the opera 'Serse', Handel appears to play up the comic element, with Xerxes sitting under the tree and regaling it in song: '*Ombra mai fu/di vegatabile/cara ed amabile/soave piu.*' I looked it up in my book of operas, which translates it rather uncharitably as, 'No shade is more sweet than the shade of this dear and lovely vegetable.' It was originally scored as 'larghetto' but became universally famous as 'Handel's Largo'. Its innumerable renditions remain blissfully ignorant of its original satiric intent.

Xerxes was, as it turned out, on his way to defeat at the great Battle of Thermopylae and it is with the Greeks, rather than the Persians, that the tree remains inextricably linked. Every Greek town and village has its square, the centre of both its civic and its social life, and every Greek square has its plane. They cast their shade over the chairs and tables that spill out from the fringing tavernas, over the groups of men talking or playing *tavli*. On one side of the square there is generally an old and whitewashed church which, like the plane, is part of the very fabric of the place. It is often the plane, however, that is the more venerable of the two. Always large and usually aged, there is one in Crete that is said to be a thousand years old; whilst on the Pelion peninsula, the tree at Tsagarada is thought to be at least 1,500 years old.

The Pelion peninsula projects southwards from Volos and Mount Pelion on the eastern coast of the Greek mainland and it was there, in the course of a family holiday, that we went to search out this tree. This is the land that Apollo loved, a leafy, hilly country where figs and fruit fall lush and uncollected from the trees. Until more recent times they were harvested and distributed on the ancient cobbled donkey tracks that criss-cross the country, but are now falling victim to neglect and, worse, to the bulldozer and the ubiquitous concrete track. The peninsula's west coast frames a bay so calm that the sea is a glistening sheet of still, spun silk, broken only by the occasional leaping of dolphins. The east coast is steeper, sloping down through chestnut woodlands to reach busy, local resorts on the rougher Aegean Sea.

Above these slopes stands Tsagarada, a village so straggling that it has four different centres linked by a network of stone footpaths. In the Agia Paraskevi, the largest of its squares, stands the old plane, whitewashed around the massive trunk, which is some fourteen metres in circumference. It soon splits into several great trunks, each one itself the size of a very respectable tree, one of them leaning massively and horizontally across the square, where it is supported on its own purpose-built brick column.

The classic Greek name for the plane is *platanus* and the Pelion peninsula is dotted with place names such as Platania. *Platanus* also gives us the modern scientific name for the tree as well as its common name. The word means 'broad' and is said to refer either to the shape of the leaf or to the spread of the dome. I find the suggestion unsatisfactory and prefer to seek a derivation from the *plateia*, the Greek square with its accompanying plane that stands at the heart of every village.

The educational system in Georgian England, for those who could afford it, was classical to the core. To the gentlemen who built and lived in those first city squares, the plane would have seemed an inspired choice for planting. The earliest and still the most famous example is Berkeley Square, where the trees are now over 225 years old. Though they cannot compare with the planes of the *plateia*, they are the prototypes of what was to become the iconic tree of the capital. Having previously travelled all the way to Tsagarada, it seemed only courteous to pay these more local trees a visit.

Berkeley Square is in the heart of Mayfair, the most expensive district of the metropolis, as it is of the Monopoly board. It is built on inherited wealth, the London homes of the landed rich, and the approach I took from Piccadilly and along Berkeley Street, still displayed, in its seven- and eight-storey blocks, a bland and self-accepting attitude to wealth. But among the jewellers, the Land Rover salesrooms and the physiotherapist studios that line the ground floor, the Palm Beach Hotel betrays the changing pattern of property ownership in central London. 'Arabic night every Sunday', announced a board on the street outside, 'Arabic DJ, belly dancers, Arabic mezzes and electronic sheesha'.

The 'square' itself is not actually square. It is a rectangle of streets surrounding an oval piece of parkland. Nor is it, despite its reputation, tranquil. It is a noisy throb of constant, and constantly impatient, cars and taxis. It is a circulatory system set on a busy through route that successfully separates the open space from the pedestrians who might want to use it. It is a device for traffic regulation; a glorified roundabout.

The four fringing streets further contribute to this malaise by lacking any form of architectural integrity. The east side is dominated by an ugly yellow-brick block, its low towers rising in steps like a pseudo-ziggurat. It has the air, and the anonymity, of the modern municipal office. Along its ground floor is a row of featureless glass frontages; a Bentley showroom, an obscure bank, an Ancient Arts Centre selling antique carpets and, the one deviation from the general depression, a glass atrium on which a large engraved plane tree echoes the real ones in the square. It seems to be a case of brash modern cash confronting the sedate respectability of old money: for the opposite, west, side of the square is lined with older houses whose one-time occupants included George Canning, Britain's briefest-serving Prime Minister. Today they are occupied by offices, though what business is transacted within them it is hard to say, for they are obviously far too important to bear nameplates. Those who need them know what they are, and of such people, men in anonymous suits carrying significant briefcases, there was great coming and going.

On the south side, below another contrasting frontage, this time in art deco style, I bought myself a noodle 'potsu' for sustenance. It was, a sign assured me, 'a healthy, low-fat lunch', and having thus improved my life chances I proceeded to lower them again by crossing the aggressively busy road to get to the gardens. Broad gravel paths dissected and surrounded the large, grassy oval within, densely lined with brown municipal benches. At the southern end a half-clad nymph clutched a water jar and, at the centre, a fat square pillar, topped with a stone urn, was fringed with an undulating metal canopy that was trying, unsuccessfully, to mimic drapery.

It was a grey day, something I am not necessarily averse to, but on this occasion even the pigeons seemed to lack enthusiasm. Half were asleep on the grass whilst the rest wandered over the gravel in an amnesiac way whilst trying to recall what they were there for. Equally desultory were some pieces of instantly forgettable public art and the scattering of signs that forbad me from either playing ball games or 'drinking from the water feature'.

But then there were the trees, some twenty-seven of them and all with the presence of mind to overtop the surrounding buildings, even the tallest blocks, and to look down on them with an aloof, and rather superior, dignity. Though they were all alike in stature, they differed widely in shape. Some rose slender and erect like tall forest trees on a single bole, whilst others split early into several separate trunks. Some had a strangely fluted base, like the stem on a fancy wine glass. Some bore entirely upright boughs, whilst others were fringed with a trailing curtain of twigs as though wrapped in a crocheted stole. Beneath them a few cyclamen had struggled into flower. There was a smattering of autumn leaves, a wood pigeon, a magpie and a strutting crow. The nightingale, however, was conspicuous by its absence.

They might have been there when the area was first developed, skulking, as nightingales do, in the scrub and the meadows that surrounded the Tyburn stream. By 1747, however, when the 4th Lord Berkeley began laying out the streets and houses, the stream had already become an open sewer. As part of his project, Berkeley entered into an agreement with his son, and with two local carpenters, to enclose three and a half acres of the site as gardens. Whilst this undoubtedly added an initial dignity, it was clearly not maintained, for within thirteen years the surrounding walls and fences had collapsed and the gardens within them gone to ruin. It took an Act of Parliament to re-establish the square, this time with the addition of an equestrian statue of George III. In a more rapid version of the ruin of Ozymandias, this, too, was not to last. By 1772 the weight of the royal rider had proved too much for the horse and its legs buckled under the strain. The statue was removed and replaced by the current feature, the draped central pillar rather unrealistically known as a gazebo. It was not till 1789, when the square had already been in existence for some forty years, and as the gift of a local resident, that the trees were added.

Unlike their predecessors, the reinstalled railings of the refurbished park were to last for nearly 200 years. In this case it was the Second World War that was their undoing. They were removed and melted down for munitions and the park itself first filled with air raid shelters and then adapted as the base for an American army unit. The most enduring impact of the war, however, was not to the appearance of the park but to its reputation, for it was in the first year of the struggle that two British composers, Eric Maschwitz and Manning Sherwin, published the song that both romanticised and immortalised Berkeley Square and linked it, inextricably, to the song of the nightingale.

A nightingale singing in Berkeley Square is, of course, as ornithologically unlikely as a bluebird over the white cliffs of Dover. I have read earnest articles in the wildlife press arguing that the song really referred to is that of the robin, which can often be heard singing by a street lamp at the dead of night. But that is to miss the point of the song. It is the very improbability of a nightingale serenading Mayfair that creates its magic.

By the end of its first year, the song had already been recorded by both Vera Lynn and Ray Noble. Innumerable versions were to follow, casting a lasting spell over the name of the square. It survives today in what might be thought of as a striking example of reputation outliving reality. The song of any contemporary nightingale in the square would be drowned in the din of the traffic, and anyone dancing Fred Astaire-like along its surrounding streets would be felled in short order by a taxi.

But the association persists. It is perpetuated in the romantic inscriptions of many of the commemorative plaques on the benches that line the square:

> *'This lovely garden, two hearts reunited from 9000 kilometres away'*

> *'For Libby, where I proposed and you accepted'*

'Danny and Ron who rekindled their love after 30 years. We sit here in love and happiness'

'Berkeley Square is such a romantic affair. We love this London Town'

Like the nightingale, the 'romantic affair' and the 'London Town' are both phrases from the song. Just an energetic stone's throw from Berkeley Square there are other tree-lined London squares that are perhaps more beautiful and more tranquil but it is Berkeley Square that retains its reputation for an almost other-worldly peace and calm:

'Home is tranquil Berkeley Gardens, or wherever we gather together'

'With thanks for many moments of tranquil contemplation in this beautiful square'

'A place of calm. A place to reflect'

Despite the surrounding traffic, despite the busy streets, there are some, it seems, who are still listening for the nightingale.

Having found early use in the London squares, the planting of planes was also to be adopted in the city's streets. The Regency architect John Nash used them in the grand boulevards that made up his vision of a redesigned London but they were soon to spread beyond the wealthiest areas and out into other parts of the city. From being the private developer's tree of choice, it became a symbol of the municipal vision, even, or especially, in the very poorest parts of London.

It was in the vestries, and after them the metropolitan boroughs, in places like the East End and Bermondsey, that they were embraced most enthusiastically. The annual report of the vestry of St. Matthew, Bethnal Green, records in 1879 a £100 donation by a 'gentleman ... to plant trees in thoroughfares'. With the help of an additional donation by the churchwardens and overseers, sixty-six plane trees were planted. The vestry then passed a further resolution 'expressing approval of planting trees in thoroughfares and their willingness to consider applications for permission to do so'. This approach was not without its critics. Across the river in Bermondsey where Alfred Salter, one of the greatest of London's unsung heroes, was lining the streets with new plantings, it was being slated by some as a waste of money on working people who would be unable to appreciate their benefits. The socialist burghers of Poplar, however, betrayed no such qualms. The 1927 *Official Guide* to the borough praises the results of past tree planting projects as well as revealing the still-lingering nostalgia for the countryside that the spread of the city had replaced:

> *The Council has set a good example in fostering a love of the beautiful in Nature and, thanks to its enterprise, over 2000 trees have already been planted within the Borough and no less than 54 thoroughfares are shaded in summer by their foliage. This verdure, bringing a sensation of the country into what before was*

> *a wilderness of bricks and mortar, is an innovation that*
> *is keenly appreciated by residents and one that never*
> *fails to appeal to the casual visitor.*

The greater part of these new plantings was of planes and I found them in many corners of contemporary Poplar. A fine group stood on the East India Dock Road, harking back to the days when this was a new thoroughfare lined with Poplar's wealthier dwellings. Others formed avenues on the older housing developments, such as the Aberfeldy estate, created on the East Marsh once it had been infilled with the diggings from the nearby dock basin.

Increasingly the plane became part of the municipal endeavour, bringing life and colour to streets that had been treeless or where early 'slum clearance' had taken place. In such places, the planting of planes continued well into the 20th century and I found them lining stretches of the Blackwall Tunnel approach road, decorating the post-war Chrisp Street Market and dotting the surrounding Lansbury estate. They were present in parks and recreation grounds, and they marked out the boundaries of schools and church-yards and of vicarages – like our own, where they were to cause such grief to the rector's wife. And I was to find 'ghost trees', too; planes whose location could be used to detect the sites of buildings that no longer existed.

St. Gabriel's Church, which once stood with a small parish school nestling next to it in its own small grounds in Violet Street, was so badly damaged in the Blitz that its demolition became inevitable. Today the site is covered with the flats of St. Gabriel's Court, but I found I could make out the trian-gular site of the long-vanished churchyard from the line of large planes that curved around its northern apex. They raised the possibility of a new form of arboreal archaeology. Just as the yews in a rural churchyard can provide evidence of the existence of an earlier, pre-Christian site, so perhaps the urban plane can provide the traces of earlier, long-lost sites or buildings.

Although its classical and aristocratic associations contributed to the early use of the plane, the real secret to its success was its reputation for withstanding pollution; its ability, as Alan Mitchell puts it in *A Field Guide to the Trees of Britain and Northern Europe*, to remain 'remarkably vigorous even under very trying conditions'. According to popular account, the most important reason for this is the tree's habit of continually shedding its old bark, thus sloughing off the accumulated soot that would have been such a feature of the 19th and early 20th centuries, and 'allowing the tree to breathe'. Other sources suggest that the tree stores toxins in the bark then rids itself of them by shedding it. They are ideas that have been repeated from source to source and become the received wisdom, part of the popular imagination.

The *Poplar Parish Magazine* of 1905 provides an irresistible local example. The 'Honourable Cordelia Leigh' keeps alive the lost connection with the countryside by writing a regular column of 'Nature Notes' with the strapline, 'Through Nature Up to God's Nature'. 'Dwellers in large towns,' she tells us, 'are fond of plane trees because they stand the soot and smoke better than any other tree. This is owing ... to the outer bark of the stem peeling off continually, being pushed aside by the soft, inner bark so that the tree is constantly getting, so to speak, a fresh, clean skin.'

A fresh, clean skin it does have, but the role of this in helping the tree to survive pollution is now doubted by botanists. There are, after all, other trees that can cope in the city without such a device; the poplar, ash, ailanthus, sycamore and the lime, among them. The leaf of the plane may be just as important: their smooth, glossy surfaces remaining free of accumulated grime and easily washed down by the summer rain, whilst Mitchell puts their success down to the ability of the roots to survive in compacted and covered soil. Though the story of the peeling bark and pollution is repeated in many tree books, there have always been those who questioned it. In his book *The Nature-World of London*, written in 1924, Walter Johnson not only dismisses the idea but begins to provide an explanation of why it has been so persistent:

> *Everyone has noticed that the plane periodically throws off flakes from its outer bark and thus exposes the clean yellowish or olive-green under-surface. This property is vulgarly believed to account for the healthiness of the tree in our tainted, sooty atmosphere. Why this should be is not evident. The function of the lenticels, or breathing organs, which are scattered over all the twigs is generally overlooked. If these were clogged, no removal of the outer bark could compensate for their loss ... The dirty bark scales off, the piebald tree looks clean and smart and popular opinion deems the change curative or remedial whereas it is a sign of past and present health. The*

> *removal of the bark causes the plane to look clean, and*
> *the fact probably gave rise to the legend.*

Perhaps, as Johnson suggests, the truth of whether the shedding of bark does or does not help resist pollution is less important than the impression it gives. It is certainly crucial to the personality of the tree and to the Londoner's perception of it. The mid-1800s through to the 1960s was, in London, a century of soot. It blackened the brickwork, corroded the stone, obscured the windows, coated every surface, made dark silhouettes of the trees. Life was a continual struggle against it. It changed the colour, and the character, of the city. Here, though, was a tree that was self-cleansing, that was repeatedly sloughing off the soot, that was perpetually renewing itself, that presented a bright and cheerful face in a world of cloying grime. Like London itself, it was a phoenix rising from the ashes.

It is likely, therefore, that the 'London plane' gets its name not just from the abundance of the tree but from its place in the psyche of the Londoner, just as the Mancunians related the flying seed of the poplar to conditions in the cotton mills. Here, though, the significance was restorative; it represented the ability to survive in even the harshest conditions, to put a brave and cheerful face to the world even in adversity. It was exactly the same reputation as was afforded to that other symbol of London, the 'cheerful' Cockney sparrow.

The plane is one of just three plants that have earned themselves the London epithet. All of them share this same association of a plucky survival against the odds. *Sisymbrium irio* is a smallish, yellow-flowered member of the cress and cabbage family. It was once, and it is again now, a scarce plant of walls and waste places, but that changed after the 1666 fire that consumed the City of London from Pudding Lane to Pie Corner. In those scorched streets and burnt-out buildings it appeared in a sudden abundance, a fact commented on in his diaries by Samuel Pepys. So common did it become that it was believed to have generated spontaneously from the ashes. It was then that it took on the name that it retains to this day, the 'London rocket'. To the ordinary Londoner it would have been a symbol of regeneration, of the possibility of life rising, literally, from the ashes. To the 17th-century mind this would have had an even deeper significance that is largely lost to us now, for it was from ashes that the alchemists of the time were trying to create spontaneous life. Here was proof that just as death returned us to dust and ashes, so was it from dust and ashes that life could again arise.

Unlike the London rocket, the London pride is a garden plant, a member of the saxifrage family originating in the Pyrenees. Its great virtue is its adaptability, its ability to thrive, and to multiply itself, in even the poorest of soils and the harshest of conditions. Where most other plants might fail, it produces spreading rosettes of succulent leaves from which spring masses of wiry stems, carrying star-like sprays of dainty, five-petalled pink flowers. It was the plant that any Londoner could grow in the polluted city soils. So it was in my childhood garden in Bermondsey, a prefab site hacked out of a London bomb site, and so it was in the vicarage garden tended by Eileen Baillie's mother in Poplar, in 'the unproductive earth' where 'little could withstand the infertility of the soil or the chemical content of the atmosphere'. Nothing would grow here save 'purple flag-iris, tiger lilies,' and, appropriately enough, 'a flourishing crop of London Pride'. Here again is a plant that defies its surroundings, not just surviving but spreading, its leaves evergreen, its flowers a splash of summer brightness. It was exactly this spirit of defiance, of flourishing against the odds, that was picked up by Noël Coward when he wrote, in the middle of the Blitz, his sentimental song, 'London Pride'. It describes a plant that grows in pavement cracks and flowers unfailingly, a plant that stands for freedom and represents the city and the character of its people.

The rocket, the pride and the plane bear their London epithet like medal holders in the same campaign. As for the plane, there is more evidence of its relationship with the perceived spirit of the Londoner in the poetry of that sooty century. Edith Nesbit was a prolific children's author, many of her abundant books now completely forgotten, but she pioneered a new approach to children's writing, one in which events are seen and explained from a child's point of view. She is best known today for works like *The Railway Children* and *Five Children and It*. She regarded herself primarily, however, as a poet. I came across her poem 'A Child's Song in Spring' in a 1905 edition of the All Saints' parish magazine. It had a suitably sanctimonious air, ascribing virtues to a number of tree species:

> *Such a gay green gown God gave the larches –*
> *As green as he is good!*
> *The hazels hold up their arms for arches*
> *When spring rides through the woods.*
> *The chestnut's proud and the lilac's pretty*

> *The poplar's gentle and tall;*
> *But the plane-tree's kind to the poor old city*
> *I love him best of all!*

The identification of the beloved plane with the poor old city may have been strengthened by the fact that Nesbit was also a life-long social activist and a supporter of the early Labour Party. She knew the East End well and had a strong connection with Poplar. She had met her second husband, Tommy Tucker, at a socialist lecture in Poplar. Tucker was a Poplar man, working in the Isle of Dogs shipyards, and had attended our own church of All Saints', so we can lay claim to some small connection.

Nesbit's poetry is too sentimental for today's taste but another poet, writing at almost the same time, adds a more personal, and perhaps more poignant, touch on this relationship between the plane tree and the city dweller. Amy Levy's poem 'The Plane Tree' is said to be among the first English poems to be influenced by the French symbolists:

> *Green is the plane-tree in the square,*
> *The other trees are brown;*
> *They droop and pine for country air;*
> *The plane-tree loves the town.*
>
> *Here from my garret-pane, I mark*
> *The plane-tree bud and blow,*
> *Shed her recuperative bark,*
> *And spread her shade below.*

It is easy to picture Levy looking from her attic room out onto a London square, and perhaps in the 'recuperative' shedding of the bark she is looking to her own survival as much as to that of the plane tree. Just a few years earlier she had composed 'A Minor Poet', a long poem in which a (male) poet is interrupted during his third attempt at suicide. Here too is the window from a small room looking out on the London scene:

> *Up, you creaking thing,*
> *You squinting, cobwebbed casement!*
> *So, at last,*
> *I can drink in the sunlight. How it falls.*
> *Across that endless sea of London roofs,*
> *Weaving such golden wonders on the grey,*
> *That almost, for the moment, we forget*
> *The world of woe beneath them.*
> *Underneath,*
> *For all the sunset glory, Pain is king.*

Pain is what Levy wrestled with for much of her life. Born in 1861 to an Anglo-Jewish family in Clapham, south London, she became only the second woman to attend Cambridge University, and the first at Newnham College. But she never completed her studies, dropping out in her fourth term there. Although she was part of a circle of other young women writers, including Eleanor Marx, she always felt something of an outsider in Victorian London, not just as a Jew but also as a lesbian. Her most significant relationship, with older, fellow-writer Vernon Lee, ended in despair. The 'health in adversity' represented by the plane tree was, in her case, to prove unattainable. In 1889, suffering from major depressive bouts and an increasing deafness, she took her life in her parents' house in Bloomsbury by inhaling charcoal fumes. The poem was published in a volume, bearing the same title 'The Plane Tree', a few months after her death.

In the course of its 250 years in the country, the plane has been on a strange journey. From an early predominance in west London, it spread to the east. From the richest London squares, it spread to the poorest quarters of the city. From its use by the first private developers, it became a mainstay of municipal planting. And from its early classical and aristocratic associations, it became the tree of the Cockney and the ordinary Londoner, their symbol of survival and 'recuperation' amidst the grinding hardship of their everyday lives.

Chapter Four

A Year Observed

From tiny wall-top mosses to the tall limes of the Balfron Tower, it was as Gilbert White had suggested: that 'that district produces the greatest variety that is the most examined.' I was walking and examining and enjoying, and the parish had formed its own new map in my mind. It was made up not so much of road names or the location of shops or swimming baths, but of the bush where the chiffchaff fed, the corner where the ragwort bloomed, the street that was lined with Turkish hazel. I was beginning to see both differently and more deeply, and to develop a shared ownership of the place, along with the blackcaps and the beetles, the hoverflies and the hornbeams, and everything else that lived there.

What, then, if this focus on location could be drawn even tighter? What if it were to feature not the local landscape as a whole but just a single feature within it? The idea had come to me that, alongside my parish walk, I would under-take another, parallel journey, and one that would take me through time as much as space. Not in a science-fiction, time-travelling sort of way, but alongside time, taking time to be with time. I would, I had decided, spend a year observing a single tree: its life and the lives it sheltered; its constancies and inconstancies; its furlings and unfurlings; its aspects in every weather; its moods at different times of day.

Perhaps it would be less of a 'journey' than a matter of being still and letting time happen, but it also seemed an act of defiance in an area so cut up by major roads that the requirements of those who move through it have clearly been given priority over the needs of those who stay. Here, by contrast, was something that would require more 'staying', more being, than going or doing. It brought to mind a quote from Franz Kafka's *The Great Wall of China*: 'You don't need to leave your room,' he wrote. 'Remain sitting at your table and listen. Don't even listen, simply wait. Don't even wait, be quite still and solitary. The world will freely offer itself to you to be unmasked. It has no choice. It will roll in ecstasy at your feet.' I cannot claim to have witnessed the deep rolling in ecstasy, but I did find a gradual and deeply fulfilling unfolding.

The choice of a specific tree was not difficult. There was, after all, one that shaped and shadowed my garden, that confronted me every time I opened the kitchen door, that turned my study window into a large, framed picture of a plane tree.

January

At its short swelling base – before it splits into two, then into two again, and then, recklessly, into six or seven – the tree takes on a reddish hue. Up that first length of trunk it is unexpectedly tinged with the colour of a desert

153

sand. The bark here is corkier. It has a cracked and crusty consistency and, unlike the smoothness of the upsweeping boughs beyond, reveals the true age of the tree and the many seasons it has weathered. Contrasting with this edgy angularity are a series of successive, softly contoured folds. It is as if the weight of the rest of the tree bears down on this supporting pillar, causing it to bulge here and there more like a slumped soft toy than a solid wooden trunk.

The folds get smaller as they ascend the tree. They become like the last ripples of an incoming wave exhausting itself as it runs over the sand. Higher up, with that strange propensity of a tree to be young and old at the same time and in the same body, the bark is paler and patched and picked out, on the upper boughs, in lime and yellow in the clear winter sun. In this defining crispness, it has the precision of a draughtsman's drawing. It is an impression that passes as the early dusk arrives and the daytime display of sharpness and certainty subsides into something more moody and subjective.

It is at this brooding time of day, with all the individual details disappearing, that almost any belief about a tree becomes possible: that it has a silent, slow consciousness; that it is linked to life beyond its own; that it is the repository of ancient, earthy memories; or, most persistently, that it knows something deep and deeply distracting. Watching with the tree at this turning light engenders a sort of yearning, a desire to be admitted into its secret, silent company. I found myself wanting to walk deeper into some mysterious wood where brown leaves crackle underfoot, branches lace and lock above the head and darkness settles on the shoulders like a cloak. It was a desire to be enwrapped in tree; a feeling that was simultaneously alluring and disturbing.

The Greek personification of death was Thanatos. His name was purloined by the post-Freudians, though not by Freud himself, and applied to the concept of the 'death-wish' which they saw manifest in risk-taking, in an addiction to speed or danger. But the real Thanatos seems something far drowsier. He was the son of Night and Darkness and the twin brother of Sleep. His allure is the sleepy forgetfulness of death, the sort that Keats wrote about, and the release of complete self-abandonment. It is not so long since life led us to hack and cut and hew our way out of the all-encompassing woodland. Perhaps Thanatos is the lingering desire to be drawn back in again. The real primeval fear of the forest may be its allure as much as its menace. Thanatos, I think, should be the god of the winter tree.

Sylvia Plath knew about winter trees. In her poem of that name she describes them as having an 'otherworldliness', with their 'ring doves chanting'. I have heard those ring doves in the early hours. We know them more prosaically as wood pigeons, birds which have become so abundant in urban areas that they are said to now outnumber the common, feral pigeons. In my garden, it is still the reverse that remains true and the feral pigeons predominate. So while the wood pigeons remain less common, they also remain more welcome; guests but not yet pests. Before first light, not long after the wren had sounded the first alarm, I can hear one uttering over and over its soft five-syllable call.

Later, when I go out to the tree, the sky is a pale duck-egg blue, creased with feathery cirrus clouds. Towards the east, however, the clouds are thickening, and it seems certain that the day will later bring more rain to the already saturated soil. But for now the plane tree is framed in bright sunlight, its boughs casting distinct dark shadows across the trunk. A light breeze waves the tasselled outer branches so that the seed balls, those persistent hanging baubles, dangle to and fro on their long stems. The wood pigeon sits in the tree so high and so still that I do not notice it at first. Normally it is a Tweedledum among birds – fat, waddling, a bully for bird table food – but today it sits so quietly that it does indeed seem otherworldly; and beautiful, too, in its subtle shades of pink, pale blue and grey. Its stillness, except for an occasional slow turn of the head, is absolute and contrasts with the exasperated squabbling of starlings on the feeder below. And then, suddenly, with an explosive clap of the wings, it takes flight, losing height at first so that it can the more effectively rise again and soar away over the surrounding rooftops. There is no hint of what has prompted its departure. It is as if there is something it has very suddenly remembered, the urgency of an appointment it has only now recalled.

February

February is the month of Imbolc, the Celtic feast of spring's awakening. It is the month of Candlemas and of St. Bride, when the coltsfoot flowers open on wasteland and catkins appear on the alder and willow. But the plane tree remains locked in absent-mindedness, deeply wrapped inside itself, unstirring.

With the hawthorn beneath, it is a different matter. Despite the earliness of the season, its buds are breaking and a few leaves have already appeared. The small tree snuggles so tightly beneath the plane that their roots must be interlacing. The larger tree arches its boughs over the hawthorn and they huddle together like a mother bird sheltering a fledgling. I have seen plane trees on local estates where hawthorns, undoubtedly bird-sown, are springing up between the junctions of boughs high up the tree. Perhaps there is some silent encouragement, an affinity between the species, for, in its early leafing, this hawthorn is way ahead of others in the neighbourhood. Or perhaps, like the mother bird's wing, the plane tree's enclosing boughs create a warmer, more sheltered condition. But the plane tree itself remains far behind its protégé; indifferent, and perhaps wisely so, to any early signs of spring.

The month becomes windy and twigs and small branches are scattered across the garden. I gather them and take them indoors as tinder for the fire; it is a small but meaningful harvest. Stronger winds arrive and the boughs sway backwards and forwards over the fixed point of the firm trunk. I have been reading the 8th-century Sufi poet, Rabia of Basra, and come across a description of the wind in the trees as 'God … trying to coax the world to dance.' 'Look how the wind holds the tree in its hands,' she says, 'helping them to sway.' It is the contrast of the sturdy trunk, unmoved by the storm, with the flailing boughs above, that heightens the impression of dancing.

Though branches are torn from the tree, the dangling seed balls remain undislodged, despite the thin and fragile threads they hang from. Perhaps they offer less resistance to the wind, moving with and not against it. And strangely, the crow's nest also remains secure. It is no more than a precarious pile of twigs balanced in a crook of thin branches, but it has some secret engineering of its own, an invisible anchoring that enables it to ride out the storm. There are other planes along the East India Dock Road that have been the victims of savage municipal mauling; a pruning that has left them scarred and skeletal. On one of these a crow's nest remained isolated and totally exposed at the very top of the main bough, without any other visible support or protective surrounding growth. For weeks we looked out for it every time we passed and it remained inexplicably firm. It resembled the lookout at the top of a mainmast, the very image of its maritime name-sake.

Back in the garden, two crows appear and sit close to the nest, occasionally uttering a contented high-pitched churring. Crows have a far greater vocabulary than the basic 'cawing' we usually attribute to them. I have heard them utter more plaintive notes and hollow hoops and this churring, a sound like the winding of a giant watch. One of them is breaking twigs from the tree as if to repair the nest, though I never actually witness it adding anything to the pile. A group of starlings lands on another branch and one of the crows lumbers over to drive them away. Clearly there is something proprietorial going on; the crows aren't nesting, they are not even preparing to nest, but they are mooning about in the general vicinity of the nest, getting used to the idea of it, re-establishing ownership as the season approaches; acclimatising.

The squirrels too have become more active. They chase in pairs up and down the tree, jump the garden wall and leap from bough to bough of the planes on the opposite side, turning our separate trees into a single small forest. Like the crows they are creatures of a bright intelligence. Crows have been shown to adapt twigs as simple tools, whilst squirrels can learn to overcome almost any obstacle placed between them and a source of food. Perhaps intelligence is a requirement of any creature that is to survive in the hostile surroundings of the city; not just the squirrel and the crow but the tits, which learned to steal the milk from doorstep bottles, the sparrows with their resourcefulness and the fox with its reputation for cunning. Cunning is, after all, just the word we apply to the intelligence of those who outwit us.

The squirrels may be intelligent, but efficient they are not. For much of the autumn they have been taking peanuts from the bird hangers and burying them in the garden. They favour my planters and pots where the soil is soft, uprooting whole plants as they establish their caches. Now in winter, when they need them, they can only remember a fraction of these hiding places. This seeming carelessness is, in fact, in the long-term interest of the squirrel. It is the forgetfulness that helps the woodland thrive; in the process of caching they have moved the seed to new sites, carefully planted it, then left it to form the forest's new growth. They are the agents of regeneration, establishing the tree that will produce food for the young of their young and for generations to come. Clearly, then, efficiency is over-rated. It is the great imperative of continual economic growth, it is the cost and corner-cutting that fuels the expansionist machine; but it does not necessarily serve survival.

March

The month has begun with a spell of fine weather and I feel an excited impatience. The ivy which climbs the plane is throwing out new shoots and their fresh, pale green fingers inch up the bark. The nestling hawthorn in its shelter is enthusiastically opening leaves. The chickens are egg-laying with abandon, there are cowslips and violets in bloom in the lawn and the local cherries are shedding showers of early blossom. But the plane tree continues to keep its silent counsel, to bide its own time and no one else's. Ash Wednesday has passed and the tree is observing its Lent. It is the anticipation in the fast that will fuel the feast. We are balanced on the brink, in the period of pause before that leap into life that will mark the tree's own exuberant Easter.

Above me the boughs and twigs and branches form an intricate network in the air. They are an airy sieve through which the city's sound is filtered. The winter winds continue to cast twigs and small branches to the ground and I have come to see this as a natural form of pruning; not so much damage as a natural process that will promote the health of the tree by removing the weakest growth. As I gather the twigs I am surprised to see that several of them bear crusts of lichen. The overlapping leafy patches with their spreading rounded lobes are golden yellow in colour, with discs of a deeper orange. With their wavy, turned-up rims, which will come to hold the lichen's spores, they look like tiny fluted flan cases.

The species is *Xanthoria parietina* and although it is common enough, I am pleased to see it on my plane. Lichen favour trees like the poplar, willow and sycamore, whose bark is least acidic, so its presence here places the plane within that group. Lichens are notoriously slow growers and patches of *Xanthoria* have been shown to expand at just over three millimetres a year, a rate of growth which slows down to less than 0.2 millimetres once they become established. Consequently I have only ever found the lichen on the upper twigs and branches of the tree, or on the corkier older bark around its base. Elsewhere, it would be sloughed off along with the peeling bark before it could be established.

The lichen must be a fairly recent arrival, for it would not have been found on the tree at all in the years when the Reverend Preston's wife was tending the plot beneath it. Then, the masses of sulphur dioxide pumped into the atmosphere by factory chimneys and domestic fires would have raised the acidity of the bark and eliminated the lichen altogether. In the sixty years since the Clean Air Act there has been a remarkable return of urban lichen, and *Xanthoria* is one of the beneficiaries. It is a lover of nitrogen and obtains a plentiful supply from airborne urban dust, another reason perhaps why it favours the high twigs, which act as a filter for more than the sounds of the city. It is also a demonstration that environmental damage can be undone if the will is there.

We generally overlook our lichens, beautiful though they are, and few of them have common or country names. But not *Xanthoria*. It is the 'golden lichen', 'golden shield', 'yellow scale', 'sunburst' or 'bronze moss'. For its striking colour it was once used in Derbyshire for well-dressing, and it has its place in dyeing too. As part of the long tradition of dyeing from lichen in Scotland, *Xanthoria* was used by children in the Borders to stain their eggs for Easter. This way of marking the great feast of spring's fulfilment is one that we have tried to share. Though our children become more reluctant with each year that passes, we still paint or stain boiled eggs in preparation for Easter Sunday and our great, afternoon egg-rolling contest. Being in the Thames-side flatlands we have few hills around us and are forced to construct our own; a Heath-Robinson affair put together with garden furniture, spare timber, ladders dragged up from the cellar and old lengths of guttering. We take care to conceal our proceedings from the chickens, though I secretly suspect that this act of seasonal propitiation will ensure their laying for a further year. One year I tried staining the eggs with natural dyes, onion skins, blackberries and the like, but the results had a pale and washed out look. Even by dint of the scraping of many twigs I doubt that my efforts with *Xanthoria* would fare any better.

The month progresses with the whispering suspicion that something big is about to happen. I pick up another of the small branches dislodged by the wind and its tight, elongated buds are beginning to fatten and to turn a deeper shade of green. I take the branch indoors and within a few days the swelling buds are splitting their russet-brown caps and pushing them aside to uncover a second sticky, inner wrapping. This, too, is breaking open to reveal a layer of scales beneath, as densely furry as a miniature pussy willow. Soon, these too are being pushed out of shape and beginning to split as tiny green balls emerge on projecting stems. They are not quite circular as they have one flattened edge, a legacy of the way they have been squashed together in the bud. It gives them the appearance of tiny, stalked toadstools.

Taking my binoculars outside, I study the buds on the tree itself. They are, I can now see, a few days behind those indoors, but swelling nonetheless. Or rather, it is the balls and the leaves within them that are swelling, bulging against the cases and pushing them into new shapes. We have it all wrong about these buds. We think of them as parting politely when the spring signal is given, but this is no willing opening of the gates. It is the energy and the urge within that drives the emergence; an uncontainable swelling, an outbursting of the life within. It is the force 'that through the green fuse drives the flower', as Dylan Thomas would have it; the same force that cracks the ice, that stirs the cloud, that empowers the seed, that drives this whole peculiar planet. It is the over-coming of Thanatos; it is life reasserting itself.

And now, at last, perhaps in response to the same set of signals – the rising temperature, the increasing day length, or both – the old seed balls are beginning to shed. It is as though the arrival of the new generation has marked the completion of their task and given them leave to let go. They are uttering their 'Nunc Dimittis'. There are fallen balls about the garden, some unopened on soft ground, some burst or half-broken where they fell. There are, too, small drifts of the separated seeds and a regular blocking of drains. Then, one day as I watch the tree, I catch sight of a falling ball that suddenly explodes mid-air. One moment it is entire, the next it puffs into a khaki-coloured cloud of parachuting seed plumes. Small excitement it may be, but it seems precious to have caught sight of this one ball bursting with ripeness mid-flight.

April

With the decisiveness of something long but secretly planned, the leaves are with us literally overnight. Yesterday, it was new weeds that I was noticing, their tiny cotyledons suddenly evident in the rough, brown earth and sending me off in search of a hoe. Today is the first of the month and the plane tree is marking its onset. Stepping into the garden I notice the backyard is scattered with bud scales. Looking up I find the leaves unfurling from their cases in a single emerging mass. It is happening simultaneously on the other planes around us, those in the narrow churchyard and those on the street beyond; their previously sharp lines blurred with young and half-formed foliage, a fuzz of sandy yellow smudging their previously sharp silhouettes.

Though the tide of spring seems unstoppable, there is something improper about it. The plane is said to be a late leafer, opening in late April or early May, but here it is, several weeks ahead of itself. Perhaps it was encouraged by the recent days of milder weather, or perhaps by the night rains, the strange showers that have brought down Saharan dust to coat our streets and cars. Or perhaps it is an April Fool's Day reminder of our warming climate and of the year-on-year advance of spring.

Up to this point in the year, change in the tree has been almost imperceptible. Or it has happened during absence, just as you notice the growth of a child only when you are away for a while. It is a game of Grandmother's Footsteps in which something advances whilst your back is turned. But this month is different. There is a hurry for change and the tree is making no secret of it, advancing literally while you watch. The new leaves are not only emerging, they are changing their shape and texture daily.

They open with a covering of soft golden down, thickest on the back of the leaf and creating the appearance of a pale mist cloaking the tree. To begin with they are longer than broad, for they are rolled as reverently as scrolls within the buds, rather than folded in, as in most other trees. Then they begin to expand, stretching out their characteristic long and exquisitely pointed lobes. Gradually they lose their felt and their transient pallor and take on a deeper, brighter green with a glossy upper surface. The tree is filling out before me, revealing substance from nothing, as in a conjuror's trick. It casts new patterns of light and shade in the sunshine, intricate traceries of spiky leaf shapes that change throughout the day and that will disappear once the canopy is full.

During these same days of spring-watching, the female flower-balls are taking on a crimson shade and pushing out their bristly, hooked stigmas, eager to be fertilised. The smaller, male globes, however, take on a greenish-yellow tinge. They are transient structures; once their pollen is shed, their job is done and they will be impatiently discarded from the tree. As is so often the case in nature, the male is dismissed once its brief fertilising role is over. But the female balls will continue to extend their stems until they are hanging proud of the new leaves. They will remain there for a year or more and for a while both old and new seed balls are on the tree together, the new ones fresh and swelling, the old ones grey and dried and brittle.

A plastic bag appeared a few days ago, lodged towards the very top of the tree. It must have been borne up, balloon-like, in the wind and snagged in the network of twig ends. It is tree-wrack, an airborne jetsam, and like the plastic detritus thrown up on the tide-line it is an intrusion, the insertion of manufactured matter into a realm where it does not belong. It was only recently that I first heard the term 'witch's knickers' used to describe such trapped and torn bags and, though it may be offensive to witches, I was pleased at such evidence of a living folklore. We already have 'witch's broom' as the name given to the twiggy bundles, regularly mistaken for birds' nests, that are caused by galls on a birch tree, and perhaps these bags are the modern equivalent of a gall. This one will be hidden beneath the leaves for the summer and, neither rotting nor decomposing, may well reappear when they fall. And then it will be shredded by the winter winds into jagged threads and strips like the monstrous equivalent of a Buddhist prayer flag.

May

The canopy is still filling out, a month after that first efful-gent opening and it has yet to reach its fullness of cover. It remains an open lattice with the gaps between leaves providing a pleasantly patterned shade on sunny days. It is a shade for which the word 'dappled' could have been invented, a shade which Gerard Manley Hopkins could have included in his catalogue of 'Pied Beauty'. But as soon as leaves are opening, leaves are falling too. It sounds like a grim Calvinist dictum, but it is true. Whilst many leaves are yet to reach their full size and retain the soft texture of a child's Fuzzy Felt picture game, others are already dropping from the tree. Many of them seem perfectly healthy, with no apparent reason for their shedding, but others are dry and crinkly, or already turning brown.

These are the signs of anthracnose, the fungal disease *Apiognomia errabunda* that affects almost every plane tree in London. Though its name carries a disturbing echo of anthrax, it is disfiguring rather than disastrous and I have seen it in varying intensity year on year. It is most apparent in a warm, wet spring when blight will turn the young leaves brown at the twig ends. If it takes a greater hold, some of the larger leaves will develop angular brown patches and these too will fall. I can remember summers in London where so many plane leaves littered the ground that it resembled a premature autumn, but this seems a relatively mild attack.

Examining some of the healthier fallen leaves I am struck afresh by their elegance. There must be few other trees whose leaves can match the architectural symmetry of the tapering lobes, each tipped with a graceful curving point. These fine projections are the continuation of the veins that radiate across the leaf like a river delta. Turn the leaf over and the veins project from the leaf in raised tubes, spreading from the single central vein in the silhouette of a winter conifer.

It has been squally for several days and the wind, whipping across the garden, is bringing down the old seed heads in abundance. As I watch from my study window, the air is full of them, a brown hail scattering across the wet grass. When the wind calms, I go out to look at them. They have taken on the form of shoals, or of sandbars reshaped by a storm. There are deep drifts in the alleyway, softening the shape of obstacles in their path. They drape the cobwebs around the downpipes, and, of course, they are blocking the drains. Clearing up beneath the tree is not just an autumnal task, for there is always something being shed: the wind-sheared twigs in winter; the bud scales, the little male flowers and the early leaves in spring; the drifting seeds and unbroken plane balls throughout the summer; and, only after all this, the great autumn leaf fall. It is a perpetual task and the effort to keep on top of it is an attempt to undo nature. I have come to see it as a battle with entropy and a lesson in inevitability. It is the Second Law of Thermodynamics that is against me.

After sweeping and scooping up drifts of seed I come indoors feeling a tightness in my chest, like the warning of a coming cold or the soreness I once experienced when living next door to a field of flowering rape. The plane seeds and their spicules have an irritant quality, a fact which children have exploited, dropping them down each other's clothes as 'itchy balls', a practice I have also seen with rose hips and with the spiky seed balls of the burdock. I check in my books and find that, aside from these innocent pursuits, plane balls have been held responsible for a comprehensive list of ailments including inflamed eyes, skin irritation, sore throats, coughs, colds, pneumonia, bronchitis and asthma.

In his 1920 book *London Trees*, A.D. Webster recounts a 'notable case' afflicting 'one of the occupants of an official residence at a well-known public building in the West Central district of London'. I have little doubt that, in this coy and rather circumspect manner, he is pinpointing Buckingham Palace. Apparently a 'lady' who lived there was troubled with a throat irritation, which immediately ceased whenever she left for the countryside. Her medical advisor suggested that the cause might be a plane tree growing close to the house. Sure enough, 'with the removal of the tree which stood fully seventy feet high and within a few feet of the building, the health of the patient was restored, and there was no recurrence of the evil'. Arboreal grandeur, it seems, is no protection when the Queen's throat is under threat.

June

The leaves and branches above me are now forming overlapping layers, piling up through the canopy and allowing only a small mosaic of light between them. The tree is ripe with leaves, full to bursting with them, and the shade is as dense as it will get. Its shifting shadow encompasses much of my garden and I wrestle to find the crops that will withstand it. I blame it for the spindly cabbage, the bolting spinach, the lack of fruit on the raspberry canes, the refusal of flowers to flourish.

But sitting one day as the sun breaks through the morning's mist and I feel its heat upon me, I am reminded of the enormous importance that was once attached to shade. There was a time when everyday work took place almost entirely outdoors, when in a day of sowing, hoeing or harvesting, the opportunity to rest beneath the shade of a hedgerow or field-side tree would be welcome in a way we can hardly now envisage. It was a time when walking was not a leisure pursuit but a daily necessity, when miles were covered on the way to and from work, to reach the next town or village, to purchase goods or to get to church on Sunday. It was a mark of the importance of shade along the way that the herbalist John Gerard named the wild clematis 'Traveller's Joy' – 'by reason of the goodly shadowe which they make with their thicke bushing and clyming'. Such shade, for the agricultural labourer or the weary wayfarer was more than an absence of summer heat and glaring light, it was a positive restorative and refreshment.

The significance of shade becomes even more marked in climates such as those of the Mediterranean and the Middle East, where heat is the greater and trees the fewer. In the regions where shade can be a positive lifesaver, the trees that bestow it take on not just a benign but almost a blessed significance. It was beneath the shade of a Bodhi tree that Buddha sat for forty-nine days before reaching Enlightenment – and then spent another week staring at it with unblinking eyes in gratitude. A traveller in the Talmud gives a shade tree the blessing that all its seeds may grow up to be exactly like it. As a young boy, Guru Nanak, the founder of Sikhism, is said to have watched the family's cows from the shade of a Jal tree. In a miracle witnessed by the headman of his village, the shade did not move with the sun but remained in the same place all day to protect the meditative boy. In a lesser-known part of the story of Jonah, God makes a tree grow up over the reluctant prophet to provide him with shade and 'to save him from his discomfort', though he later reinforces his point by appointing a 'worm' to attack and destroy it. At about the same time, Hosea, another of the 'minor' prophets is railing against the idolatrous backsliding of the Jewish people. 'They sacrifice on the tops of mountains, and make offerings upon the hills, under oak, poplar and terebinth, because their shade is good.'

In all of these accounts, shade is sacred, miraculous, the source of salvation. It makes an interesting contrast with the regions of the far north, where trees are plentiful but the sun is not and where the darkness beneath the trees becomes more menacing. Here, beneath the vast coniferous forests that span a hemisphere, the shadow becomes a threatening place of fierce beasts and mischievous spirits, a place that one can be lost in, forever. The stories that emerge from this shade are therefore darker, and they include many of our fairy stories. It is in the forest that Hansel and Gretel are lost, that the menacing Rumpelstiltskin dances, that Red Riding Hood must travel to reach her grandmother's house. In these forest regions, religious ceremonies were not about the sacred shade; they were, like the midwinter fire festivals, designed to stave off darkness and to implore the return of the sun. Even in our own time they echo still; in the coniferous Christmas tree, domesticated for us by the Victorians; in the tradition of the Yule Log; in the Christmas ghost story; in the family gathering around the domestic hearth. The same communal, fireside circle that emphasises the warmth and security within, highlights the dangerous, unfathomable darkness that lies immediately beyond.

As the canopy has filled out and thickened, as the shade of the plane has deepened, so, too, its sound is changing. Sometimes it is a gentle sifting, a reassuring background noise that is easily overlaid by the rumble of passing cars or the diesel coughing of a bus at the nearby stop. Sometimes it is more a restless shifting of twigs and leaves in the breeze, a sound which rises and falls in the eddying air, pausing and returning like waves. Sometimes it is just one part of the tree that is moving; high branches waving whilst the lower remain still. Then the sound is of a small mountain waterfall.

Other sounds emerge invisibly, mysteriously from within the now deep cover. The song of a wren erupts from a density of leaves, a series of mechanical phrases, strikingly loud for such a tiny bird. They are, to me, the wheezings and whirrings of an old grandfather's clock working itself up to strike the hour. Or a robin, that year-long songster, produces its more upbeat summer song. A blackbird bursts out full-throatedly, but this being June its music soon becomes lazier; slow and measured phrases with pauses between each. The urgency of the early season is over; it is trying neither to attract a mate nor to define a territory. It is simply passing the time.

July

I have moved my seat to a different position under the tree, next to the scruffy patch of 'wild' flowers, where the cornflower and scabious are in bloom. The weather is warm but cloudy and the tree is restless. It illustrates how the air has eddies, for it does not tremble evenly. At one moment it is the near side of the tree that is shifting and shaking the extremities of its pendulous outer branches. Then a different, higher, section of the tree comes alive. And then that too stilled, and the movement shifts to the far side where the branches trail. It seems a form of choreography.

With each gust a few more leaves shake loose, yellow and dried, and hurry slantwise to the ground. My lawn is littered with them and I rake them up a couple of times a week. Among them I find a few ends of twigs, still with some leaves attached, with brown oozing scars where they have broken off. It is probably another form of the anthracnose, the shoot blight instead of the leaf blight. Despite it, the tree seems, whenever the sun emerges, to be literally glowing with health, the glossy leaves bathing the whole form in a glistening, reflected light.

The next day the tree is calmer, and with fewer leaves falling, though still it shivers slightly. It has a nervous trembling at the edges, like a man restlessly tapping his fingers on a table. The chickens beneath it are fretful too, though in a self-absorbed sort of way. Their run is part of the garden that is reamed in by the shadow of the plane and they are under its protection. Their busyness is matched by a twittering of goldfinches hidden in the tree. Theirs is an inane sort of burbling, so consistently cheerful as to be irritating. Beyond the chicken run, trailing branches hang low over the road. So many of our planes are heavily pollarded that we don't often see how graceful these pendulous outer branches can be. Their clear silhouettes are as spiky as maples and have a perennially youthful character.

As the month progresses so a stillness grows. The days get hotter and summer settles like a heavy stole. It soaks up both energy and sound. There are days when nothing stirs in the tree and the slow drone of an airplane overhead only emphasises its silence. There are no babbling finches in the branches, no coming and going of tits to the feeders, no pigeons loitering on the house ledges or lining the fences in anticipation of something unspecified. There is a consensus of stillness and silence. At the heart of it stands a tree at the height of its confidence, at the peak of its year. It gathers sunlight and it radiates shade.

It is the 22nd day of the month and all is still. A few bees are investigating a leaf high on the tree and beneath it some hoverflies come and go. A young robin, still deep brown and spotted rather than red, is confidently exploring the garden and will fall prey to the cats if it does not learn more caution. And then, suddenly, unexpectedly, a woodpecker bursts from the plane. It makes the briefest of stops at the bird feeder, describes a circuit and disappears back into the dense foliage uttering its characteristic, loud 'twerp'. Five minutes later it appears again, lands on the garden fence, defecates, flies into a holly bush and then returns to invisibility in the plane.

The great spotted woodpecker is a common enough bird. We have as many as 30,000 breeding pairs in the country, and that number is increasing. In urban areas, in particular, they are becoming commoner. But none of that matters now. The point is the excitement of seeing it here. It is something different and unexpected, an East End woodpecker; this legendary and dramatic bird among the ordinariness of our streets. Welcome though it would be anywhere, this is no countryside encounter, no sighting in a large suburban garden. It is a woodpecker-with-us, and therefore a special form of magic.

I can remember the first time I saw a blue tit. In my Bermondsey childhood I was accustomed to sparrows, pigeons and the occasional blackbird, but not much else. My first sighting of a blue tit stands out as if something remarkable had happened. How could a bird so bright, so delicate, so lively, exist in the city? It was too exotic with all its blues and yellows to belong here. It was as if a black and white film had suddenly burst into colour. Though I would never see a blue tit with quite the same excitement again, it was a little of this feeling that my woodpecker recalled. It was, I suspected, a young bird, probably one of this year's brood, old enough now to leave the area where it had been reared and to search out a territory of its own. It was out exploring and for a while my plane tree was its base. It stayed for a week and then, as abruptly as it had joined us, it was gone.

August

The tree grows tired in August. It is out of sorts. The leaves look dustier and lose their youthful gloss. They hang more limply and move in the slight breeze as if panting. The sun is slightly lower in the sky and the little hawthorn sheds a longer shadow over its protector's trunk; a new and intricate pattern complicating the already patterned bark. The great tit still calls, the goldfinches occasionally chatter, the chickens fuss and another airplane drones overhead, but there is nonetheless a sense that change is not far off. This is not autumn but its anticipation. The tree is preparing itself to let go.

There seems such inevitability about this seasonal change that it is hard to imagine an Earth without it. But it has not been a constant feature: there was a time before seasons and there may well be a future without them. It was in the Cretaceous era, between 145 and sixty-five million years ago, that the cooling of the Earth created a greater seasonal emphasis. Coincidentally, it was towards the end of this same era, while dinosaurs still ranged through forests of cycad and fern, that the first ancestral species of plane were to appear.

The Earth would need to cool still further until, in the Miocene epoch, just twenty-three to five million years ago, the seasons would become much as we know them today. By then, more modern species of plane had evolved and were growing in forests with a strange admixture of ginkgo, catalpa and the tree now known as the Japanese cedar. During this epoch, too, the first human species were separating themselves out from the chimpanzees. The human race, over much of the Earth, has therefore grown up with the seasons. They have shaped us in fundamental ways; how we work, feed and socialise. They influence our art, our faiths and our festivals. They impact on the state of our health and the state of our minds. They are in the way our blood flows.

Now we are blurring the seasonal boundaries; bringing spring forward, setting autumn back, warming ourselves back into the Miocene and beyond. Despite our brightly lit, centrally heated, largely indoor lives, with any type of food at any time of year, the seasons still influence us in ways we are hardly aware of and we tamper with them at our peril. We are part of their rhythm and the year's annual pattern remains at the heart of our mental, physical and spiritual health.

I spend some time, one sunny, late-summer day, looking more closely at the surface of the tree. A few minute mites run rapidly across the bark. A lone ant wanders around in circles looking lost and desperate. Cut off for some reason from the rest of its kind, it is totally without purpose and meaning. Slime trails left by slug or snail head straight up the trunk showing, by contrast, that these creatures have set off somewhere with real determination. Though washed away here and there by rainfall, I can trace the trails some fifteen or so feet above me and heading still higher. I am at a loss to know what they are seeking.

Peeling off a flake of loose bark, I find a single grey woodlouse. It is a miniature armadillo in its heavy armour of overlapping crinkled scales. Its association with decay has given it, in some parts of the country, the sinister name of 'coffin-cutter', but this is a creature for which I have always had an affection. Woodlice were my very first 'pets' and I kept some in an empty fish tank, trying them out on different foods and watching their movements, which, if truth be told, were not many. Most of all I was fascinated by the fact that they were crustaceans, the only land-living relatives of the crab, the prawn and the lobster. They were seafarers washed up on the warm shore. The woodlouse is something of an experiment in living, a sort of halfway house in evolution, an animal that emerged from water but has not yet broken free of its influence. It must keep to the dark and the damp and never dry out, and hence my woodlouse heads for the nearest loose flake of bark, with an instinct that drives it to cover. Prising up another piece I find two centipedes. They are not the tough, glossy brown creatures I am most familiar with but thin and anaemic, and nearly two inches long. Uncovered, they scurry anxiously down the tree, turning their heads from side to side, a curling ripple passing up the body as they move, until they find another flake loose enough to squeeze their length beneath.

What I do not find is the thing I am looking for. In 2006 an entomologist who worked in London's Natural History Museum was eating his packed lunch in the gardens when he noticed a distinctive black and red bug that, despite his profession, he was unable to identify. In what must have seemed an annoying act of provocation, it turned out to be the most numerous species in the grounds that summer, yet he was unable to match it with any of the twenty-eight million insects in the museum's collection. With the help of European entomologists, he was eventually to identify it as *Arocatus longiceps*, a bug from the eastern Mediterranean. In a westward spread it had reached the museum's gardens where it had found a home in the plane trees, feeding on the seed balls and taking refuge beneath the peeling bark. Here, too, it would hibernate and sometimes groups of several hundred sleeping bugs would be found closely clustered together. Since that first discovery *Arocatus* has spread rapidly across London where it is said to be now abundant on plane trees in many parts of the city. Apparently, it has not yet reached Poplar.

There are seedlings, threatening to become saplings, that have escaped my attention in the garden. They are thin and leggy, topped with just a few leaves, but already becoming woody in the stem. They are also surprisingly difficult to uproot and give up their leaves and shreds of skin rather than release their grip on the ground. Despite its reputedly hybrid status, the plane seed can be fertile, especially in London. But there is also a sugar maple just beyond the garden fence and this is prolific too, its helicopter seeds twirling to destinations at some distance from the tree. At this early stage of their growth it is hard to decide which of the trees I am dealing with, plane or maple.

It is a relief to know that I am not alone in my confusion. It is embedded in their very names. Scientifically, the London plane is *Platanus x acerifolia*, literally, 'the plane with leaves like maple'. Conversely, the sycamore, the commonest of our maples, is *Acer pseudoplatanus,* or 'the maple that pretends to be a plane'. This cloud of confusion thickens when you take into account their common names, for the Americans call their plane the 'sycamore', whilst the Scots call their sycamore the 'plane'. Whichever way round, the seedlings will still be uprooted.

September

From early in the month a faint flush of yellow creeps across the tree. At first it seems it could be a trick of the light, but soon it is a colour that radiates from the leaves rather than rests upon them. There is nothing dramatic about it, nothing sudden or showy, but a slowly spreading pallor, a settling in to the inevitability of autumn. I am not able to follow it for long. It is the appointed date for the vicarage to undergo its 'quinquennial'; the ordained five-yearly repairs to its fabric. Scaffolders arrive early, as scaffolders always do, and conceal the house behind poles and platforms, breaking pots and crushing bushes as they go. Builders and decorators follow and fill the garden and house; white-overalled, loud and larger than life. They are a decent, cheery bunch but neither their presence nor their appetite for tea is conducive to moments of quiet contemplation, and I am reduced, like a secret lover, to stealing glances of the tree from an open upstairs window.

After three weeks they are gone, but by then the month is almost over. More leaves have leached to yellow, while some have skipped straight to a withered brown. A few, torn off by the wind, have been entrapped in twigs on their way to the ground. Others have already made it all the way down and lie, unswept, among the cabbages or across the lawn. They are like an autumn advance guard, tentatively scouting out the terrain.

We tend to think of trees as being bullied into autumn, that autumn leaves are torn from the reluctant tree as they succumb to wind or cold, or what the rail services insist on calling 'adverse weather conditions'. The truth, however, is that this shedding is a very deliberate act. The tree is not being sundered from its leaves; it is dumping them. It 'lets them go' like redundant factory workers and then closes the gates against them. And it does so before the cold can kill them or storms damage them, before short days and little sunlight make them less productive, before the frozen ground means that they are releasing moisture but taking none in; before, in short, they are a liability.

It is the early stages of this process that I am witnessing. The tree is withdrawing nutrients, especially nitrogen, from the leaf. It will not jettison all that valuable material that has cost it so much energy to accrue but, instead, pull it back inside itself for recycling. Once this is done the leaf will be sealed off from the rest of the tree by a wall of dead cells at the base of the stem. Nothing can now move into or out of it and the leaf is condemned to its fate.

The falling leaves reveal the buds. They are a deep mahogany red, pointed and slightly curved, giving them the look of tiny rhinoceros horns. Buds are not formed in the spring, as we might lazily imagine, but in the summer when food and energy are at their most abundant. All those devices that enwrap and enclose them – the scales, the caps, the sticky covering of the horse chestnut, the inner fur coat of the plane – are there to get them through the winter, and whatever it will throw at them, before they can swell and burst in the spring.

But there is something different about the buds of the plane. In other trees they form on either side of the base of the old leaf stalk; in the plane they form inside it. Pulling a fading but unfallen leaf free from the twig, I can see how the leaf stalk swells towards its base, creating within itself a tapering, hollow chamber lined with a pale furry pith. It is safely inside this that the bud sits, protected until the leaf falls. It is a small feature but one with a great deal of significance. It is a subtle clue which shows that the plane is not like other street trees but has a far more exotic ancestry. In one of those strange taxonomic leaps, like the relationship between the little hyrax and the giant elephant, it turns out that the closest relatives of the plane are the Nile lotus, and the ancient family of the proteas, those flame-red flowers of the South African veldt. That simple act of pulling off a leaf has made more real the image of ancestral planes in the hot Cretaceous forests. It echoes of a time beyond human history.

October

Autumn is in no hurry. In April the leaves came all in a rush. They opened in what seemed a single day, as if someone had fired a starting gun for spring. But this autumn shedding is a lingering, drawn-out affair. The days of the early month are still and unseasonably warm. There is a little more yellowing of the leaves, a few more hanging brown and dead on the tree, but no great drifts of leaves or shifts of colour. The canopy is thinning like a balding man, but one who manages largely to conceal it. Sometimes, as I watch, a single leaf breaks free and begins a slow descent. It is in no great rush to get to the ground but shifts lazily from side to side as it sinks, as if trying to make itself comfortable in the cradle of air that lowers it.

The passage of seasons seems briefly suspended. It is as though there were a pause at the turning point of the year, just as there is between the coming in and going out of a tide, the magical quiet moment that falls between things happening. Virginia Woolf describes just such a moment in her long essay 'A Room with a View'. It is October 1928 and she is watching from her window. 'At this moment, as so often in London, there was a complete lull and suspension of traffic. Nothing came down the street; nobody passed. A single leaf detached itself from the plane tree at the end of the street, and in that pause and suspension fell. Somehow it was like a signal falling, a signal pointing to a force in things which one had overlooked…'

By the second week of the month a different sort of change has become apparent. The tree is rapidly shedding bark. Fresh pale areas of a custardy yellow are appearing all over the upper boughs as the older olive-grey covering peels free. It is not just my tree; as I look across the fence or walk up the street I can see that all the other planes are sharing this suddenly accelerated shedding. While the rest of the tree appears to age, these upper boughs, when lit up in the autumn sunshine, take on a young and jaunty look. It is a striking effect and I cannot recall when I have seen it happening in such a co-ordinated way.

Not all parts of the trees, I notice, are equally affected. They are shedding more on one side than the other and it seems to me that it is the side exposed to the sun that sheds most, the shadier side retaining its old bark longer or sloughing it off in smaller, thicker pieces. In fact, it is the trees most open to light that are shedding most; those open to the south or standing free of shade or that have been pruned in the last year or two.

Unlike the leaf fall, this is not part of a regular annual process and varies in intensity from year to year. Certain years have been picked out by commentators as particularly worthy of note: 1922, for example, and the summer of 1897.

It seems likely therefore that it is a response to a certain set of conditions and is said by some to follow a period of rapid growth, in which case it would relate to conditions in the preceding season. Perhaps the combination of wet weather and warmth over the summer we have just had, has enabled the trees to put on vigorous growth. Perhaps, as the boughs expanded, they are sloughing off bark, just as a growing lizard sheds its skin.

The naturalist Henry Irving described the pattern left by this peeling bark as 'a reversed leopard's spotting'. For me, another animal came to mind. I remembered travelling in Sudan and seeing groups of feeding giraffe, their long necks stretched out to pull leaves from the tops of the thorn trees. It was this I was put in mind of by the strong upsweeping boughs with their reticulated pattern of dark and light. As appropriate for a writer of murder mysteries, Ruth Rendell gives a far more sinister description in *Put On by Cunning* (Hutchinson, 1981), a book I had only recently finished. For her, bark-shedding plane trees are 'half stripped to flesh colour', looking like 'shivering forms whose nakedness was revealed through their rags'.

By the end of the month the leaf colour is beginning to change more rapidly. It is not however a single, even flush, or a co-ordinated, all-over colour change, but a far more random dotting of faded leaves across the tree. Overall, the display of autumn leaf colour is one of the great pleasures of the English natural year, not just in the countryside but here too, in the heart of the city. Clearly, however, not all trees contribute to it to the same extent. As appropriate for any piece of theatre, there are main players and there are bit parts.

The transformation of the narrow-leaved ashes down Bright Street is a work of pure alchemy, a bronze flush starting in the crown and working its way down until the whole tree takes on the sheen of dark metal. The sugar maple beside our front gate turns a single straw yellow, so pale that the light seems to shine straight through its leaves, while the small-leaved lime on Dewberry Street is still bearing flowers even as its leaves are fading. The common limes, on the other hand, are thinning unevenly and look simply untidy. The sycamore leaves are an unhealthy nicotine brown mixed with tar spot, and the poor horse chestnuts are so disfigured by the leaf miner moths that it seems a relief to them to let the leaves go. Much though I would love my plane to be one of the major players it seems to lack showmanship. Though some of the individual fallen leaves are a beautiful honeyed brown, overall it has taken on a blotchy appearance that is more measles than mellow.

Across the neighbourhood it is yellow, the colour of both hope and cowardice, that has become predominant. It appears like a side-effect of fading, like a person sickening with jaundice, but in truth it is the revelation of a colour that has always been there. As the leaf ceases to produce chlorophyll and the dominant green pigment disappears, so others become visible. The yellow and golden carotenoids have been present all the time and fulfilling their function of capturing sunlight. Only now, however, and only briefly at that, are they uncovered.

What is missing in my local display is the shades of red, though I have to walk only as far as the Recreation Ground to see the ornamental maples burst into spontaneous flame, or take the underpass to the Millennium Green to see the young American oaks flush a shameless scarlet. These fiery reds and purples arise in a different way. They come from the anthocyanin pigments that are produced by the action of bright light on any sugars left in the leaves once they have been sealed off. Though the reds and the yellows are, therefore, the result of different processes, recent research suggests that there is a functional relationship between the two.

It is a strange but well-known fact that the colour yellow seems peculiarly attractive to a wide range of wildlife. Blackbirds and sparrows, for example, will attack yellow flowers in winter, whilst gardeners will know that yellow crocuses are far more vulnerable to bird attack in spring than those of any other colour. Many insects, especially aphids, are also attracted to yellow and will collect, inconveniently, on yellow washing hanging on a line. Scientists have traditionally made use of this attraction by using yellow pan traps when capturing insects for study.

Could it be then, as scientists at Imperial College have suggested, that the red pigment is produced as a ploy by the tree to mask the 'attractive' yellow and to protect the tree from aphid attack? If this is so, one might well ask, why aren't more trees doing it – as opposed to the mere 10% of tree species that can produce red pigment? The answer, I suspect, is that the production of anthocyanin is highly energy intensive. Each species has to strike a balance between these energy costs and the potential costs of aphid damage. Perhaps because it attracts so few aphids anyway, the plane tree is one of those that has 'opted out' of anthocyanins. There will be no glowing reds or moody purples in my garden, just a rather sad decline, one leaf at a time, from green to yellow to the final pale brown.

November

The light of the street lamps that perennially bothers the city's sleep, penetrates our thin blinds also. I lie and listen to rain, thrown in gusts like handfuls of gravel at the window. Something outside, I think in my half sleep, has a message that desperately needs to be delivered. An occasional shrill shearing marks the passage of cars through the water that sheets the road. The morning, when it comes, brings a bustling sky, busy with black and purple-bellied clouds. They are perforated here and there by clear blue patches which admit a light with an edgy, electric intensity. The high winds rise and fall, the stronger gusts shaking the thinning leaves of the plane into a frenzy. They are quaking as if spirit-possessed and speak in loud, hissing tongues. Leaves are stripped from outer branches and hurtle vertically across the garden. The same scouring wind leaves the seed balls in place, though they bob up and down in agitation like floats on a stormy sea. The hawthorn beneath the plane, which still shows little sign of seasonal colour, shakes dementedly, whiplashed to one side as the gusts pass through it.

Plant pots and compost bins are overturned and my fine Cape gooseberry is snapped in several places. Twigs and branches are scattered across the garden and the cabbages lean collectively to one side like a performing dance troupe frozen in mid-manoeuvre. When the storm subsides, the tree settles back into itself as if exhausted. It has also passed a milestone in the year, for it has clearly lost more leaves than those it has remaining. Rather than a full tree that is thinning, it has become a bare tree with a few last leaves attached.

As I rake and sweep this shedding, and load leaves by armfuls into bins and garden sacks, I can't help but wonder at their sheer quantity. It is perhaps only in this ritual of clearing that I really begin to understand the tree's profligacy of production. I search in books and online for an estimate of how many leaves a tree may bear but it is hard to find a source that would be foolhardy enough to put a figure to something so variable. A large spruce, I learn, can bear three million, but these are the narrower 'needles', held in bunches, and they are shed continuously across the year rather than in a single season.

The oak is the most commonly studied of the deciduous trees and its leaves, on a large, healthy specimen, are variously estimated at somewhere between 200,000 and 250,000. Working on the unscientific assumption that my plane tree must carry something similar, I bring some of the fallen leaves indoors and weigh them. Using twenty leaves of various sizes I come to an average of two grams each for the dry, dead leaves. Taking the higher of the two estimates of leaf number gives me a weight of 500 kilos, or around eighty stone, for the leaves fallen from my plane. Add to this the three planes that stand on the other side of the churchyard wall and some two tons of leaves are being dumped annually in and around my garden.

Though no part of the garden is immune from this onslaught, there is one spot where the leaves assemble in great quantity. Blowing down the blind alley at the back of the house they collect at its far end, as if the sheer weight of numbers might give them some sanctuary against sweeping.

It is in this alley that we hang the washing and store all the clutter that gardeners accrete on the unlikely assumption that it might one day prove useful. Along here the leaves best love to twist and tumble, leapfrogging each other, scraping the ground or lifting free of it in brief exuberance and becoming finally enmeshed in old equipment, rolls of wire or piles of pots. Following the storm, they have formed drifts here thigh deep.

Their propensity to flee down this eastward extension of the garden seems affirmation of a basic geographic fact: that our prevalent winds are westerly. The 'national' winds are those that have crossed the great expanse of the western oceans, that have reached us across open salt sea, high waves and swelling tides, and that carry on towards the narrow North Sea and across to the continental land mass. It is not only a physical force but a sociological one as well for it has played a part in shaping London, and this part of it in particular.

When the city became tired of its 'noxious' industries – the smelly, the smoky, the messy or the downright dangerous – it passed an ordinance expelling them from within its boundaries. And so they came here; the slaughterhouses, oil boilers, gut spinners, varnish makers, chemical plants, calico printers, glue makers, distilleries and manufacturers of gunpowder. They concentrated on the east side of town where the westerly winds would carry the smell and the smoke away, rather than blow them back over the city that had expelled them. It was wind direction that first brought this toxic concoction, and with it the concentration of poverty and deprivation, to what was to become the East End. In the social mapping of the city it became a rough rule that wealth declined from west to east, and the wind had helped make it so. The storm-torn leaves, as they congregate at the untidy eastern end of our alley, are re-enacting social history.

Picking up some of the less withered leaves I can see large blotches, with the leaf skin brown and tightly drawn above them. They are mostly on the underside of the leaf and sit compactly between the junctions of veins. The few I find on the upper side are arranged differently and run across the veins rather than slotting between them. I know them as the marks of the plane leaf miner. Like the horse chestnut leaf miner before it, it is a new arrival in the country, first found in London as recently as 1989. Since then it has spread rapidly across the southern counties, though never achieving quite the concentrations of its horse chestnut equivalent.

Both these species are moths that inject their eggs into the leaves, the larvae that hatch from them eating their way between the upper and lower surfaces. These blotches are both their protective home and their food supply and within them I can see the characteristic 'frass', the scattering of droppings that the feeding larvae leave behind them. But the larvae themselves have gone. They have pupated in the leaf, emerged as moths, and cut their way out of their chambers.

They look, as adults, something like tiny chips of freshly chopped wood; pale beige in colour with white streaks on their narrow, elongated wings which swell at the end to bear a large black dot. It also has the effect of reversing their appearance, so to speak, so that the rear end appears to be the head. It is a common enough device in camouflage; an attempt to delude a predatory bird into attacking the wrong end, thus giving the insect enough time to make its escape.

December

The last stubborn leaves still cling to the tree. They form the rearguard of an army now driven into retreat. The hawthorn beneath has also finally changed. Previously almost untouched by autumn, it has turned yellow and shed its leaves in just a few days. Once protection from the plane was removed, it seemed to suddenly lose heart. High above, the loss of leaves has revealed the full, fine tracery of twigs in the canopy and the intricate silhouette they form against the sky. Within it, the mass of dangling balls on their seemingly fragile threads now stand out clearly in their full quantity. The impression, as we enter Advent, is of a tree hung with its own Christmas decorations.

They are not the only element of celebration. As the month begins, the stripping away of cover, the revelation of the tree within, seems only to emphasise the amount of life it is supporting. Despite its bareness, it is busy with birds, with tits flying from branch to branch, goldfinches in gossiping flocks and starlings stopping off on their way to squabbles at the bird table. A mistle thrush sings from a topmost branch and another flies in, uttering its chur-ring, football rattle call. A solitary wood pigeon sits stolid and still, brooding until something better should happen. The old crow's nest has become visible again, its untidy twiggy pile having survived wind and rain and winter storm. It shares some secret of secure construction with the football-shaped squirrel drays that have now become apparent in the neighbouring trees. They seem virtually dislodgeable. It is with the tree itself that they stand or fall.

In 1961, the ecologist Richard Southwood published an article in the *Journal of Animal Ecology* that considered the number of insect species associated with different trees. It was to become hugely influential in conservation circles and to have a wide application. It was also widely misapplied. Quoted and misquoted, especially by those who had never read it, it came to be regarded as a yardstick with which to measure the 'value' of a tree.

Southwood's article was never intended as a full measure of the biodiversity of a tree. It dealt specifically with foliage-feeding insects, excluding those that fed on other parts of the tree, that bored in its wood or burrowed beneath its bark or fed on its flowers or seeds. It did not include species that used it for other purposes: sheltering within it, tunnelling in its leaf litter or associating with its roots. It looked at species that were specific to each tree but excluded those that were generalists, feeding on a wide variety of trees. Although an updated article in 1984 included mites as well as insects, other invertebrates were left out; as were fungi, lichen, mosses, mammals and birds. Above all, it consisted of a species count rather than a measure of the overall biomass – the total quantity or weight of organisms to be found on the tree, whether they are from two species or twenty.

Despite these acknowledged limitations, its listings for each tree species came to be viewed as a sort of league table with which to form judgements on which trees are 'good' and which are 'bad'. Since the majority of trees nearer the top of the list were native species, it also came to fuel the unthinking but commonly repeated mantra of 'native' good and 'alien' bad. Despite its frightening echoes of a chant from *Animal Farm*, or worse, it was to inform much of 'pop' conservation and to launch a thousand 'alien-bashing' work parties.

This association between ecological worth and 'English-ness' reached its apex in the oak. This was the tree at the top of the role of honour, with 284 insects and a further 139 species of mite to its credit. But its position as 'the most important tree in the country for wildlife' stood alongside its role as the most English of trees. It was the tree of both commoners' rights and royal prerogative. It was the tree from which our navies and our houses were built. It was the tree which saved the life of Charles II, preserved the monarchy and had a national celebration named after it. And it was the tree that came to represent the solid sturdi-ness of the English character, and the 'hearts of oak' of our fighting men.

Way below it, at the bottom of the list, came the plane. It was listed as supporting one solitary species of leaf-feeding insect and was, consequently, the least useful of trees. It suffered the twin stigma of being both urban and alien. Yet here was a tree that had brought light to the smoke-bound Londoner, and I knew it to be bristling with life. I had seen the centipedes and the woodlice beneath its bark, the bees that investigated its canopy, the midges that did their mating dance beneath it. I had seen the lichen that lived on its twigs and the ivy that ascended its trunk. I had watched crows build their nest in it, tits feed in it, finches fuss in it, and the woodpecker burst out of its summer density. I had watched the squirrels dash up and down it and I had observed, across the year, its protective relationship with the hawthorn in its lee. The leaf miner moths were evidence, too, that nature is dynamic and that new species will arrive, or evolve, to feed on new species.

The tree in my garden radiates a form of sturdy self-sufficiency that I find almost inspirational. It lives at the heart of a complex web of relationships, both visible and invisible. Sometimes, in their interweaving ways, they seem to be not so much separate organisms but different elements in a single whole. This winter baring of the branches, this new vulnerability, has simply revealed some of the constituent parts. Low though it is in the 'official' tree table, it is the central support of a whole community.

It seems appropriate that as the tree turns inward for winter, as it becomes increasingly self-absorbed, that there should be this burst of life about it. Before the real cold comes it has already done its regenerative work. Next year's buds are formed and will overwinter in waiting. The seed balls are in place and in their slow ripening will ready themselves for spring. If it dreams during the winter months, its dreams will be haunted by the birds in its branches and the burrowers beneath its bark. The deep pull of Thanatos is balanced by this bursting affirmation of life now, and this confident preparation of new life to come.

Chapter Five

After the Fire

It is mid-January and a bitter wind blows from the river. Such really cold days are now a rarity and we have come, almost, to miss them. Absence makes fond memory of even harsh weather and the year feels incomplete without it. It is something missing from the cycle, like a wheel that has lost several spokes.

On Sunday morning I make my way to church with the children. When Jane first raised her tentative plan to train for the priesthood, I consoled myself with visions of a walk to some eventual Sunday morning service. As bells rang out from a steeple-topped tower, we would follow the footpath across frosted fields where stationary cattle exhaled steam, towards a ragstone church held in a clutch of ancient, churchyard trees. In real life I walk a puddled pavement alongside the A12, passing a car park with a burnt-out motorbike, and descending the underpass with its acrid smell of urine. But we do have our trees. Not old oaks or dark yews but a eucalyptus that leans out from the little open space of Jolly's Green and forms a natural arch over the top of the underpass ramp. The pavement around it is scattered today with what looks like a mass of little, dark beads. At first, I take it to be grit thrown up by passing traffic but, looking closer, I find it is not. In the heart of winter, it seems, the eucalyptus is shedding its seeds.

There are hundreds of species of eucalypt, perhaps as many as a thousand, but I know this one to be the blue gum, a tree now widely planted in our parks and gardens. Elsewhere in the parish I have found the commoner cider gum, and I have seen a florist on Chrisp Street adding sprays of the round young leaves of this same species to her bunches of gerbera and chrysanthemum. They remain evergreen throughout the English winter and strike something of an incongruous note, for these are the iconic Australian trees and endemic to that continent. From there, however, they have conquered the planet. The blue gum, especially, though once restricted to the island state of Tasmania, is now the fastest and the biggest-growing tree in almost every hot country in the world. If brashness is an Australian characteristic, it was modelled by the blue gum. It forms copses in Italy and glades in Greece. In Peru I have seen it make up whole forests, and in California it has displaced many of the native oak woods. It provides incontrovertible evidence that a global economy is leading to a global ecology, and that both will be to the eventual detriment of diversity.

Mr. Jolly, on whose Green my local specimen grows, was the local butcher and with inevitable irony was known as a rather miserable man. The eponymous green is appropriately glum. It is a dour and put-upon place, plagued with traffic noise and used by the locals solely to loose a dog or two. The blue gum does its best to cheer things up, rising from the roadside edge on three twisting trunks. Their loose spirals give the impression of long-compressed springs that are now uncoiling. The bark is a very pale blue-grey, peeling off to reveal dun patches underneath. These peelings are not like the thicker plates shed by the plane but long, thin, untidy shreds that drape themselves over branches or litter the ground beneath. The dense foliage takes on a tufted look. It is not the single continuous leafy cover that constitutes our usual image of a tree, but forms itself into several separate, shivering bunches. When shaken by the wind, as they are today, they resemble nothing so much as a collection of cheerleader's pom-poms.

At rest, the individual leaves hang rather limply from the tree. Each has a sickle-shaped curve and, influenced by the Australian connection, I see them as shallow boomerangs. There are a few of them on my table as I write. They have stiffened and dried and crumble easily to the touch but still they release their distinctive fragrance, a smell that sits somewhere between the medicinal and the aromatic, like a cross between camphor and honey. The volatile oils that produce it evaporate freely into the atmosphere so that on a warm, still day the fragrance hangs languidly all about the tree. It was not any peculiarity of local rock or soil but the effect of these evaporating oils, clothing the eucalyptus forests on sunny summer mornings in a fine blue haze, that gave the Blue Mountains of Australia their name.

It was eucalyptus seeds, or, strictly speaking, seed cases, that had drawn my attention on the pavement and I collected some to take home, just as, a few months earlier I had gathered conkers from a few yards up this same pavement. Just half a centimetre or so across, the eucalyptus seed cases were the shape of miniature goblets but topped with a pierced cap. Examining them more closely, these perforations took on very precise arrangements. Sometimes they took the form of a Celtic cross with four short, equal arms, while others were pierced with a perfect trefoil like the upper light of an old church window. Though green on the tree, the cases had turned dark on the ground, with a skin wrinkled like that of a brown avocado. And, despite their tiny size, they were tough enough to tolerate our trampling.

There is a point to these toughened cases: in its natural state, the eucalyptus has a life that is inextricably linked with fire. Though we experience them as disasters, the forest fires that sweep the Australian bush are an essential part of its natural cycle. They remove old growth and all that which is dead, dying, damaged or diseased; they reduce the quantity of pathogenic fungi; and they clear the way for new growth. This is a purging heat, equivalent, perhaps, to the purging cold of the English winters we are losing. They are the phoenix flames of natural regeneration and in the course of several million years of coevolution, the eucalypts have become perfectly adapted to fires, and even dependent upon them.

The hardened seed cases withstand the flames, the heat of which softens them in readiness for germination, while the trees themselves contain protected buds, buried in the bark, that can shoot from the charcoaled stools. The relationship is so significant that not only does the eucalyptus tolerate fire, it actively promotes it. The evaporating aromatic oils are highly inflammable, waiting to catch and spread the flame, and the shed peelings of skin, building up on the forest floor, form a perfect natural tinder. It is an attribute once exploited by the native Australians in fire-making and still, today, some species of eucalypt bear the name of 'kindling-bark'.

Climate change and inappropriate development have increased the frequency of the Australian forest fires, as well as their extent and their impact. It is hard to think of them as 'natural', a necessary ecological process. But fires – and floods, earthquakes and volcanoes – are part of a wider pattern, wonderfully terrifying, but vital to life on Earth. According to Robert White, a professor of geophysics writing in his book *Creation in Crisis*, 'far from being unwelcome intrusions, (they) make the earth a fruitful, habitable place where humans and indeed the whole biosphere can survive. Without them the earth would be barren'.

It was volcanoes as sources of carbon dioxide in the atmosphere, helping to warm the planet and protect it against UV rays, that made life possible. It was the strange drifting of the cooling planetary crust, and the crashing and grinding of plate tectonics as they threw up our mountain systems, that determined and distributed our rainfall. It is the continuation of that building and erosion of mountains that maintains the supply of nutrient-rich soils, and it is the continuing volcanic eruptions that cycle to the surface huge quantities of the minerals essential for life, just as our floods still redistribute them as fertile soils. It is the dreadful human dilemma; that the very forces that threaten our lives are those that also make it possible.

'Australia,' the ecologist Oliver Rackham once said, 'is the planet of fire.' That may be the case, but London is its capital. Like the eucalyptus forest, it has been regularly scoured by flame. And, like the forest, it has regenerated too. At least until the late 17th century, when much of it was rebuilt in stone, London was a tinderbox town. 1666, the year of the Great Fire, must run second only to 1066 as the best-known date in English history, but this memorable conflagration was in fact preceded by at least fifteen other major city fires.

As early as 60 AD, Boudicca took her short-lived revenge on the Romans by burning London to the ground so comprehensively that the resulting ash formed a layer still used in archaeological dating today. Subsequent Roman, Saxon, Norman and mediaeval cities were all subject to major conflagrations and two of them, in 1135 and 1212, had both already been entitled the 'Great Fire of London' before a greater one came along to eclipse them. By 1666, fire was so familiar to the citizens of London that the Lord Mayor refused to be bothered by it. Roused in the early hours to see a baker's shop in flames, he dismissed it contemptuously with the remark that 'a woman could piss it out'. He was famously wrong and, from Pudding Lane to Pie Corner, 13,200 houses and eighty close-packed parish churches were destroyed.

Among the dozens of public buildings that were also lost, St. Paul's Cathedral was the largest and the most iconic. It was at least the third time that this, too, had been burnt to the ground. The Wren building that arose from the ashes became the City's magnificent centrepiece, at least until the late 20th century when the new bland glass blocks were allowed to dwarf it and when mammon rather than God came to mark out the skyline. This 'new' cathedral was also to be tested by fire and to become a symbol of fortitude and, ultimately, of survival, during the next and greatest of the London conflagrations: the Blitz of the Second World War.

In Poplar the bombing had begun somewhat earlier, for the parish already had bitter experience of it during the First World War. On June 13th 1917, fourteen Gotha biplanes took off from Belgium for the first ever daytime raid by fixed-wing aircraft. Their bombs hit East Ham and then the eastern edge of the City, including Liverpool Street Station. Turning homeward, they dropped the rest of their load on the East End. At around noon, a 110-pound bomb crashed through the roof of the Upper Street School in Poplar and fell through two floors before exploding in the ground-floor nursery. When rescuers arrived, the children, both living and dead, were invisible beneath a layer of ash and debris. Though severely injured herself, their teacher remained on the spot, pointing out the places where the children were most likely to be found. Eighteen of them, mostly five-year-olds, were dead. Another twenty-seven were seriously injured, many losing limbs. One girl, Rose Symmons, was not found till three days later. Her twelve-year-old brother had refused to leave the site and had continued searching for her. The children are buried in the East London Cemetery but their memorial forms the centrepiece of the Poplar Recreation Ground and is still commemorated with an annual wreath. When the centenary arrived in 2017, the Queen came to Poplar to mark it with us.

This was, of course, but a terrible foretaste of the things to come. The Second World War bombing of London began on August 24th 1940 but got into its stride in the September. Seventy-one major aerial bombardments were to follow, including one period of fifty-seven consecutive nights. By the end of it, at least 20,000 civilians were dead and over one million houses destroyed. Since it contained London's largest concentration of docklands, Poplar was at the very heart of the storm. The website www.bombsight.org maps every bomb dropped on London between October 7th 1940 and June 6th 1941. It shows a total of 543 high explosive bombs and seventeen parachute mines falling on the areas that made up the old borough of Poplar. This is without the huge quantity of incendiary sticks that would have accompanied them.

An account from the archives of the Imperial War Museum gives a taste of what it would have been like to live here at the time. A boy is returning with his mother from the Chrisp Street Market when the sirens begin to sound. They dash the last few yards home and into the Anderson shelter in the garden where they are joined by his father, who, he wryly comments, is as scared of the spiders as he is of the bombs. As the bombardment begins

> *the noise is horrendous. Every time a bomb falls near, everything shakes. Above us there is the 'voom, voom, voom' sound of the planes. The ack-ack guns make a hollow booming noise and the Bofors make a rapid staccato rattle. It seems to go on for hours and then, suddenly, there is a pause, then the 'all clear'.*
>
> *Stunned by the noise, we emerge. The house is still standing and doesn't seem damaged. We go out through the front door to see a scene which even now I recall as vividly as when it happened. The entire street is choked with emergency vehicles — ambulances, fire engines — all clanging their bells. The gutters and pavements are full of writhing hoses like giant snakes, and above … the*

sky. The sky – to the south, still a deep, beautiful blue, but to the north a vision of hell. It is red, it is orange, it is luminous yellow. It writhes in billows, it is threaded through with wisps and clouds of grey smoke and white steam. All around there are shouts and occasional screams, whistles blow and bells clang.

The neighbours stand around in small groups. They talk quietly and seem as dazed as us. … The gutters run with water, soot and oily rainbows and the reflections of the fiery sky … About 20 minutes later, another alert, we are back in the Anderson, and it all begins again.

Though the massed night-time raids subsided by late 1941, this was not the end of the East Enders' miseries. The raids were followed by the first of Hitler's two secret weapons. The V1 was a stubby, short-winged flying bomb that passed overhead with a distinctive buzzing sound. My mother, who lived through the Blitz in the south London docklands just across the river, described the strange security to be had from the sound: as long as you could hear the buzzing, she said, you were safe. Once it ceased, that was where you did not want to be. The engine had cut out and the bomb was gliding down to its explosion.

The V1s were nicknamed 'doodlebugs' and I was intrigued to find that this was originally a London name for the cockchafer. I had dug one up one of these insects, in its larval form, in the garden; a fat white grub curled into a distinctive C shape, an ungainly, blubbery thing with a sandy orange head. It spends its first three years like this, burrowing beneath the ground and grazing on plant roots before emerging in early summer as a large brown beetle with fanned antennae like miniature moose antlers. It has declined in numbers over recent years, like our entire insect fauna, but it was once a familiar creature, even in the heart of the city. Appearing at dusk and attracted to light it was renowned for blundering into rooms and for bumping repeatedly into window panes. It became the 'doodlebug' from a distinctive humming flight caused by its rapid wing vibrations, a sound which stopped abruptly when the beetle alighted. For this aspect, its name was transferred to the lethal new weapons.

The V2s that followed made no such sound and were all the more sinister because of it. They were also far more destructive. As a man from East Bow put it, 'The bombs took out one or two houses, the doodlebugs a whole street; with the V2s, a whole neighbourhood was destroyed.' It was one of the very last of the V2s to fall on London that had destroyed the streets behind our All Saints' Church. The rector had insisted on continuing a daily mass, whatever else was happening, and it was in the course of this midday office that the rocket fell. As an enormous glow lit him up from behind, he interrupted the liturgy with the comment, 'Friends, I think this is it.' As the church roof caved in, the small congregation dived beneath the pews. It was the sturdiness of those benches, and the fact that a balcony above them had taken much of the weight of the falling roof, that saved them. Behind the church, two whole streets were obliterated in what was one of the worst bombing incidents of the war. It was to take another forty-eight hours to dig out the dead and injured.

I had grown up, almost literally, on these London bomb sites. Our home in Bermondsey was one of a row of prefabs set down as emergency housing on the site of a blitzed terrace. We were at the end of the row, next to the dry-cleaning factory that had somehow survived and whose smell, along with that of the Peek Freans biscuit factory, permeated my childhood. Immediately opposite our kitchen door was a high brick wall, three storeys high and formed from the suddenly truncated terrace. It still bore the ghostly traces of the homes that had been there; the shape of staircases, the indentations of first and second floor fireplaces, the peeling paint of a kitchen wall, the last flaps of wallpaper from what had once been a bedroom. It was our daily landscape and it never occurred to us to think about those who had lived there or to ask what might have happened to them.

Another bomb site ran adjacent to our back garden, fenced off and as yet unbuilt on. There was a gap in the fence that, when not too closely observed, we would climb through and go exploring in the rubble. This, and other Bermondsey bomb sites, had been our playground ever since we had been allowed to walk to and from school unaccompanied. There were fragments of wall, broken timbers, piles of London red brick and mysterious stairs that led down into stinking and water-logged cellars. And around it all there was also new herbage, the green and vigorous growth of the 'weeds' that came to clothe these open spaces. This really was our 'countryside' and though I was neither old nor interested enough then to learn their names, I remember them now as the yellow of ragwort, the

pink of Herb Robert, the purple of buddleia and the deep
red ranks of rosebay willowherb.

The Great Fire of 1666 had been followed by an amazing
botanical outburst when, among the ashes and the charred
spars, the exposed cellars and the fallen roofs, the scattered
domestic debris of homes that had been suddenly fled,
there sprung up the mysterious abundance of the 'London
rocket'. In a similar way, the Blitz was to produce its own
botanical aftermath with the rapid colonisation of acres of
London bomb site. Scarce species were to become abundant, old species were to change their habit of growth and
others were to appear for the very first time.

The dramatic reclothing of the ruins of London with a
newly exuberant flora was documented by Professor Edward
Salisbury, then the Director of Kew Gardens. Observing
it as he travelled to and from work in the final years of
the war he became fascinated by the rapidity of spread,
describing in scientific papers and in his book *Weeds and
Aliens* the processes that allowed it to happen. Altogether
he was to record 126 different species – from bracken to
buttercup, and groundsel to Gallant soldier – describing
their arrival rather tactlessly as 'a good dig-over writ large'.
Many of these species were to remain common even after
the redevelopment of the bomb sites; the buddleia, for
example, continuing to seed itself on railway bridges, waste
sites, neglected walls and even rooftops, up to the present
day. The war was to have a permanent effect on the distribution of plants in London. And it was not only the wild
plants that were to be affected. A gradual but permanent
change to street tree planting was now in the offing.

Like the fallen galleries of the parish church, the small terraces demolished by the V2 would never be replaced. On their ruins, and on those of many others like it, a new, and significantly different, city was to arise. In Poplar two thirds of the housing had been damaged or destroyed by what local people had labelled, with typical East End irony, 'Hitler's slum clearance'. And what the Luftwaffe had left, the planners and the politicians continued to sweep away. Theirs was a vision of a municipally-managed collectivism; a brave new world of centrist social planning. Away went the tight grids of terraced homes, each with its little backyard, and in their place came the new estates. Outdoor space was about to become communal.

Though the housing crisis meant that a great deal had to be put up very quickly, some very significant architects were involved. The concrete blocks of Balfron Tower, which bucked the trend of low-rise development in much of the Poplar area, were designed by Ernö Goldfinger. He lived in them for a month, inviting other tenants to a sequence of champagne suppers, before returning to his permanent Hampstead residence. It was probably an insufficient sojourn to realise that his concept of 'streets in the sky' had failed. Not far away, perched above the Blackwall Tunnel entrance, the two brutalist blocks of Robin Hood Gardens, designed by Peter and Alison Smithson, faced each other across a wide, landscaped open space. Severe in appearance, and with the undoubted air of a penitentiary, they are flanked by a raked concrete wall with a disturbing similarity to the one that divided Berlin. Though the blocks have their defenders, they now face demolition, with the even more intensive development to be put in their place meaning that much of the open space between them will also go. Within fifteen years of being declared a Millennium Green, the slopes of flowering gorse, the little raised-bed allotment sites, the groves of cherry, alder and ailanthus, will all be lost.

Of all the new estates, the largest and most ambitious was the Lansbury, named after the great social reformer and socialist politician, local man George Lansbury. As well as various national and international roles he had been the first Labour Mayor of Poplar. A convinced pacifist, his efforts to prevent the outbreak of war had led him to hold meetings with both Hitler and Mussolini. It was ironic therefore that the estate named after him covered nearly sixty acres that had been destroyed or damaged by wartime bombing.

The site was laid out by Frederick Gibberd, also known for his designs for Heathrow airport, Harlow New Town and, most famously, Liverpool's Catholic Cathedral. The construction of the new Lansbury estate was to be included in the 1951 Festival of Britain as an exhibition of 'living architecture' and an example of futuristic housing. Under the strapline 'New Homes Rise from London's Ruins', visitors were bussed from the main South Bank site to view the Poplar estate under development. Though the new flats were popular enough to begin with, they were soon to reveal failings in terms of sustainability and long-term maintenance and, above all, in their negative impacts on social cohesion. Community, it turned out, was something that could not be easily engineered. The tower erected by Gibberd in the new marketplace at the heart of the estate came to serve as a metaphor for whole endeavour. Planned as a public viewing point and an eye-catching centrepiece, a shortage of money mid-project meant its height was truncated. It was closed shortly after completion on the grounds that it might be used by people trying to commit suicide. Its sole remaining function was as a clock tower, a function that was soon compromised by the fact that its four different faces were showing four different times.

A decline in community cohesion, and in personal open space, was a price paid for a necessarily rapid replacement of homes. It was true, however, that most were now living in better conditions and in a greener Poplar. There were new parks and the new estates were dotted with grassed squares, planted with trees or set within areas of landscaped open space. And along with the radical realignment of streets was to come an equally radical new approach to tree planting. Among its most obvious characteristics were the huge increase in the range of species involved and their increasingly international origins. A flood of new species was appearing and, with the obvious exception of Antarctica, they represented every continent in the world.

I had, in my walks, recorded ninety-four species and cultivars of tree in Poplar, and there were undoubtedly others that I had missed. From Australasia, along with the blue and cider gums, there were the New Zealand cabbage palms, more reminiscent of the Italian Riviera than of the windy Thames riverside. From continental Europe there were Swedish whitebeams, Italian alders and Turkey oaks, tamarisks and laburnums, with their yellow waterfalls of blossom. The Americas provided maples, honey locusts, robinias and the confusingly named Indian bean tree. Asian trees were particularly well represented with maples and cherries from Japan; white-barked birches and red-berried tree cotoneasters from the Himalayas; dawn redwoods, ginkgos, tree privets and Pride of India – another misleading name – all coming from China. Together they represent the fruits of early botanical exploration, of a century or more of Empire and of the post-war growth in trade. To walk, with awareness, around the parish had become a botanical world tour.

I had my own favourites among them. One was a sugar maple that I would see when walking the children to school. It filled its own street corner magnificently, shooting up so exuberantly that it looked like a firework exploding. Smaller and more exotic was a moosewood beside the old dock wall in Naval Row. It had the most striking pattern of creamy stripes set against an unusual pale green bark. And in the grounds of the local secondary school a golden robinia had leaves of a buttery yellow that seemed, in summer, to collect and radiate the sunshine. I passed it every time I carried the shopping home and it never failed to cheer me.

There was, however, a further feature that distinguished this list of new trees, and especially those among them that had been planted in the greatest number. More than anything else, the post-war tree was smaller. The pre-war trees had been architectural in scale: the broadly spreading chestnuts, the monumental planes and the abundant limes were giving way to the smaller cherries, crab apples, ornamental birches, rowans, whitebeams and cockspur thorns.

It was not that there was anything wrong with these new species individually, and there were many beautiful trees among them, but collectively they represented a significant change. Big trees make a big statement. They provided avenues with attitude. They had added significance to streets and grandeur to public buildings. In their size and solidity, they bestowed a sense of permanence and place. The new trees, by contrast, were becoming little more than street accessories, a sprouting form of street furniture.

To an extent, there were practicalities attached to this change. Smaller trees require less maintenance, an important consideration for local authorities whose budgets have been decreasing year on year. They require less pruning, cause less shading and produce less obstruction. They have smaller root runs and are therefore less likely to be held responsible for undermining nearby buildings. It is compensation and insurance claims that are, in our litigious society, the curse of the modern tree officer and they determine their choice of tree species accordingly.

Beyond this, however, it is possible to see in these changes reflections of broader social currents. This was a post-war world, altered forever by the impact and implications of two global conflicts. The years that followed marked the end of Empire, of industrial world dominance and of municipal ambition. After initial experiments in corporatism, both local and national, collective responsibility began to be replaced by pragmatism and a greater individualism. A certain self-confidence disappeared from the public realm, the market replaced the municipal and the role of local authorities gradually transmuted from that of local leadership to that of facility management. The change from the semi-permanent and statuesque to the shorter-lived and less substantial street tree seems to mirror this. The tree is no longer a statement of imperial stature, nor, like the grand Town Hall, a reflection of civic ambition. It has become a form of decoration, like those wispy adjuncts in an architect's drawing.

This can be seen clearly in the decline of the avenue. Their planting requircs a faith in the future that we no longer have. Not only do they now rarely feature but the ones that we do have are being diminished; 'gapped up', as older trees die, not with younger specimens of the same species but with whatever happens to be available in the nursery. Fine avenues of lime or plane are infilled with a birch or an alder or, worse, a muddy-leaved ornamental cherry. The overall concept and impression is forgotten, there is only now an assortment of individual trees. We have lost a sense of permanence – and permanence, according to Kenneth Clark, is the essence of civilisation.

Caught between practicality and a shrinking sense of the collective, it would be unsurprising if the choice of post-war street tree lacked any cultural resonance, but, against the odds, connections persist. They do so because trees have a meaning for us that runs deeper than the demands of everyday decision-making, connections that we are barely aware of and associations that have built up over the hundreds of generations that we have lived alongside them. They persist, and have influence still, in the cultural unconscious. One clear example of this is the rowan.

In 1989 the Forestry Commission carried out a survey of 3,600 street trees in thirty towns and cities throughout England. The average age of all the trees surveyed was twenty-five, an indication of the increase in planting in the post-war years. Nearly 20% of all trees recorded in the survey were members of the genus *Sorbus*; the whitebeams and the rowans. In particular, the rowan, which rarely exceeds thirty feet in height, has become the typical small street tree and almost an urban cliché. In some boroughs it lines street after street; in Poplar I recorded it more commonly on estates and in car parks, public parks and gardens.

The wild rowan is a tree of the woodlands but it can also grow at altitudes of up to 3,200 feet, higher than any other tree in the country. It is this fact, together with a similarity in leaf shape, that has earned it the alternative name of 'mountain ash'. In this setting it is, perhaps, at its most beautiful, growing as a single specimen on a stony mountain slope, or wind-bent beside an upland track. On the Poplar pavements it could, too often, be a weak or wispy thing, with a frail and undernourished look or displaying dead and dying branches in its thinning crown. Where it was well established, however, it displayed its full character.

I had seen the rowans on the Pennyfield estate set against a grey autumn sky, their bunches of red berries framed with leaves of dark green and an almost metallic blue, reflecting the bruised colour of the lowering clouds and bringing back memories of walks on wild days in the moorlands. In spring, by contrast, the same trees appeared feathery, almost frivolous, with their bunches of frothy white flowers. By summer these would turn to green berries, gradually reddening as the foliage too ran through a whole chromatic scale. There are species and cultivars on the local streets with berries in purple, white, pink and even gold, but none of them quite matches the fiery red of the native tree. Towards winter they add an extra light to the street, an internal glow, as though the trees have been hung with lanterns, even as the leaves about them begin to fall.

A further virtue of these berries is their great attractiveness to birds. They are too big for the warblers, and just at the limit for robins, but many larger birds love them. Liming the twigs of a rowan was a technique once used by bird catchers, a practice reflected in the tree's specific name of *aucuparia*, derived from the Latin for 'a bait for catching birds'. In the less threatening context of our streets, a variety of birds will gather to feed on them from late summer onwards, often in large numbers.

It begins with the wood pigeons, which seem able to digest the fruit while it is still green. Their bulk makes them ungainly in the small trees and the slender branches bow beneath their weight, causing the birds to shift and flutter awkwardly in order to retain their balance in the tree. It does not stop the determined efficiency with which they strip the fruit.

Starlings follow them and, as October turns to November, sociable flocks of these grassland foragers increasingly turn to feeding in the rowan trees, chattering and arguing vigorously amongst themselves like a noisy party in a fast food restaurant. Blackbirds become occasional visitors about this time and later, if the crop has been sufficient, they will be joined by mistle thrushes, announcing their arrival with a guttural churring like the waving of old-fashioned football rattles.

All these are regulars but a good year will produce other

species, especially in harsher weather. I have seen redwing, those beautiful small thrushes with Christmas-red underwings, foraging in the trees when early snow lay on the ground around them and, on one magical occasion, a flock of twenty waxwing. I had waited years to see these beautiful charcoal grey and yellow birds, exotic in their black eye-masks and coiffured crests, and, when it finally happened, they were feasting on rowan berries just yards from my own front door.

There is another, deeper, magic to the rowan. No British native tree has such a widespread and deeply ingrained reputation for its protective powers. It features in English, Celtic, Irish, Scandinavian and even Icelandic folklore. In Lancashire, it was used in divining. In Cornwall, a piece was carried in the pocket to avert rheumatism and lumbago. In Yorkshire, May 2nd was regarded as Rowan-tree witch day, a day when witches were particularly active and twigs of the tree were placed in byres to protect against them. In Scotland, sprigs of rowan were tied to the halyards of fishing boats. In Ireland, it was planted in graveyards to discourage the dead from rising. In Wales, it could counteract the power of a fairy ring. Across the country, twigs of rowan were made into crosses, put over doorways, tied to gates, hung in barns or byres, put in the milk churn, suspended over the hearth or attached to the yokes of oxen.

A belief in rowan's protective properties spread with British settlers round the world and survived in distant parts of the old empire long after it had ostensibly died out here. I worked for a mayor of Islington once who was a New Zealander by birth and who came up with the idea of planting rowans around the entire local authority boundary.

Just what it was in the surrounding boroughs that she was protecting us against she never clarified, and the scheme was never implemented. Perhaps, however, in its planting today, some hint of its magic persists. Something deep has stirred in the air-conditioned offices of architects, town planners and tree departments as they unwittingly chose our major protective tree for street after street and block after block of estates. It is another type of 'ghost tree', exerting its influence, and that of the long-held beliefs that surround it, even when they are seemingly lost to our conscious and rational minds.

There is one well-known example where the power of the rowan was invoked not for protection but in order to deliberately inflict harm. In 1949, the poet Kathleen Raine was introduced by her publisher to Gavin Maxwell, later famous for his books but then a struggling painter and failed shark farmer. According to several sources, including her autobiography, *The Lion's Mouth*, Raine developed a passion for him that was to lead to a seven-year relationship, punctuated by a series of tempestuous rows. The intensity of her feelings was not reciprocated and the relationship was never physically consummated, Maxwell himself being ambiguously homosexual. Nonetheless the landscape around Maxwell's house at Sandaig, on the coast of Wester Ross, was to feature in many of Raine's poems and it was a phrase from one of them that Maxwell came to use as the title of his most successful book, *Ring of Bright Water*.

In 1956, in the course of one particularly angry encounter, while a storm was raging theatrically outside, Maxwell banished Raine from his home. She took shelter under a rowan tree and, taking hold of it, cursed him with the words 'Let Gavin suffer in this place as I am suffering now'. Within a few years his house had been destroyed by fire, his beloved otter had been killed, and he himself was diagnosed with terminal cancer.

'Whether or not your curse has been responsible for this terrible disaster,' he wrote to her of the fire, 'I don't know or should never know. If it was, I can only say God forgive you…' Raine herself seemed to have been more certain about its influence and came to bitterly regret her action. The curse, she thought, had rightly rebounded on her and she suffered from depression and self-loathing, before reaching some resolution in her later years.

Another of the small number of native tree species that make up the post-war urban forest is the hornbeam. It made a slightly later appearance in Poplar than the rowan but is growing in popularity and is now nearly as numerous. But, unlike the rowan, it has almost no role in our national folklore. This is something of a puzzle, for though it has few timber uses it once played an important part in the life of the poor, being extensively harvested for firewood. Its connection, however, remains one not so much of lore as of location. The hornbeam is a peculiarly local tree and while the black poplar was characteristic of the Poplar marshlands, the hornbeam was the typical tree of the forests that clothed the hills beyond.

It is distinctively a tree of south-east England. Though not fussy about the soil it lives in, it loves the local clays and, for twenty miles around London, it becomes the commonest woodland tree. Apart from one or two outliers, such as that on the Suffolk/Norfolk borders, it is fairly safe to say that the further north and west you travel, the less common the hornbeam becomes.

Long before he was recording the flora of the London bomb sites, Edward Salisbury was studying hornbeams in the Hertfordshire woodlands. From that county they run eastwards, leaping the Lea valley to reappear again in Essex, where they formed an important component of the once great forests of Epping, Hainault and Hatfield. Travelling northwards up the Lea from the village of Poplar, at the time when black poplars still fringed the waterside and lined the ditches of the Bromley Marsh, you would have seen the broad, damp valley gradually giving way on either side to a ridge of higher ground dense with hornbeam woodland. The contemporary fashion for planting hornbeams feels, therefore, like a recolonisation; a reassertion of its ancient rights and an incursion of the ancient forest into the modern city.

The urban hornbeams do, however, have a different appearance than those in the Essex forests. There was one that stood close to a footbridge over the Docklands Light Railway, squeezed between the railway wall and the estate, and, having discovered it on my walks, I paid it regular visits. In spring its opening buds were long and thin, with a characteristic inward curve that gave them the appearance of overgrown fingernails. Later, I would find them unfurled into a dense foliage of oval, toothed leaves with parallel veins that were so deeply incised they resembled pieces of unfolded origami. From surprisingly early in the summer I would see its fruit, hanging in bundles of green spiky sepals, the shape of pagoda roofs. As the year progressed, so they became paler, increasingly coming to resemble drying bunches of hops. And in autumn I would cross the railway bridge to see the leaves putting on their display of yellow, orange and russet tones before finally giving way to winter. It was then that the bark was seen at its best, smooth and silvery-grey and streaked with sinuous, paler patches.

In all these details the urban tree is similar to its forest equivalent; it is in its overall shape and character that the difference appears. Street hornbeams are purchased from the nurseries in the cultivated form known as 'Fastigiata'. Fastigiate trees have an erect shape formed by parallel, upsweeping branches. They are, in other words, the ideal shape for the limited space of the city street and the epitome of post-war planting. The fastigiate hornbeams begin with a columnar shape but widen somewhat as they grow to form neat, dense cones. They have the smart appearance of snappy dressers that have wandered over from the offices of Canary Wharf, well turned out and with the confidence that comes from a good suit. The forest hornbeams are the very opposite; not just broader in outline but sprawling and spidery. They are eccentric, raggedy trees, their distinctive appearance arising from the way which, for hundreds of years, they were used.

For generations, the commoners of Essex cut the forest hornbeams for firewood. Since they also had rights to the grazing of pigs, sheep and cattle in the woodlands, the trees were cut just above the level where animals could browse, a process known as pollarding. This technique, used on both the hornbeams and the larger beeches that interspersed them, came to an end in the 1880s. Instead of being harvested at a manageable size, every seven or eight years, the many stems shooting out of the thickening bole were suddenly left to themselves, growing to become large unstable boughs which gave the trees a top-heavy and lop-sided look. Impractical though they had become, their contorted appearance gave the forest its character and I determined that I would complement my observations of street hornbeams by visiting their forest cousins. Earlier in the year, whilst searching for the rare marsh fern, I had noticed interesting groups of hornbeams at Gernon Bushes, a detached northerly part of the Epping Forest. It was there, I decided, that I would return in order to examine them more closely.

Walking the hornbeam thickets of Gernon has the disconcerting air of being on the inside of someone else's imagination; a Palmer painting perhaps, or a Fuseli nightmare. The trees have a fantastical appearance, their ageing trunks deeply fluted into strange and twisting patterns. They resemble bunches of knotted muscles or one of those anatomical illustrations that used to hang on laboratory walls showing human bodies with the skin stripped away revealing the complex pattern of sinews and tendons below.

The short trunks are topped with swollen and contorted boles in which it became easier, the more time I spent in the forest, to see peering, knobbly faces. It was an impression heightened by the boughs that shoot upwards from them, like Struwwelpeter's hair. Few of the trees remain completely upright under the weight of these outsized boughs, and they lean at a variety of contrasting angles like a group of drunks staggering home from a party. Some are completely hollowed out, some split at the top, others broken open at the bole with rainfall penetrating to ensure their rapid rotting. One or two have toppled completely, taking with them great plates of dried and crusted clay. Still they live on, their branches now growing up at right angles to the trunk.

It was bright beyond the wood and looking up I could see that the leaves were almost translucent; the sunlight pouring through them to produce a golden green light in the upper canopy. None of this reached ground level, however, and the glow in the canopy seemed only to heighten the depth of the shadow below. It was from places like this that the Victorian illustrators of scary children's books must have drawn their inspiration. I had walked them before, I was sure, in cautionary childhood tales of the dangerous, dark wood where the trees are alive and suspicious and menacing. If any woodland were to be inhabited by witches, it would be this, and I would not have been surprised to stumble across a gingerbread house in a clearing.

Apart from the pollarding of poles for fuel, the extreme hardness of the hornbeam means that its wood has few uses. It is worked only for the most hard-wearing of items, such as the percussive keys in pianos or the crossbeams of yokes between ploughing cattle. According to some accounts it is this that gave rise to the name of 'hornbeam', but this is almost certainly fanciful. Since 'beam' is an old English word for tree, the name is more likely to mean, 'the tree that is as hard as horn'.

Hornbeam does have one more recorded use. It was carved for the cogs of the interlinking wheels that work a mill. For this work, it was said, hornbeam was the only suitable wood. It would have been present here in Poplar, alongside the fire-resistant black poplar, in the tidal mills that once stood on the banks or straddled the River Lea.

Apart from the rowan and the hornbeam, most of the new generation of street planting involved exotic cousins of some of our familiar trees. The common ash, probably the most abundant tree in the English countryside, is now less common on our local streets than its narrow-leaved Caucasian relative, planted for its beautifully bronze autumn foliage. The birch, another abundant British tree, is increasingly outnumbered by exotic mountain relatives from the Himalayas that display a bark so preternaturally white that it seems to have sprung from an old-fashioned advert for washing powder. And the hazel, perhaps the most historically significant of all British trees, is represented more by the Turkish hazel, a relative from western Asia, than by its native form.

To be fair, the Turkish hazel does have the advantage of being indisputably a tree. Our native hazel seems more ambivalent about its status. Sometimes growing from a single short trunk but far more often formed of multiple shrubby stems, it has left foresters and the writers of tree books uncertain as to how it should be categorised. There are several of these native hazels, coarse-leaved and bushy, in the nature garden of the local secondary school, from where they push their vigorous growth through the chain-link fence and across the pavement of St. Leonard's Road. I have planted several more in my own garden where they grow with equal speed and vigour and need to be taken to task at the season's end. In one rather odd little Poplar park, beside the Further Education College on the High Street, their shrubbiness has been put to good purpose, the shady site being divided up into 'rooms' by diagonal hedges of hazel.

The Turkish hazel harbours no similar doubts about its status. Growing rapidly from a single stout shoot, it can put on as much as 1.3 metres in a year, forming a shapely, leafy tree that will thrive in even the most difficult situation. Its leaves are similar in shape to those of our own hazel, and just as coarse to the touch, and its somewhat twisty branches form a conical dome. Its really distinctive feature, however, is its bark. Marked with corky corrugations, it has an attractively shaggy look.

Its appearance on our streets is very recent, later even than that of the hornbeam and the rowan. My well-thumbed 1978 edition of Alan Mitchell's tree guide describes it as 'infrequent' and found in 'collections, some large gardens and a few parks'. Just thirty years later it can be found in streets all over London. It was the Americans who first discovered its usefulness in urban planting schemes, and it is clearly now popular in Poplar, with newly planted rows on several of our streets. On Ricardo Street, its saplings line the pavement behind the Lansbury-Lawrence Primary School. On Ada Street, they form a neat row outside the newly refurbished flats. On Kerbey Street, they run down the west side of the market and on past the Salvation Army Hall, the place from where, each Good Friday, a dwindling band sets out on a 'March of Witness', following a big bass drum and a large wooden cross, a tree of a more symbolic kind.

Both species of hazel bear nuts and it is from the nut that they get their names; both common and scientific. The hazel genus is *Corylus,* from the classical Greek name for the tree, which itself is said to derive from *korys,* a helmet. It describes not so much the nut as the leafy husk that surrounds it, in the same way that a helmet surrounds the face. In a similar, but rather less militaristic manner, the common name 'hazel' derives from the Old English *haesel*, meaning a hat or a cap. It represents a far more English sensibility, calling to mind those old illustrations in children's books where the fresh-faced elves wear caps of hazel cups, the stalk projecting as a peak.

It is significant that all these names have origins relating to the nut, for its importance in the survival of the human species can hardly be overstated. Exploring in the British Museum, I came across a single case devoted to the Palaeolithic era in Britain; those tens of thousands of years of the 'Old Stone Age' and of the wandering hunter-gatherers who preceded the development of agriculture, permanent settlement and the smelting of bronze and iron. Among the items displayed within the case was a small petri dish filled with pale grey ash; the remains, I read, of the burnt shells of hazelnuts.

According to the pollen record, hazel was abundant at this time. Its nuts would have been an important food source; portable, easily stored and providing a rich source of protein, particularly significant for surviving the lean winter months. Even the shells were put to use, saved for kindling, or thrown onto the fire in handfuls for an extra burst of heat and light. It was the remains of just such a fire that sat in a dish in the British Museum, forming perhaps, the earliest surviving record of the long relationship between humans and the hazel.

Its cut poles could be split lengthwise and were supple enough to bend, without breaking, almost into two. They were facets that made it adaptable for many uses. Across the ages they appear in hurdles and fencing and wattle-and-daub walls, in furniture and in ties for faggots, in spars for thatching and in stakes for nets, in walking sticks and pea and bean sticks and in a multitude of other ways. Rods of hazel appear even in the legal system where, from the 13th century, they were notched by 'quit rent knives' to record the payment of rents and services. As early as Neolithic times, hazel poles were being cut and laid down as part of the trackways that criss-crossed the Somerset marshes. The Mesolithic peoples deliberately cleared or burned areas, including the Thames valley, to encourage the growth of hazel. And as late as 1905, such was the importance of the tree, there were still half a million acres of managed hazel coppice across the country.

It was the nut, however, that was its most crucial product. The Middle Ages saw the hazel wildwood being turned into managed coppice, and the planting of the first hazelnut orchards with cultivars, cobs and filberts. The collection of wild nuts also continued and became, for many, an important source of income. For villagers in Dorset the collection of hazelnuts was said to earn enough money to pay off a whole year's rent. But, above all, they were a free source of food for the poor, providing essential nutrients at a time of year when little else was available. Weight for weight, hazelnuts contain 50% more protein, seven times more fat and five times more carbohydrate than chicken eggs. The success of the hazelnut harvest could, at times, mean the difference between survival and starvation.

Given their importance, it is unsurprising that the gathering of nuts was subject to regulation. It was not the written law of the ruling classes; such formal codes were for the privilege of the rich, not the protection of the poor. It

took the form of taboos and warnings, rhymes and impre-
cations, sayings and superstitions; the communal regulation
of a community asset. Together they made up a code that
protected the crop from being expropriated by individuals,
from being picked without the knowledge of the rest of
the community or even from being collected too early.
Here was a body of local lore not as a form of the primitive
simple-mindedness, as we sometimes like to think it, but
as a means of ensuring fair distribution and the welfare of
the community as a whole. In this respect it was like the
regulation of the commons, a social institution designed to
ensure both equity and sustainability.

Crucially, the hazel had its own protective spirit. Its name
varied from region to region, whether Melsh Dick, Hind
Etin or Milk Churn Peg. To pick nuts without seeking
permission from the spirit would invoke it, and the consequences could be dire. The famous 'Child Ballads', collected
at the end of the 19th century by American scholar Francis
James Child, contain a typical example. Intriguingly it is set
in a 'Mulberry Wood' and it involves both the Hind Etin
and a woman by the name of May Margaret:

> *May Margaret stood in her bouerdoor,*
> *Kaiming doun her yellow hair,*
> *She spied some nuts growin in the wud*
> *And wishd that she was there.*
>
> *She has plaited her yellow locks*
> *A little abune her bree,*
> *And she has kilted her petticoats*
> *A little below her knee,*

And she's aff to Mulberry wud,
As fast as she could gae.

She had nae pu'd a nut, a nut,
A nut but barely ane,
Till up started the Hynde Etin
Says, Lady, let thae alane!

In his wrath, he takes her by the hair, ties her to the hazel and threatens to kill her. When she pleads for her life, he agrees to spare her as long as she remains with him in the woods. She does so, bearing him seven children before, many years later, being restored to her family.

Such was the power and persistence of the spirit that Christianity could hardly ignore it. It responded, as it so often did, by replacing the spirit with a saint: St. Philibert. A 7th-century Dominican priest who had founded the abbey of Jumièges on the Seine, his main qualification for this patronage seems to be that his name day fell on August 22nd, the time of year when the nuts begin to ripen. It was a corruption of the name Philibert that was to give us 'filbert' for the largest and best of the cultivated nuts. St. Philibert continued to protect the tree against unlicensed nutting, especially if it took place on a Sunday, and it was the Devil himself who was now summoned to deal with transgressors. In another echo of the Hind Etin and May Margaret, an unwanted pregnancy was one of the potential consequences of untimely nutting. This process of the 'Christianisation' of older symbols and practices was not necessarily the aggressive elimination that is sometimes portrayed but a process of gradual acculturation in which the older beliefs survive in the newer religion, taking on new forms whilst their meaning remains essentially the same. Their echoes can still be found in the prayer book or heard in the Anglican liturgy today.

It was an event in the liturgical year that was to come to mark the opening of the 'approved' nutting season. Holy Cross Day, or Holy Rood Day as it was earlier known, falls on September 14th. It had, from the 4th century, been set aside for the veneration of the sacred tree, and it was on this day that the collection of hazelnuts could begin. The gathering was an enterprise in which the whole community would participate, taking to the trees together. In a practice that continued right up to the First World War, many village schools would close for the day so that children could join their families in the woods.

There is a well-known children's song, sung to the tune of 'Here we go round the mulberry bush' and first recorded in written form by the folklorist Alice Gomme in 1894:

> *Here we go gathering nuts in May*
> *Nuts in May, nuts in May*
> *Here we go gathering nuts in May,*
> *On a cold and frosty morning*

The suggestion that nuts should be gathered in the month of May is something of a puzzle. At this time, last year's nuts will have long been stripped, whilst the new ones are only at the earliest stage of formation from the recently fertilised female flowers. It is a contradiction for which two explanations are conventionally given, and they are equally unconvincing. According to some accounts, these 'nuts in May' are a corruption of 'knots of May'; bunches of blossom cut from the May, or hawthorn, tree, perhaps for some part in the May Day celebrations. According to others, the reference is not to the hazel but to the pignut. This is a small relative of the cow parsley, a fine-leaved plant that grows in the light shade of open woods, field edges and hedgerows. Three or four inches below the ground it produces a brown tuber that can be skinned to reveal the white flesh beneath. I have grubbed them up myself on occasions and shared their crisp, nutty taste with friends and family. Once this practice would have been more common, especially among children, but I cannot see them as more than a casual or wayfaring food, lacking the real significance of the organised nutting outings. The real answer to this puzzle lies, I believe, in another aspect of our long-term relationship with the hazel.

Many of the old fairs and festivals, whatever their religious origins, soon became opportunities for boisterous and exuberant behaviour; some of them falling foul of church and state because of it. The Holy Cross Day nutting expeditions seem to have followed a similar trajectory and developed a reputation for heavy drinking, horseplay and licentiousness. It is hardly surprising, in a society where privacy was hard to come by, that a sanctioned excursion by both sexes into the woods should lead to some extracurricular activity. The phrase 'to go nutting' was to become a euphemism for courtship, whilst cruder sayings related the size of the hazel crop to the number of children born the next year, or to the number of bastards in the village.

By 1826, the owner of Hatfield Forest was complaining that 'under the pretence of gathering nuts, the idle and disorderly men and women of bad character from Bishop Stortford' – a town on a branch of the River Lea – 'are afforded an opportunity for all sorts of Debauchery'.

In this respect, the Holy Cross Day outings seem to be reinforcing a deeper link already existing between the hazelnut, sex and fertility. It is there in the sexual threat emanating from the spirits of the hazel against anyone who trespassed on their domain. It is there in the story of May Margaret, ravished by the spirit of the Hind Etin; and it is there, when the Devil supplants him, in the threat of pregnancy against the woman who goes, untimely, nutting. It is there in the divinatory rhymes surrounding the eating of hazelnuts and the burning of their shells on the fire. And it is there, further afield, in the old French custom of throwing hazelnuts as 'confetti' at weddings, a possibly painful way of ensuring fertility. It is there, perhaps, even in the use of the word 'nuts' for testicles.

An old folk song called 'The Nutting Girl' makes the connections perfectly explicit:

> *So come all you young women, this warning by me take*
> *Oh, if you should a-nutting go, don't stay out too late.*
> *For if you should stay too late for to hear that ploughboy sing,*
> *You might have a young farmer to nurse up in the spring.*

The outcome for the nutting girl was not a happy one, as the chorus makes clear: 'Whatever nuts that poor girl had, she threw them all away.'

Against this background, the words of 'Here we go gathering nuts in May' take on an entirely different connotation. Here is no rhyme of innocent rural children digging for pignuts or of white-smocked young maids gathering bunches of May blossom. Here, instead, is a smutty sexual reference, something like an earlier version of the rugby song. The reference to nuts is entirely ironic and it is set in May because it was the fullness of spring, the month of sexuality and fertility and the time of the May Day excursions into the woods.

The connection is borne out still further by the children's game that once accompanied the rhyme. It would be sung by children holding hands in a circle, with one child selected to stand at the centre. On reaching the second verse, 'Who will you have for nuts in May?', the child would respond by choosing a partner of the opposite sex. They were, in their innocence, illustrating the hidden history of 'nutting'.

With the increasing number of Turkish hazels on the streets, I was tempted to wonder whether we might one day be able to resurrect the communal harvesting of hazelnuts. There was, of course, the risk of a similar descent into collective indecency, but the streets of Poplar are a less enticing setting than an autumnal woodland and I was reasonably confident that it could be avoided. A much more serious objection came from the fact that a ripe hazelnut seems almost impossible to come by. Outside of cultivation they have, in modern times, almost completely disappeared. Oliver Rackham had no doubt as to where to point the finger of blame. Grey squirrels, those relatively recent arrivals on the British scene had, he said, managed to do what centuries of protective lore had prevented: to strip the nuts too early in the season.

When Holy Rood Day came round again I happened to be on a few days' walking break with a friend and it seemed an ideal opportunity to check the reality of this shortage for myself. We were camped near the village of Silverdale, on the Lancashire/Cumbria border and alongside the huge expanse of Morecambe Bay; stunning in its beauty and terrifying in its power. This should have been good country for finding nuts: 'The hazel still fruits in the damper western woods of Cumbria,' claims Edward Milner in *Trees of Britain and Ireland*. Our explorations led us through wood after wood: Eaves Wood and Cringlebarrow Wood; Warton Crag, with its Three Brothers stones; Gait Barrows, with its limestone pavement; Arnside Park and Grubbins Wood, both on the coastal path; and the tree-clad hillsides of Arnside Knot and Middlebarrow. We must have walked past several hundred hazels and all day, in this totally unscientific survey, I scanned them for nuts. My final haul was exactly five.

Would this paucity also apply to the Turkish hazel? Returning to Poplar I tested it out with a walk on the parish streets. Down Kerbey Street and alongside the Salvation Army Hall, the Turkish hazel leaves were turning yellow and, forming at the twig ends, were the thin shapes of next year's catkins. Taller than the woodland hazel shrubs, they were harder to scan, but my inspection produced nothing. Along Ricardo Street there were six more trees and here I began to find a few, not as single or even paired nuts, but in tightly bundled and heavily hooded clusters. A curious passer-by was parking his car beneath the trees and I had to explain why I was examining them so intently. Perhaps mistakenly, I went for the totally unconvincing truth. Gathering a few of the bundles, I continued to the Penny-field estate where another eight trees stood on an open expanse of grass. In the litter beneath them lay clusters that seemed to have been stripped from the tree, as well as the scattered shells of individual nuts.

From examining the way a hazel shell has been opened, it is possible to identify the creature responsible. The common dormouse, which is also known as the hazel dormouse, leaves a neat round hole with no teeth marks. The wood mouse makes a more irregular hole towards one end of the nut showing fine tooth marks. The bank vole opens the nut at one end, and birds like the great tit or the nuthatch drill a smaller hole altogether. The grey squirrel, as one might imagine of this irrepressible beast, has a gung-ho approach, splitting the nuts completely in two or opening them with a very large hole. I have some of the Turkish hazel shells beside me as I write. They are completely split, with irregular edges and no sign of the nut. It was clearly the work of grey squirrels.

Though greater than that from the native wild hazels, my haul from the Turkish trees remained very meagre. My route home took me past one more stop, on Ada Street. Here a line of the trees stood along the fence beside the newly renovated flats. I collected two or three more bundles of nuts, but it was on the ground near the trees that I found a harvest of a completely different kind, for the grass was dense with shaggy ink caps. The elegant mushrooms, tall and slender like rockets on their launch pads, stood in masses on the grass, their white caps peeling back in the curling white shreds that earn them their alternative name of 'lawyer's wig'. They had, I assumed, been imported as spores in the turf but I could not recall ever having seen them in such number and density. Here on this little estate lawn I counted nearly 200 of them, in all stages of growth from young crowns, just pushing their way free of the soil, to large specimens now doing the inky dissolve that eventually overtakes the firm, white flesh. I was gathering a few of the younger and more edible specimens for next morning's breakfast when the caretaker came out and stumbled across me. I had expected to be reprimanded but he was charm itself, interested in what they were and why I was collecting them. My explanations, however, failed to convince him to try a few.

The shaggy ink caps were, it turned out, not just more numerous but more edible than nuts of the Turkish hazel. These Turkish nuts had thicker, tougher shells than the native hazel, a fact which became all too evident as I tried to open them. The use of a nutcracker would, of course, have helped significantly, but having put in an appearance at Christmas it had decided to absent itself for the rest of the year. I was reduced to hitting the nuts with a hammer, which sent the majority of them spinning skittishly across the floor. Those that I did manage to hit shattered into a mass of inconveniently tiny pieces. When, eventually, I had successfully extracted a few, I found them much smaller as well, still soft and therefore rather bitter. It was becoming clear that, come the collapse of civilisation, the local crop of Turkish hazelnuts would not provide my alternative noisette.

Probably I shouldn't have been eating them so close to Holy Cross Day. Though traditionally collected at this time of year, they were normally hardened off with a few weeks' storage before eating, an occasion that would provide another opportunity for celebration. This was Nut Crack Night, a final element in the ritual year of the hazelnut and one which returns us to the recurring theme of fire. It was celebrated on different dates around the country but most commonly occurred on October 31st, providing an alternative name for Halloween.

On this uneasy night it would have been especially comforting to gather round the fire in good company, eating the nuts and throwing their shells onto the flames, and joining in the traditional Nut Crack Night games. Versions and variations of these are found everywhere from Devon to Scotland, where Robert Burns recorded several. A typical example involved throwing a handful of nuts onto the fire whilst giving each the name of a would-be lover. The one to burn the brightest would reveal the identity of one's true sweetheart. The process is described in 'The Spell', a poem by John Gay, best known as author of *The Beggar's Opera*:

> *Two hazel-nuts I threw into the flame,*
> *And to each nut I gave a sweetheart's name:*
> *This with the loudest bounce me sore amazed,*
> *That in a flame of brightest colour blazed;*
> *As blazed the nut, so may thy passion grow,*
> *For 'twas thy nut that did so brightly glow!*

In another version, each of the single people in the

party would throw a nut onto the fire simultaneously. The first nut to catch fire would indicate which of the company would marry first, with various other interpretations attached to the rest. In a game played in the northern counties, a couple would place two nuts into the fire together. If the nuts burnt quietly side by side, a successful outcome to their courtship was indicated. If they jumped or hissed or moved apart, then a different conclusion could be drawn. In a clear indication of the North/South divide, the same game was played in the southern counties with a completely different interpretation:

> *If he loves me, pop and fly*
> *If he hates me, lie and die.*

These youthful courtship games almost certainly hark back to the much older associations of the hazel with sex, survival and fertility. They were the reworked remnants of ancient divinations or, as the title of John Gay's poem makes clear, they were spells. No wonder that these games were played at Halloween, the night when the influence of the spirits is most potent and the veil is thinly drawn between this world and the next.

Perhaps the spirits were those of our Palaeolithic ancestors who had, in their own time, burnt hazel shells upon the winter fire. Might they too not have read the brief bright flames for some indications of the year ahead and its likely impacts on the tribe? It seemed an old and venerable tradition and, having come so far in my journey with the hazel, I felt that I should revisit it. I would celebrate Nut Crack Night with my family.

Halloween had passed and it was already November when I lit the fire in our living room grate. Given the regional variations in the date for Nut Crack Night, I hoped this late one would not matter. Neither can I really say that the family were sharing my enthusiasm. The fact that they participated at all felt like an act of resigned but commendable tolerance. My sister was staying with us at the time and had brought with her a bag of filberts from her greengrocer in Emsworth. We sat on cushions around the hearth, eating the nuts and aiming the shells at the fire. The nutcracker was still missing but the nuts were brittle enough to crack with our teeth, a difference with the Turkish hazelnuts of which I made a mental note. We tried the different games in turn, or our own makeshift variations of them. Sometimes the shells burned with an orange, and sometimes with a bluer flame; sometimes they burned steadily and sometimes they lay dormant before issuing a long soft sigh as though giving up the ghost without a struggle. Mostly, however, they waited on the coals, as though weighing up their various options, before suddenly and determinedly bursting into the same bright yellow flames.

It was all most hard to interpret and the presence of the hazel spirits remained open to question. Perhaps the fact that it was not Halloween had, after all, been a disadvantage, or maybe a certain element of incredulity amongst those present had served to deter them. The names the children had provided for their putative sweethearts had, after all, given me some doubts as to the seriousness they were affording the occasion. Did they really know a Fatima, a Veracity and a Tatiana? But it didn't matter. There were games and flames, and words and warmth. There were no screens, no distractions, no technological addictions. There was a brightness here to contrast with the greater darkness beyond; a passing closeness in this otherwise overwhelming world. And there was a link with our 18th- and 19th-century forebears, and through them, with more ancient ancestors, a link scanning more than 6,000 years.

Chapter Six

Dowsing the Black Ditch

It would seem careless to lose meadows and fields and farms. It takes another level of determination altogether to eliminate a river. That, however, had been the fate of the Black Ditch, the East End's own river, not a single stretch of which remained visible above ground. For much of its short length, it had run through Poplar and I was keen to retrace this lost element of our local landscape. Here was one of the area's most significant natural features, one that would have played an important role in its ecology, and I wanted to reconnect with it.

Its course was almost synonymous with the western boundary of the parish, separating it from Limehouse, and the fact that this was the last place where the wild black poplars had been recorded had further engaged my attention. I liked to imagine them clustered along the river's bank, leaning conspiratorially together over the flowing water as it made its tranquil way towards the more turbulent Thames. I wanted to know the parish not just as it is, but as it had been, and I decided to track this lost river's route through the modern East End. I would look for clues in street names and in contours and wherever else I could find them; but I was not going to rely on logic alone. I was going to dowse the river.

My decision to dowse was not just to do with the river. Having spent some time studying the hazel I wanted to try out another of its traditional uses. Just as I had gathered nuts at the appropriate season and played those family games at the fireside, so too I would put to the test this ancient usage of the tree. And this being modern, multicultural Poplar, I would attempt it with both the native hazel that grew in my garden and with the Turkish species that flourished on the streets outside. I would use the local trees to dowse for local water.

To be fair, the hazel is not the only tree to have been set to this purpose; the rowan, the birch and even the mistletoe, each with their own magical associations, have been used in dowsing. But the hazel was by far the commonest. Locating water seems to have been only one of its powers. It has been used to find treasure, to track criminals and to eliminate snakes. According to the British Society of Dowsers, dowsing in general can be used to locate archaeological features, cavities, tunnels, oil, mineral ores, underground building services, missing items – golf balls get a particular mention – and even missing persons. A friend of mine went on a dowsing course and found herself trying to detect the course of drains beneath houses solely by dowsing their architectural drawings.

The magical associations of dowsing were to become something of a problem for the early dowsers, creating the possibility of a dangerous conflict with the all-powerful church. By 1518, Martin Luther had listed dowsing as a violation of the first commandment, and therefore a form of occultism. During the 17th century, with the fear of witchcraft becoming a national obsession, dowsing was seen as evidence of heresy and denounced by the Jesuits as both superstitious and satanic. It had become one of the darker arts.

There is, however, a story that traces the origin of dowsing to Moses. It was, perhaps, a story devised by the dowsers in response to this attack on their 'art'. After all, when accused of being an agent of the Devil, what better response than to cite a Biblical authority? In the great liberation story of the Exodus, which has inspired generations of the oppressed, Moses becomes a dowser as he wanders in the deserts of Sinai. He has confounded the Egyptians and led the Israelites out of their slavery but now they are living as nomads, wandering endlessly and aimlessly, as it seemed, and looking back almost nostalgically on their time of suppression in an alien land. At least, there, they had shelter, food and water. Thirst is now a perennial problem and as the complaining swells, Moses begins to worry that his leadership, perhaps even his life, is threatened. He confesses to God his fear of being stoned and God responds by instructing him to walk ahead to the rock of Horeb. Reaching the rock, he raises his staff and strikes it. Immediately it gushes water.

It is a powerful image: Moses brandishing his wooden staff, the symbol of his authority, the conduit of his power. With it he summons the plagues that torture Egypt. With it he parts the Red Sea as the Israelites pass dry shod. With it he closes the waters again to destroy one of the world's mightiest armies. At Morah he uses his staff to turn the bitter waters 'sweet' and drinkable. At Rephaim, while the battle against Amalek rages in the valley below, he stands atop a hill all day, holding his staff aloft to ensure that the Israelites triumph. Here, surely, is the model for wizards to come, from Merlin to Dumbledore, his main tool throughout, a simple shaft of wood. It is no wonder that in English folk-lore it became equated with the magical hazel, just as the fruit with which Eve was tempted had become, in English interpretation, the apple.

There is something magical, too, about the subterranean. As a potholer for many of my earlier years, I had known the strange appeal of those darkly sacred spaces. The under-ground setting appears time and time again in the popular imagination; in stories of secret tunnels that link unlikely places, of sea caves and hidden treasures, of deep bunkers and subterranean mining peoples. It suggests the forces that work beneath the surface of things, the blood that beats in the buried vein, the underground services that criss-cross and power the city. It represents the strange workings of the subconscious, the dream that emerges from darkness, the source of creativity. With whom better to explore this liminal world, where physical and fantastical worlds collide, than an artist? An artist of water, in fact.

Up to a few months previously, I confess, I had never heard of a 'water artist'. But then I had been invited to curate an event for Tipping Point, the organisation that brings together artists and scientists around the issue of climate change. It was here that I met Amy Sharrocks, whose past projects included mass dives and group swims. She had led fifty people in a journey across London, using every lido on the way and travelling between them on public transport; still, as far as I could determine, in their dripping costumes. In a work entitled 'London is a city river', she had engaged groups of people in dowsing the routes of seven of the city's lost rivers. This included leading sixty-five people, tied together, along the route of the Walbrook during rush hour. In her most recent work she had become the self-styled curator of the 'Museum of Water', a growing collection of publicly donated phials, every one of them telling a personal story. Over two years she had accumulated more than 700, touring with them and sharing their stories both in this country and abroad. Their origins were as diverse as an Indian holy river and the condensation from a Falmouth window. They included water from a burst London water main, the liquid remains of a melted snowman, a newborn baby's bath water and water from a bedside glass, said to be infused with dreams. If I could persuade her, Amy would be my ideal companion.

In fact, she required very little persuading, and we convened on a rainy autumnal morning at Shoreditch station. I was equipped with two Y-shaped lengths of twig, one cut from the native hazel, and one from the Turkish. Accounts on how to cut your rod, I had discovered, varied widely. It should be done on a holy day, or on the night of a new moon, or taken from an east-facing branch at dawn and presented to the rising sun. I had failed on every one of these variants but hoped that cutting one from a tree outside the Salvation Army Hall might give it an equivalent aura. Amy was to point out later that I might have done better to cut the Turkish hazel from outside the local mosque. Clearly I hadn't thought this through sufficiently.

Amy's own equipment, I was surprised to discover, wasn't wooden at all. She had brought a couple of L-shaped metal rods, each with a little ball at the end of its shorter arm. Whereas the hazel rods would, I hoped, vibrate or convey some other physical message at the presence of water, these metal rods responded in a different way. 'You have to feel the river,' she told me, 'to go with it.' And you had to ask questions of the rods, framing them carefully with only a yes or no answer. They would swing together for a positive response and move apart for a negative. But, she explained confusingly, 'It doesn't work if the questions are spoken aloud.' Armed with our different equipment and our different approaches we set off in a drizzle through Shoreditch streets that were busy with black umbrellas, into the area that had once been old East End but now was the heart of hip.

Short though it is, the Black Ditch falls into two distinct sections. On maps from the 18th century onwards it is shown as rising in the heart of Stepney, close to the parish church, from where it flows eastward before describing a distinctly hook-like loop and turning south and back west to reach the Thames. More conjectural, however, is a stretch before this, further west in Shoreditch and with a supposed source in what had once been the grounds of the Holywell Priory. It seems, for most of its later years, to have been little more than an open sewer and was covered over long before the rest of the river.

It was this initial stretch and its source that Amy and I set off to locate. Within a couple of minutes of our departure, a rather strange thing happened. Perhaps I was showing too little confidence in the efficacy of dowsing, but I had researched the river's route in advance and marked it off, as best I could determine it, in an A–Z Atlas of London. Within a very short distance from the station, the book had disappeared. It was not in my pocket nor in my bag. I retraced the way we had walked and it was not on the pavement. Neither was it to be found at the station, the last place where I had consulted it, and even an enquiry at the ticket office was to prove unfruitful. My map, like the river itself, was missing. To Amy, this was a sign. I was being too logical, too dependent on my book knowledge, too little trusting of the rods. She quoted the German artist Joseph Beuys at me and told me to 'think with my knees'. I did my best and with rods alone, and with thoughtful knees, we found our way to Holywell Close.

Holywell Priory, or the 'Priory of St. John the Baptist at Haliwell', was founded by the Bishop of London for the benefit of the Augustinian canons in 1152. It must have fallen into disuse in the subsequent centuries, for it seems to have been later 'refounded' by Sir Thomas Lovell, a powerful administrator who served as Chancellor of the Exchequer under both Henry VII and Henry VIII. He repaired and expanded the buildings and added the chapel in which he was to be buried in 1524. His body, I thought, might still lie somewhere under these sodden streets.

Like most religious establishments of its day, the priory was excessively wealthy. Returns from ten years after the death of Thomas show that it owned land in six different counties, as well as farms in Finchley, Hoxton, Hackney and Edmonton. It also extended its influence into Poplar for, listed amongst its possessions, was one of the tidal mills on the River Lea beneath Bow. Despite, or more likely because of its wealth, it wasn't to last. In 1539, just five years after the publication of these returns, the priory was dissolved, another victim of Henry's religious purges. Its 'valuables, moveables, jewels and base silver' were seized, and the lead was stripped from its roofs and used in repairs of the palace at Westminster. By 1541, the remainder of the buildings had been sold off or demolished. The last surviving remnant of this once imposing ecclesiastical establishment was said to be a fifty-foot length of stone wall located in a timber yard off the Shoreditch High Street. We looked for it, but that too had now disappeared.

On April 13th 1576, a portion of the site was leased to the well-known actor-manager and impresario, James Burbage. This lease contains the first evidence I could find of the source and early stages of the river. The land, it says, is 'on the moor from which the spring which is called Halliwelle arises'. Among the buildings on the site was a 'Great Barn', some eighty feet long, along the southern end of which ran 'a brook or sewer'. It was against the side of this Great Barn that Burbage was to build what was described by his son as the first purpose-built theatre in London since Roman times. It was to evoke the splendour of the ancient Roman *theatrum* that he named it 'The Theatre'; a name which was to take on a much wider connotation. Burbage was a member of the Lord Chamberlain's Men, as was his friend William Shakespeare. Shakespeare would have performed regularly at The Theatre, albeit in minor roles, and some of his plays were premiered here.

But Burbage had a difficult relationship with his landlord and it seems to have descended, eventually, into a series of legal disputes. These continued beyond his death and, when matters intensified, his sons were driven to drastic action. On the night of December 28th 1598, and with the help of a small team of carpenters, they secretly dismantled the entire theatre and carried its timbers away to storage in Brideswell. As soon as the weather improved in the following spring, they ferried them across to the south bank of the river and used them in the building of a new playhouse. And thus The Globe was born.

Even at the start of the lease the Great Barn had been in poor condition and when Burbage built his theatre next to it, it had been necessary to support it with a system of props running between the two buildings. When The Theatre was moved, it left the barn in danger of collapse and a new series of props had to be installed, this time sunk into the adjacent ground. It was at this time that Shakespeare was writing *The Merchant of Venice*. When Shylock attempts to take a pound of flesh from Antonio in settlement of his debt, his effort is foiled by Portia, in the guise of a lawyer. His entire estate is forfeit, though his life is spared. But what's the point of it, he asks, without the means to sustain himself?

> *Nay, take my life and all. Pardon not that*
> *You take my house when you do take the prop*
> *That doth sustain my house. You take my life*
> *When you do take the means whereby I live*

It is a speech believed by Shakespearean critics to reflect

the separation of The Theatre and the Great Barn, as well as the anxiety and uncertainty of the actors moving to their future home.

The source of our little, sometime stinking river might be just a ditch, but it was a ditch over which Shakespeare had stepped, and Amy was keen to locate it. Holywell Street seemed a good start and dowsing along it led us into a car park. An attendant came out of his hut to ask if we needed help but we reassured him by telling him we were dowsing the Black Ditch. He walked off without a further word, as if this were a regular occurrence. One of the walls surrounding the car park had been extensively covered in colourful graffiti and bore, in large, flowing letters, the legend 'End of the Line. Rock Well'. I have no idea what it meant but for Amy it was a sign. It was also an early indication of the way that she would see things, her imaginative antennae attuned to any incidental connection or tangential reference to water. She seized excitedly on the name of Waterlow Buildings, of Salmon Lane and Hare Marsh. It was surely not coincidence that at Tapp Street a roadside tree hung over the street sign, obscuring the second 'p'. There was, too, a beautiful old building that had clearly once been a bath house. Built in bright red brick with white stone courses and decorative semicircular windows, it had tall chimneys rising from a black slate roof. The separate entrances were still signed with 'Men's Bath' and 'Women's Bath' and beside them stood sculpted semi-naked figures draped only in towels.

Appearances of the word 'black' were just as important.

Outside Blackman's Shoes she asked the bemused owner if his cellar ever flooded while later, beside a street tree, we came upon the most curious of our finds. The tree was a white poplar, its shed leaves littering the pavement around us, anaemic greeny-yellow on the upper surface but still a felty white beneath. Discarded in the pit below its trunk was a pile of discarded CDs labelled 'Noir Music'. I took one home and am playing it as I write. It is electronic dance music, insistent and repetitive, and a couple of tracks will probably suffice.

All of this had an unintended connectivity, a synchronicity that the Surrealists would have loved. 'It was,' Amy told me, quoting Beuys again, 'all about the plurality of experience.' These were evidences from the imagination, cabalistic clues that we were on the right track. And, by and large, we were. This, I have to say, was all to do with Amy's metal rods and nothing to do with my hazel. Try as I might, I could get nothing from them, and my English and Turkish sticks were equivalent in their ineffectiveness. Occasionally a passing lorry deceived me into detecting a tremor but any other communication was disappointingly absent. It would be wrong, however, to blame the hazel. Dowsing may be dismissed by official opinion as a 'pseudo-science' but the fault in this instance was almost certainly mine. Perhaps I had cut the sticks in the wrong way or in the wrong place or at the wrong time. Perhaps the persistent drizzle was a form of static interference. Or, most likely, I had approached the whole thing with too much of a doubting, left-brain logic. Clearly my knees were not doing enough of the thinking.

We must have made a strange sight walking in the rain through the East End streets, holding our divining rods ahead of us; me with a forked length of hazel, Amy clutching her rods in tight-lipped concentration. Periodically she would stop to ask her silent question and then take off again, pacing forward or veering in a completely different direction. At a hot tea stand, workers with bacon rolls and steaming mugs took a particular, and bemused, interest in what we were doing. Groping for an answer I suggested that we were employees of Thames Water and that this was our latest technology, an assertion that they seemed to have no problem accepting.

But did it work? As we walked we seemed to deviate regularly from what I remembered of the 'book' route but just as regularly we would come back to it again. As we veered in different directions I would bite my tongue, but before my concern could get the better of me I would find us veering back again. We created a much more meandering river, I suspect, than the real one; zig-zagging around it and adding curious curves, and in Poplar the rods seemed committed to a short cut, omitting much of the loop in which the river was supposed to have run. And yet we somehow found ourselves at Stepney Church and the second source at Rhodeswell, and later still, at Limekiln Dock, the undisputed mouth of the river. Here, where a cul-de-sac of a creek abuts the Thames, we stood by the dock wall and looked down. The tide was out but immediately below us a little sluice was emptying a trickle of water onto the mud and gravel. 'And there,' said Amy, 'is your lost river.'

Amy has now moved on to bigger things. She took her water museum to Australia for a year and speaks at international conferences on water resources; 'next to the prime minister of Hungary,' she told me in one of her emails. I have yet to tell her that I went back to walk the river a second time. Perhaps I am embarrassed about it. I wanted to look again at the route of the river from Stepney onwards, and particularly that part of it that went through Poplar. I wanted, too, to try out a different sort of detection, to see if the land itself would yield clues to the course of the river. This time I asked an old friend, Graham Scrivener, to come with me. Graham is an accredited Blue Badge London guide, a historian and a cartographer, and he had worked with me on the maps in my previous book, *The Green London Way*. Whilst I would not want to condemn him as sensible, his approach would, I thought, provide an interesting and a contrasting one to Amy's.

It was a mild December day when we set out, the skies grey and overcast as they had been all week. It was a day that was typical of our current not-quite-winters. Rhodeswell Road, our starting point, had been split by post-Blitz development into two separate sections. We walked from one to the other across a thin strip of parkland beside the Regent's Canal where a gaggle of Canada geese ran towards a woman with a bag of bread so enthusiastically that I feared for her safety. A solitary tall, brick chimney rose from the grass ahead of us. It was covered with tags and graffiti at the base and a fossilised black crud clung to its lower sections, but it reared above all this in a display of fine disdain. It seemed slightly forlorn, there on the grass alone, as if some long past factory had packed up its business and moved on but forgotten to take the chimney with it. But it was, we found, nothing to do with a factory at all, but a sewer ventilation shaft. Here, perhaps, would be our first clue to the route of the lost river.

The London sewage system is a marvellous and mysterious thing. Vast and labyrinthine, it was designed by Joseph Bazalgette, who took the earlier outmoded network of drains and ditches that emptied directly into the Thames and moulded them into something magnificent. By 1866 almost all of the city had been connected to his new system, which intercepted the flow of foul water from the older sewers and underground rivers and diverted it along large pipes running eastward under the city. In a display of admirable foresight he had designed them four times larger than the requirement of the time so that only today, in a much larger and more populous London, are they reaching capacity. Known as the 'Low-Level Sewers', these feed into two huge encircling 'Outfall Sewers', one to the north and one to the south of London, which carry the waste beyond the city. Here is a whole world of hidden flows and tides and channels, one that has saved us from the terrible epidemics of cholera and typhoid, from filth and foul smells and from the accumulation of our own excreta. Yet we remain almost entirely ignorant of it. One of its main components, vented by this chimney, was now below us.

Tom Ridge, a stalwart of East End history, has produced a *Central Stepney History Walk* and Graham had brought a copy with him. Ridge names this as the 'Northern Low Level No.2 Sewer', en route from west London to its junction with the Northern Outfall Sewer. He also suggests that it is joined here by a smaller sewer, 'Limekiln Dock Diversion Sewer', which 'passes under the canal and cascades into the chamber below the shaft'. Knowing that Limekiln Dock was the mouth of the Black Ditch, I was intrigued and later sought out a map of the London sewage system. The Limekiln Dock Diversion Sewer is just a detail in the massive network, but it was immediately apparent that where the majority of sewers describe largely straight lines, here was one that was less engineered in shape and followed the same flowing, hook-like loop through Poplar as had the Black Ditch before it. This, then, was its final encasement, and it was flowing beneath our feet. But if Ridge is right and the Limekiln Dock Diversion Sewer 'cascades' into the Northern Low Level Sewer beneath this chimney, then there is a paradox; for the Black Ditch is not only now running underground, it seems to have totally reversed its direction.

There was a railway bridge beyond the chimney and we walked beneath it to reach the second stretch of Rhodeswell Road. This 'Rhodes Well' had been the secondary source of the river and had originally been known as the Rogue's Well. I had never been able to trace these rogues but they appealed to me. I liked the irony that I had begun one of my walks at a 'Holy Well' and the other at that of some anonymous rascals, though I hoped it wasn't a commentary on my two different approaches. The road descended gently to a roundabout and in the circular movement of the traffic Amy would have seen the swirling waters of a spring-fed well. But I was not with Amy, I was with Graham, and he was more sceptical. So we continued east instead, following the most likely route of the river, between pre-war terraces and a post-war estate.

The street was lined with winter whitebeams, rowans

and a single weeping birch. At its far end a large poplar rose magnificently beside a block of flats, almost equalling their eight storeys in its height. It was the Italian hybrid black poplar and not the native tree but even so it became, in my imagination, a relic of lost riverside. I refrained from mentioning this to Graham.

It is possible that the Black Ditch was once navigable to this point. In Saxon times, before its partial taming, the Thames was a much broader river, spilling out over large areas of the surrounding marshland. Its massive tides would have flooded and filled the little tributary. Stybba, a Saxon warrior, is said to have rowed up it and moored his boats here to found the settlement that still bears his name, Stybeney or Stepney. The 'ey' in the name indicates an island, or virtual island, in this case the parcel of well-drained gravel between the hook of the Black Ditch and the Thames.

Bermondsey, Stepney, Hackney; there are many of these 'eys' in London and they were all once islands, or higher, dryer points in the surrounding marshlands. Even Westminster was built on one, the island of 'Thorney', and the word still survives in the 'eyots, and 'aits', the 'little islands' that dot the river on the west side of London. But here, to the east, it was Stybeney that was the first of the settlements and it came to dominate the flatlands. Its church, established as early as the 7th century by those first Saxon settlers, was to become the mother church for east London and was later to spawn as many as sixty-seven separate parishes, including Poplar.

We had reached the estates of South Bow now; red brick blocks, a newly built mosque, a tyre-fitters, a cobbled lane between garages. There was less evidence of the old river channel than of the countryside it had run through. This was once Bow Common, a wild and windswept area of scrubland, dotted with bracken and brush, where pigs were grazed and washerwomen spread their linen on the thorny bushes. It is common now, without any sense of irony, for new-built estates to bear the names of the countryside they have obliterated; Bluebell Close, Cowslip Close, Elm Lane or Oak Avenue. Here was a much earlier equivalent, for Bow Common had been one of the last local areas to succumb to the 19th-century wave of development and some of the streets created then bore the names of the heathland flora they had displaced. There was Blackthorn Street, Broomfield Street and Fern Street. There was Whitethorn Street, bearing an older name for the hawthorn, and Furze Street, conveying an alternative name for the gorse.

Collectively they conjured a landscape of suckering blackthorn bushes, their early flowers white against the leafless dark wood; of the hawthorn, flowering later, its blossom forming foaming masses around the freshly opened leaves; of the slender whippy stems of broom topped with their yellow pea-flowers; and the prickly gorse that never tires of flowering, its seed pods popping audibly in the summer heat. On such sunny days the heathland would have been rich with their smells; the trodden 'fern', or bracken, redolent of cooking oil and almond, with just a hint of the seaside; the gorse of coconut and Caribbean hair oil; the broom of vanilla; and the hawthorn, a cloying and sickly-sweet combination of sex and decomposition. It is said to have absorbed the smell of rotting bodies by blooming at the time of the London plague. It was not inappropriate, then, that as we turned down Bow Common Lane we arrived at Stinkhouse Bridge.

Officially it is the road bridge over the Limehouse Cut, joining Bow Common Lane to Upper North Street, but Stinkhouse Bridge is how it has been known for as long as the locals can remember. It is a reference to the factories that once fronted the canal and the smells they produced; of varnish, fish manure and potash, of rubber and burning bones, of tar and of resin. I am a connoisseur of such smells. They are the bouquets of my boyhood; the cloying hot sweetness of a biscuit factory and the sharp vinegary smells of a pickle cannery. I knew my way from our house to the river through the sourness of the tanneries, the pepper and spice of the warehouses, the dark brown maltiness of the Anchor brewery. These olfactory memories seem as vivid still as the visual ones and I polled the older members of the All Saints' congregation as to which smell it was that they remembered most strongly from the Stinkhouse Bridge. The winner, by a margin, was ammonia from the chemical works.

The bridge seems too hefty for the small road it carries. It is pretty much an industrial structure in itself. It marks the official boundary of the parish of Poplar, sturdy, iron-clad and battleship grey, looking as if it had been put together by military engineers to defend the borders with Bow. On one side, to protect an adjacent gas pipe, it is topped with lines of barbed wire. Shreds of black and white plastic flap from them like withered flags in the wind.

Having walked for some time roughly parallel to the Thames, we were now heading south towards it. I hoped that our change of direction might provide some clearer evidence of the river's course, but the signs were not promising. On one side of us the football pitches of a municipal parkland stretched away in an unrelieved flatness, on the other there were more estates, now yellow-brick, and cut by a sequence of side roads. Graham suggested that the course of the Ditch might be a little further to the east so we turned down and followed the first of the side roads. And there, just a few hundred yards along it was, the shadow of a river: a dip in the road, shallow but distinct, a tiny vale that sloped down briefly on one side and rose again on the other. To confirm it we hurried back to the main road and down to the next side turning. It was there again, the same declivity in the same position. And so it continued as our walk took on a fitful progression up and down the side streets. It was there on Brabazon Street and again on Cordelia Street. It was on Ricardo Street and on Grundy Street, and always in a parallel position. The further south we went, the more obvious it became. It crossed the broad and busy East India Dock Road in a clear shallow valley and became even clearer on Poplar High Street, where the river had once supplied a small pond beside the White Horse Inn.

It is hard to express the satisfaction I felt at these small signs. I had, after all, walked these streets before. They were all familiar. I had hurried to the station or dragged my shopping along them without registering these dips and rises. But looking at them now they provided the fossil of a landform, cast in tarmac and York stone. These impressions on our pavements were what was left of the channel up which Stybba had rowed through a landscape of salt marsh, sprawling sea purslane and wind-bent reed; of the river in which people had fished or trapped eels or washed down their horses or splashed each other after a hot day in the fields. It was the river that had run beneath the last leaning black poplars of Poplar, its banks thick with purple loosestrife and the frothy meadowsweet. It was the river that had darkened and died, with effluent and offal, with run-off from the filthy streets and the contents of overflowing cesspits, until it became, truly, the Black Ditch and was finally encased.

We walked the final stretch westwards, passing a grate, way below which water gurgled continuously in auditory evidence of the Limekiln Dock Diversion Sewer. We passed Kiln Wharf and Westferry Station and winter cherries in bloom and a dry cleaner specialising in river-stained clothing, and we arrived at Limekiln Dock.

It seemed more Dickensian on this darker day with its hoists and derricks, its assortment of buildings in mismatched shapes and sizes, its wood and brick warehouses leaning straight out over the muddy creek. It was the same sort of setting as Jacob's Island on the Bermondsey shore, where Dickens had famously set Fagin's hide-out and the dramatic demise of Bill Sykes; and the great writer would have known this stump of a creek, for he regularly visited an uncle in nearby Three Colt Street. It was the place where cargoes of chalk were unloaded, carried here from quarries in Kent and burnt in the lime oasts to provide mortar for London's expansion. Later, the first voluntary emigrants had left from Limekiln Dock on their long journey, for good or bad, to a new life in Australia.

Though it was the mouth, the 'end' of the Black Ditch, it seemed more like a beginning, the place where the little stream was released into the greater flow and freedom of the Thames. And both my walks had led me here. With Amy or Graham, dowsing or doubting, consulting the imagination or reading the landscape, thinking with my knees or using left-brain logic, both approaches had led me to this place. Graham and I had followed the river as literally as we could. We had inspected sewer vents and gurgling grates and street names and small dips and slight slopes and had recorded the evidence of the Black Ditch as faithfully as we could find it in Poplar. And Amy and I had added magic to the everyday. We had respected the river's subterranean mystery, its route appearing like automatic writing on the blank slab of the city. We had made a map of the imagination. It seemed to me then, standing on the bridge over the creek and looking across the broad reach of the Thames towards Rotherhithe, that these approaches had been entirely complementary.

Observing and recording around the streets of the parish, I had already been creating one kind of map in my head. I walked now not so much down Joshua Street or across Jolly's Green or beside the Balfron Tower as past the place of the small-leaved lime, along the rough at the edge of the park where the mullein had flowered, and through the trees where the long-tailed tits came to feed. It was a map that reminded me where the shaggy ink caps shot up, then did their dissolve, in the autumn, where a chiffchaff had dropped down to sing in the spring and where, in the summer, the sand martins had built their unlikely nests in drains along the canal bank.

My walks along the length of the Black Ditch had given me two further approaches to mapping. Only by laying both of these and more, I realised, one on top of another could you really begin to understand a locality. We look on maps as something essentially objective. But, of course, they are no such thing. They make propositions about the world. In what they omit or include, in what they chose to represent and how they chose to represent it, they are organising a world view. To be truly accurate, to even begin to reflect the 'plurality of experience', it is multiple, diverse and questioning approaches that we need in our maps and mapping.

Now that I had seen the evidence of its existence, I missed the actual presence of our Poplar river. I liked to imagine a place where the children of the Will Crook's estate, or from the grounds of the Brownfield, could turn over stones looking for caddis fly larvae, or catch the darting sticklebacks in jars. But if the Black Ditch were ever to return, it might, I fear, be in more angry form. With climate change and with rising sea levels we have already seen the return of some of our marshlands and the policy of a managed retreat. Could we, through changing rainfall patterns, through storm or surge, through deliberate intention or through frightful force, see the resurfacing of London's lost rivers? It is the vision described by U.A. Fanthorpe in her poem 'Rising Damp':

> *At our feet they lie low,*
> *The little fervent underground*
> *Rivers of London*
> *Effra, Graveney, Falcon, Quaggy,*
> *Wandle, Walbrook, Tyburn, Fleet*
> *Whose names are disfigured,*
> *Frayed, effaced.*

These are 'the Magogs that chewed the clay' and the currents 'that chiselled the city' and though they have 'gone under. / Boxed, like the magician's assistant', their influence can still be seen; in the flooding of suburban gardens after heavy rain or in the statistics for chronic bronchitis. They refuse to remain 'buried alive in earth'.

> *Being of our world, they will return*
> *(Westbourne, caged at Sloane Square,*
> *Will jack from his box)*
> *Will deluge cellars, detonate manholes,*
> *Plant effluent on our faces,*
> *Sink the city.*

These are the words of a London apocalypse, but they are not quite the end of the poem. Fanthorpe, too, sees the subterranean river not just as a physical force but as an imaginative one as well; an unseen influence, an upswelling of the unconscious, a reference to magic and to mortality.

> *Effra, Graveney, Falcon, Quaggy,*
> *Wandle, Walbrook, Tyburn, Fleet*
> *It is the other rivers that lie*
> *Lower, that touch us only in dreams*
> *That never surface. We feel their tug*
> *As a dowser's rod bends to the surface below.*

> *Phlegethon, Acheron, Lethe, Styx.*

It is river as both route and root.

Chapter Seven

The Post-Human Tree

It is Palm Sunday and a procession has set out from the church of St. Nicholas on the Aberfeldy estate. It is the first act in the great Easter drama, celebrating the triumphant entry of Jesus into Jerusalem, and a curtain-raiser for the story that will unfold across the coming week, a story that will lead to a death, and then to regeneration. A few moments ago our palm crosses were blessed in the church hall and we will keep them until they are burnt next year for use in the Ash Wednesday service. But now we are crossing the unkempt grassy triangle of the Millennium Green. The servers and the clergy go first, resplendent in their robes of white and red and bearing a large wooden cross. The rest of us straggle behind, waving our palm fronds and trying to ensure that we are singing the same line of the hymn as those nearer the front.

Ahead we can see the disused gasworks, once a central source of employment in the area. Now the circular iron frames that supported the gas holders are being dismantled one by one to make way for more development. They were, as the East End blogger the 'Gentle Author' put it, our version of the Colosseum: 'a heroic example of an earlier age of handmade engineering on an epic scale'. Now, despite council assurances and local petitions, beam by beam and spar by iron spar, they are coming down.

We turn westward and follow Abbott Road towards the underpass. It has its perennial smell of urine but we continue singing and it sounds rather better as it resonates through the tunnel. As we head towards the East India Dock Road through the Brownfield estate, passers-by watch us with interest, or with a faint disdain, or, as can only happen in cities, affect not to notice us at all. Still, we make ourselves heard and give out our leaflets and invite people to join us for the Easter services. Eventually we will reach All Saints', the main-road mother church. As we enter it the organ will swell and the rest of the congregation will join in the hymn, though undoubtedly on a different verse to the rest of us.

There is a cryptic connection between this Palm Sunday procession and the gasworks it has just passed. Since 1976, when gas production ceased, wild plants have colonised the site and the spaces between the holders are now a rich tangle of willowherbs and Herb Robert, mugworts and mustards, sow thistle, common thistle and nipplewort. Crows pick their way amongst the tall stems, goldfinches hang from the thistle-heads and sparrows bustle in the bushes. There was once a colony of rabbits with a peculiarly light colouration, according to Richard Fitter in *London's Natural History*. They have long left us, as have the hedgehogs for which the gasworkers once put out bowls of milk. But occasionally we have kestrels, or even a peregrine, hunting over the gasworks' waste. Shrubs, too, are later arrivals, colonising the site with bramble and elder and the ubiquitous buddleia. Chief among them, here, is the goat willow, the plant that was the 'English palm'.

The practice of celebrating the Sunday before Easter with the blessing of palms seems to have become established in the churches of Palestine as early as the 4th century. From there it spread across Europe, and with it the idea of the Palm Sunday procession. An 8th-century account, in which Archbishop Egbert of York is described as 'hallowing the fronds', provides the first English record. From this time on the processions were to grow in size and ostentation. They usually began at an outlying chapel or shrine and proceeded from there, the clergy leading, the people following, to the cathedral or main church of the town. They were banned as papist manifestations under Edward VI, and again under Elizabeth I, but their popularity ensured their return and their continued survival across the centuries. They are once again enjoying a resurgence in the Anglican church, including here in Poplar where, up to a few years ago, the sum of our observance was no more than a quick, and rather private, trot around the churchyard.

For all this blessing and processing there was a practical problem. As a plant of the semi-arid plains, the palm tree is native nowhere in Western Europe. The palms we carry through the Poplar streets today are dried, imported fronds, and somewhat lacking in exuberance because of it, but this, of course, is a recent innovation. With the true palm being locally unavailable, it was customary to press some other plant into service in its place and in England this was, most commonly, the goat willow. It would not seem an obvious candidate. The palm is a stately tree, up to thirty metres in height. It grows on a single, sometimes curving, stem topped with a coronet of shapely fronds. Hardly a tree at all, the goat willow is more of a many-stemmed shrub. It is a rather nondescript bush with no well-defined shape and, for nine months out of twelve, it is easily overlooked. But for a month or two in the early spring, it comes into its glory.

In March or April, and sometimes as early as mid-December, the flowers of the goat willow open against the bare winter wood in a massive display of catkins. The female catkins are a whitish-green, becoming brighter as they ripen and eventually form a cylindrical spur of seed heads like some exotic spiky fruit. The male catkins, however, are sleek and silvery, with a coating of soft, silky hairs, opening finally into a brilliant glowing gold. They are the colour of the down on a freshly hatched goose, which once earned them the name of 'goslings'. Today they are better known as pussy willows. Against the late winter greyness they are miniature sunbursts, announcing the imminence of spring when there is little else to suggest it, and producing their defiant display of colour when the cold is sharp and the winds can still be bitter. From 'silky mouse silver', says H.E. Bates in his book *Through the Woods* (Victor Gollancz, 1969), 'they rise to a glory, a glory of colour and fragrance ... It is, with the daffodil, the true Easter flower, standing for the ascension of sunlight, for the final triumph of light over the tomb of winter darkness.'

With their flowering coinciding, more or less, with Easter, it was these golden, catkin-bearing branches that were cut and carried in the Palm Sunday processions. While all around was still bleak, and summer still a long way off, they spoke of radiance, of royalty and rejoicing, of celebration and praise. Our own procession, I am sure, would have been positively leaping along past the gasworks had we been bearing branches of glorious pussy willow rather than those anaemic imported palms.

So common was this use of the willow that, throughout the country, 'palm' became its common name. There was 'snow on the palms,' notes Frances Kilvert, a Radnorshire curate, in his journal in March 1872, whilst in March 1900 George Sturt, a Surrey farmer, records 'in Sandy Lane … the snow-white glossy tips of palm buds'. As well as their place in the processions, these catkin-palms were used to decorate both church and home, and the act of gathering them became, like nutting and May Day morning, another of those communal country outings. Before dawn on Palm Sunday, parties of young people would set out for the woods, returning bearing bundles of branches and wearing willow catkins in their hats. It was known as 'going a-palming' or in the north as 'a-palmsoning'. This was not just a rural custom and in *The Stations of the Sun* Ronald Hutton describes how 'the custom had evolved into an opportunity for young East Enders to carouse all night in the fields and woods of Essex.' The working people of Poplar may well, therefore have been a-palming but 'in the early nineteenth [century] a natural resentment grew among the country people whose land was being invaded in this fashion by people sallying forth from the city'.

Just as with the nutting expeditions on Holy Rood Day, the legitimised mass excursion of Palm Sunday morning seemed to have become the opportunity for all sorts of ancillary activities and as John Aubrey, the 17th-century author and antiquarian, put it, 'this day gives many a conception'. Unsurprisingly the outings were denounced from the puritan pulpits as debauchery.

The goat willow, known also as the sallow or great sallow or, in Ireland, the salley, is a plant of damp woodland, thick hedges and scrub. But it also has an urban presence. Those spiky female catkins produce a mass of cottony seeds that carry for long distances on the wind and spring up readily on any disturbed soil where they land. It was one of the early colonists of the bomb sites after the Blitz but it also established itself on the poisonous soils of slag heaps, amongst the ruins of abandoned industry, in neglected urban corners and on city 'brownfield' sites.

I returned to our own gasworks a few months after our procession to get a last glimpse of the goat willows before they were bulldozed into non-entity. For the most part the willow family are trees of stature and shapeliness, with slender branches and an uplifting airiness. But not the goat willows. Here they were blowsy bushes, hunkered down into a shaggy density but always with some eager, unkempt shoots sprouting several feet above the rest of the bulk and swaying unsteadily in the breeze. They could only be described as untidy, like heads in need of a haircut, but it was an untidiness that displayed their vigour and their unrestrained urge for growth.

Their leaves added little in the way of neatness for,

where those of other willows are often both elegant and elongate, these were dull and dumpy; broad and rounded with small teeth at the edges and tapering to a hooked tip. It was towards the end of the season and some had already fallen. Others were stained with orange from fungal rust or blotched white with mould or fretted with holes from insect predation. But this reflected an ecological virtue. The willow family supports over 450 species of insect, mite and lichen, more even than the oak tree, and the goat willow is among the richest of the group. On a sunny day the catkins can be humming with life; with newly emerged queen bumblebees, with comma and peacock butterflies, with solitary bees and hoverflies.

Whilst many of the creatures the goat willow supports are small and undistinguished (though none the less valuable for that), it is also, in some rare southern woodlands, the food plant for one of Britain's largest and most beautiful butterflies: the purple emperor, an insect so charismatic that its devotees are almost cultish about it, referring to it as 'His Majesty' and waiting attendance upon its appearance. It is mysterious, muscular and magnificent and, as a light drizzle began to fall on this dull grey autumn day, I fell into a brief reverie in which purple emperor butterflies flew down from the tops of surrounding tower blocks, their cobalt blue iridescence flashing against their velvet black wings, to feed on our gasworks' goat willows.

These few remaining 'waste' places are the last wilderness of Poplar: the remaining undeveloped strips of Orchard Place where buddleia runs rampant; the stretch of Blackwall Way which has turned to thickets of broom and where melilot and rocket and broomrape grow beneath it on the broken stone; and lengths of river wall where cherry and aspen and birch have seeded and grown unhindered. I had recorded them all in my parish walks but they were few and transient and always under threat.

But there was wildness, too, in those individual trees that sprang up outside the confines of cultivation; the seedlings and the saplings that appeared without permission on lawns, in flowerbeds, along the pavement edges and in pots in my back garden. They represented nature in its constant effort of recuperation. They were as irresistible as entropy and constituted, for me, a final chapter in the story of trees though time in Poplar. Should the influence of humanity somehow be eliminated, should an apocalypse suddenly depopulate Poplar, these were the plants that would supplant us. It would be these colonising the empty streets, the decaying buildings and the abandoned blocks, poking through the fractured window, demolishing the wall and blocking the disused door. This would be the wilderness returning, and these would be the post-human trees.

Across the aeons of pre-human history there have been, according to palaeontologists, at least five mass extinction events. Their causes, their exact effects, and even their number have been a matter of academic argument, but there is a generally accepted sequence which begins some 450 million years ago with the Ordovician-Silurian event. It led to the eradication of 70% of all living species including the trilobites, the brachiopods, the graptolites and all the other groups that dominated life in those swarming early seas.

More devastating still was the Permian event, the third in the sequence. It came close to ending life on Earth altogether, with the loss of a staggering 96% of species. It is from the surviving 4% that everything alive today is descended. Probably best known is the K/T or Cretaceous-Tertiary event. Taking place around sixty-six million years ago, it led to the elimination of the ammonites and the pterosaurs, of many flowering plants, and most famously, of the dinosaurs.

The causes of these incidents, though differing, seem to have been a combination of long-term stresses compounded by a short-term shock. It is the nature of these final shocks that has been most hotly debated. All of the different causes cited, and sometimes established, involve catastrophic incidents, whether asteroid impact, volcanic activity, outpourings of flood basalt, oxygen depletion, climate change or outbursts of gamma rays. Now, perhaps, we are in the throes of a sixth great event, caused, this time, by human activity. This, at least, is the view of 15,364 scientists from 184 countries who signed the 'Warning to Humanity' in the journal *BioScience* in November 2017. We have, they stated, 'unleashed a mass extinction event, the sixth in roughly 540 million years, wherein many current life forms could be annihilated'. With the current rate of extinctions running between 100 and 1,000 times higher than the 'background' rate, it is estimated that we could lose at least a half of the planet's lifeforms by the end of the century.

We think of mass extinctions largely in terms of what they have eliminated, but perhaps our focus should be just as much on what they have enabled. In each one of them it was the largest and most dominant life forms that were most affected, thus providing new opportunities for the underdogs to come out on top. These events acted as major shake-ups when evolution seemed set in its ways, allowing new and different groups of species to emerge and reshaping the nature of life on Earth. From the 'great dying' of the Permian came forth the archosaurs; from the Triassic-Jurassic event, the dinosaurs; and from the K/T event, the mammals, evolving into a greater variety of form in the next few million years than they had managed in the previous 160 million. Just as Robert White had argued that Earth's natural disasters also served to replenish its resources, perhaps we should conclude that these cataclysmic events are not so much interruptions in the course of evolution but an integral part of its process.

Darwin himself had insisted that 'species are produced and exterminated by slowly acting causes' and that the most important causes of change are 'almost independent of altered physical conditions'. In the popular conception, too, we tend to see evolution as a constant and rather steady process in which things flow gently but implacably towards a fulfilment. But as our knowledge of the past has grown, it has come to seem that the evolution of species is more a matter of fits and starts, and that one of its greatest engines is catastrophe.

In the abandoned gardens, along the empty railway embankments, on the old estate lawns of a depeopled Poplar, the fast-spreading, fast-growing herbaceous 'weeds' will come first: the groundsel and shepherd's purse and thale cress that can grow at almost any time, produce seeds in six weeks from their own germination and run through several generations in a year. They will be joined by, and eventually displaced by, the woody shrubs.

Those that currently thrive uncultivated, that grow in the interstices of our manic over-management, provide a clue as to what this future flora might look like. Oliver Gilbert, a lichenologist who was also one of the pioneers of urban ecology, produced in *The Flowering of Cities*, an account of such wild sites across a number of British cities. In Bristol, wild clematis was a leading component. In Birmingham, the goldenrod and the greater bindweed were significant. In Southampton there were firethorns, cotoneasters and Norway maples. Leeds had produced thickets of a poplar hybrid, and in both Swansea and Manchester there were swathes of Japanese knotweed.

Japanese knotweed had featured strongly in my explorations around our previous home in north London. It covered large areas of the railway lands, appeared in individual front gardens and shot up around tennis courts and playgrounds. I had even found it growing inside the cabling of a street lamp and pushing out its leafy stems from part way up the column. But in Poplar I did not record it at all. Here the goat willow would remain a component of our wild flora, for though it was about to be eliminated at the gasworks, it had already spread its feathery seeds across the parish and was springing up wherever the opportunity arose. Once I had become accustomed to looking for it, I found it regularly in flower and shrub beds even on the gritty path above the Blackwall Tunnel portals.

Occasionally I found their close relative, the grey sallow, too, with its narrower leaves and the curious little ear-shaped stipules that remain on the stem at the base of each leaf. One of these, in a shrub bed on the Brownfield estate, was doing so well that it had taken on fine, spreading proportions and I was hopeful that the gardeners would mistake it for a deliberate planting and leave it to produce its spring crop of catkins.

Other shrubs appeared even more frequently. The assertive elder was everywhere, a Jekyll and Hyde of a plant with lacy white flower-heads, moodily dark berries, foul-smelling leaves and an aggressive and straggly growth. It regularly lays siege to my garden, attempting to choke the drains and block the driveway gate. Equally vigorous on our 'waste' sites were the brambles, which seem to be a particularly stout-stemmed and fierce-thorned variety. They scramble across open ground suppressing all growth beneath them, bending down to produce new roots along the way, and curling like a botanical barbed wire.

All these are native species, but international differences will disappear in the future urban commons, where plants of many different origins will rub their metaphorical shoulders. Already along untended edges of the A12, we have self-sown honey locust forming thorny thickets, whilst on the railway cutting stand bushes of bladder senna with their strangely inflated seed pods. Further along, the Duke of Argyll's tea plant is scrambling over chain-link fences and tumbling down the railway bank between bridges. Its strange name is said to come from a mix-up over labels in the eponymous Duke's garden. It is not a tea at all, but it is the bush that bears the famous 'goji' berries, one of the recent 'superfoods' credited with curing almost everything.

None of these shrubs, however, can match the

abundance, and the exuberance, of the buddleia. *Buddleia davidii,* the butterfly bush, is everywhere in the parish. It grows on bare ground and broken concrete and stony hardcore. It grows in old car parks and abandoned builder's yards, on walls and roofs, on parapets and bridges. It grows amongst the scrapyards of the Lochnagar Street edgelands and out of the masonry of the All Saints' Church. It grows on the once grand homes of the Poplar sea captains and out of the roof of my Chinese takeaway. It grows in particular density on the far bank of the Limehouse Cut, from the top of the retaining wall down to the water line, and though that is technically outside the parish, such distinctions will seem less significant post-holocaust.

On the East India Dock Road, it grows on a vacant plot behind a line of blue hoardings. The recent high winds have blown out several of the panels and revealed the almost impenetrable growth that has developed behind them. It rises up above a tangled mass of dead twigs, concrete blocks, old planks and litter, on a site that only a couple of years ago was still bare land. The tall and many-stemmed bushes lean outwards, their long heads nodding towards me as if in vague acquaintance.

Their late-winter leaves seem reluctantly evergreen, as though they would like to fall but are awaiting further instruction. They are dark and spear-shaped except for the younger, fresher growth, which has a thin covering of silver-white down like a coating of hoar frost. The fragrant flowers, which once formed long, lax and deep purple spires, have turned to woody seed heads. These too remain on the shrub through the winter, like dark silhouettes of their former flowering selves. When I look at them closely,

I find these densely packed and desiccated seed cases are the colour of hazelnuts. It is a curious detail that where the flowers used to project at every angle from the stem, all of these seed cases seem to be pointing upwards.

I picked a length of stem with its head of dried husks and laid it on my writing desk. I very soon found that it was still shedding seeds. They spread across the coffee-stained surface, infiltrating my paperwork and getting between the laptop keys. Examining one of them under a lens, I could see that its tiny structure consisted of an elongated, transparent filament with a single swollen seed at the centre. The projecting ends would serve as wings, I thought, to assist in its dissemination. Perhaps this was why all the seed cases now pointed upwards, splitting open like rows of gaping mouths, to release their contents into the wind rather than to simply drop them onto the ground beneath.

The quantity of these seeds is prodigious. I have seen estimates of 40,000 seeds per flower, or three million for the shrub as a whole. Clearly, profligacy in seed production is one of the factors in its success. It is a plant to which I feel a particular attachment. It did not choose to live here but it nonetheless found a way of thriving. It has energy and resourcefulness. And it has a link with the parson naturalists.

Adam Buddle was born in 1662 in the village of Deeping St. James in the Lincolnshire fens. His father was a prosperous hemp dresser who could clearly afford to provide him with a good education, for he sent him first to Woodbridge School and then on to St. Catherine's College, Cambridge.

After graduating there he remained a Fellow until 1691 but, like several other parson naturalists, became embroiled in the religious controversies of his day. Following the Glorious Revolution, when the Catholic James II fled the country, he felt unable to take the Oath of Allegiance to William III, the new Protestant king, and his Fellowship was revoked. He was in company that included the Archbishop of Canterbury and at least 400 Anglican clerics, who held that they had already taken the Oath of Allegiance to James II and could not just revoke it at will. They were all deprived of their posts.

Buddle married in 1695 and perhaps it was the need to support a family that helped him change his mind. In 1702 he swore the Oath to William and was ordained shortly after. The next year he became rector to the Essex parish of North Fambridge, close to the Blackwater estuary. He was also appointed reader at Gray's Inn Chapel, attached to the London Law Courts. This might explain why he spent so much time in London, for it was here that he engaged in his 'botanising'.

It hardly seems an adequate word to express the excitement of the pursuit in which Buddle and his friends were involved. Here was a group that was pioneering a new approach to the natural sciences, one that was based on observation and the collection of data. They were making new discoveries, opening up new areas of knowledge and sharing in a ferment of findings and theories. The Royal Society, founded just a few years earlier, had given botany and zoology a respectability and social standing it had never known before, but here were people going beyond its fine words and lofty sentiments and actually grubbing about in the field. They were finding pinks in Deptford, heathers in Hampstead and mints on the Medway – one of which, bearing Buddle's name, in still to be found in the herbarium at Kew. Such was the group that, in 1689, founded the Temple Coffee House Botanic Club, the earliest natural history club in Britain, and, probably, the world.

It was more of a loose coterie of friends than a formal organisation. It kept no minutes and what we know about it comes largely from the letters they exchanged. They met on Friday evenings, and went off on Sunday excursions in pursuit of sites and species. Buddle seems not to have confined himself to this group and he also attended outings with young apothecaries who were interested in plants for their practical applications: the 'herbalising of the apothecaries' as he called it. He also attended gatherings at the Greyhound Tavern in Fleet Street, a pub at which Samuel Pepys was another patron.

It was inevitable in these circles that Buddle would eventually meet John Ray, the 'father of natural history', promoter of 'natural theology' and an inspiration to all the younger naturalists of his day. Buddle visited him several times and may well have assisted him in some of his work. Buddle's area of interest was wide and his collections included grasses, algae and butterflies, but his specialism was mosses and liverworts. Described by one of his contemporaries as 'top of all the moss croppers' he was to become one of the founders of the new field of bryology.

His most significant work, however, was the production of a 'New English Flora'. It was completed in 1708, three years after Ray's death, and though it achieved a very high degree of accuracy, it was never published. The manuscript was clearly available to his friends and was used both by contemporaries and immediate successors in their work, even being applied in later revisions of John Ray's books. It survives in the Sloane collection at the London Natural History Museum, but it seems that Buddle did not receive proper recognition for this work. As Dawson Turner, a later botanist, was to comment, 'justice was not done him by those of his immediate successors who more particularly benefited by his labours'. He died in 1715 and was buried in St. Andrew's Church, Holborn. No trace of his grave there survives.

One of the great quests of natural science of the time was to find a unifying approach to the classification of living things. Without a single taxonomic system, and the understanding of natural relationships that came with it, there could be little significant progress in the life sciences and the great work of Darwin would have been impossible. John Ray produced the first of such systems but Buddle made his own contribution, publishing an approach to the classification of plants. In this respect both men were precursors of the great Linnaeus, whose binomial taxonomic system became the accepted system and remains in use to this day. It was perhaps Buddle's contribution to this emerging science that led Linnaeus to accept a suggestion that a newly described genus be named in his honour. And so, fifteen years after his death, Adam Buddle finally received the recognition he deserved in the naming of the new, diverse and beautiful genus of *Buddleia*.

The buddleias now include more than a hundred species. The first of them to arrive here was *Buddleia globosa* in 1766. With its pom-poms of marmalade-orange flowers, it is still grown in parks and gardens as the 'orange-ball tree'. It was more than another hundred years before the first specimen of *Buddleia davidii* was sent to Kew Gardens. It came from central China, where it had first been described by the French missionary priest, Armand David. The fact that it bears his name too, gives the butterfly bush the rare distinction of being named after not one cleric but two. With one a Protestant and the other a Catholic, this is clearly the most ecumenical of plants.

Buddleia davidii is a plant of stony mountain slopes and high river valleys. Its adaptation to rooting in thin soils, flood gravels and the smallest fissures of rock ensured its urban success and it thrives here in the most seemingly inhospitable of terrains, probing seams of mortar with its roots, exploiting and expanding the tiniest of cracks and growing out of an almost soilless rubble. Describing buddleia thickets in Bristol, Oliver Gilbert quotes an early traveller to the Satani River in China where its thick growth on the valley shingle provided 'a famous harbourage for leopards'. In my imagination I have introduced them, too, to the buddleia stands of Poplar and seen them lying up beneath the bushes just feet from the people-thronged streets. It is an idea that might appeal to the proponents of 'rewilding' but we will probably have to settle for the stray cats that stalk the plot; those and the butterflies.

As its common name would suggest, the buddleia is famous for butterflies. Almost every written account of the plant includes an enthusiastic description of kaleidoscopic collections of small tortoiseshells, red admirals, peacocks and commas feeding upon the honey-scented flowers. In *Flora Britannica*, Richard Mabey describes more than fifty individuals of up to ten species feeding on a single bush in his garden. I, too, can remember these brightly-coloured congregations sipping so intently on a sunny summer's day that you could virtually pick them off the bush like brooches.

But such accounts are becoming anachronistic as these encounters become less and less common. Visitors to the bush in my own garden are now, at best, sporadic, and never in large numbers. Their absence is indicative of the disturbing decline of our butterflies, a decline which is particularly marked in urban areas. According to a twenty-year study reported in the journal *Ecological Indicators* in May 2017, numbers have declined by 45% in rural areas, but by as much as 69% in our cities. The urban 'butterfly bush' is now devoid of butterflies. The combination of these two stories – the urban adaptability of the buddleia and the decline of its butterfly fauna – means that in this one plant we have an illustration of our current inexorable loss of wildlife, alongside an example of nature's extraordinary recuperative power.

It is not, perhaps, inappropriate that one of the earliest examples of post-apocalyptic fiction comes from the pen of a naturalist. Richard Jefferies wrote *After London* in 1885. During most of his thirty-nine years he suffered from both poverty and ill-health but still managed to produce an extraordinary amount of literature, including journalism, essays, children's books, novels and an autobiography. But it is for his nature writing that he is best known.

He was one of the first of a generation to be influenced

by Henry David Thoreau, writing with a controlled lyricism that was neither sentimental nor moodily romantic. His work expresses the often harsh reality of English rural life as well as his deep love of the natural world, with an intensity of experience that sometimes borders on the ecstatic. He was, as Raymond Williams put it in *The Country and the City*, 'the most brilliant imaginative observer of trees and animals and flowers and weather in his century'.

Jefferies was brought up on a small Wiltshire farm, but he lived at various periods of his life on the outskirts of London. He moved in 1884 to Eltham, just south east of the capital, to a house on Footscray Road, the long road that runs from Eltham down towards Sidcup. Coincidentally I spent the later years of my childhood living on this same road some eighty years later. And it was here, on a hill-top overlooking the spread of suburbia, that he wrote *After London*.

It is a strange little book, set after some unspecified apocalypse in which a greatly reduced human population has regressed to a quasi-mediaeval condition, ruled over by bitter, quarrelling barons. Its second, main, section consists of a fairly straightforward adventure story in which Felix Aquilas, the rather moody hero, builds himself a canoe (hollowing it out of a poplar log, I am pleased to say), fits it with an outrigger and sail and leaves home in order to sail round the vast, uncharted inland sea that now occupies much of southern England. After various adventures he returns home a leader of men and ready to lay claim to his beloved.

The first part of the book is completely different. 'The Relapse into Barbarism' contains no narrative but sets out a detailed account of the natural history, social history and geography of this post-apocalyptic England. Jefferies seems so engrossed in this imaginative construction that you suspect the rest of the book has been written simply to justify these first five chapters. It is a world of evolved wildlife and devolved humanity. With a countryman's eye and a naturalist's knowledge, he sets out the process through which nature has recolonised the country as the humans retreat:

> *The old men say their fathers told them that soon after the fields were left to themselves a change began to be visible. It became green everywhere in the first spring, after London ended, so that all the county looked alike.*

There follows an account of the stages that, left to itself, nature will pass through:

> *Next summer the prostrate straw of the preceding year was concealed by young green wheat and barley that sprang up from the grain sown by dropping from ears, and by quantities of docks, thistles, oxeye daisies and similar plants. This matted mass grew up through the bleached straw. Charlock, too, hid the rotting roots in the fields under a blaze of yellow flower. The young spring meadow-grass could barely push its way up through the long dead grass and bennets of the year previous, but docks and thistles, sorrel, wild carrots, and nettles, found no such difficulty.*

Gradually, all trace of the old agricultural countryside disappears, as the shrubs arrive, followed by trees:

> *Hawthorn bushes sprang up among them and, protected*

> *by the briars and thorns from grazing animals, the*
> *suckers of elm trees rose and flourished. Sapling ashes,*
> *sycamores and horse chestnuts, lifted their heads. Of*
> *old time the cattle would have eaten off the seed leaves*
> *with the grass so soon as they were out of the ground,*
> *but now most of the acorns that were dropped by birds,*
> *and the keys that were wafted by the wind, twirling as*
> *they floated, took root and grew into trees.*

And what of the London that Jefferies now lived next
to? It is

> *lost in vast marshes ... For this marvellous city, of*
> *which such legends are related, was after all only of*
> *brick, and when the ivy grew over and trees and shrubs*
> *sprang up, and lastly, the waters underneath burst in,*
> *this huge metropolis was soon overthrown.*

Here is no gentle decline into romantic ruin with nature
softening and concealing like the pre-tourist temples of
Angkor Wat. In what reads like the Black Ditch returning
with a vengeance, London is not just fallen, it is deadly:

> *There exhales from this oozy mass so fatal a vapour*
> *that no animal can endure it. The black water bears a*
> *greenish-brown floating scum, which for ever bubbles*
> *up from the putrid mud of the bottom. When the wind*
> *collects the miasma, and, as it were, presses it together,*
> *it becomes visible as a low cloud which hangs over the*
> *place ... All the rottenness of a thousand years and*
> *of many hundred million of human beings is there*

> *festering under the stagnant water, which has sunk down into and penetrated the earth, and floated up to the surface the contents of the buried cloacae … It is a vast stagnant swamp, which no man dare enter, since death would be his fate.*

But our hero does, in the course of his journey, unwittingly enter the city, and only narrowly escapes with his life. The description of his later visit to this lost place, with its luminous yellow vapours, its sulphurous fumes and the skeletal relics of previous visitors, is thought by some to be the best section of the book. It has been argued that Jefferies did not really dislike London, it was just the unstoppable spread of its suburbs that he objected to. It is a view that is difficult to maintain in the face of this descriptive contrast between a recovered countryside and a poisoned, putrid city.

After London is not a great book and Jefferies' skill was never really in narrative. Its importance is in its subject matter and it is at its most interesting when detailing natural progression once humanity is no longer a dominant force. It clearly shows the influence of Darwinian theory, even though he outwardly rejected it, and has been called the first novel of the Anthropocene. As a pioneering work of Victorian science fiction, it had a considerable impact on writers in the coming decades – including William Morris, who was particularly impressed and drew from it inspiration for his 1890 work, *News from Nowhere*, even though his was a utopian vision.

But Jefferies' vision was distinctly dystopic. *After London* was written during the years of the Long Depression and it reflects both the prevailing anxieties of the time and the Victorian obsession with catastrophe. Perhaps, too, there was an outlet here for the author's personal pain, for not only was he already suffering from the tuberculosis that would kill him but he wrote it in the year that his youngest son died of meningitis. Jefferies was so upset that he was unable to attend the funeral. Most of all, however, this portrayal of a completely foul and fallen London would seem to be a projection of the problems besetting the Victorian city. Here was 'the Great Wen' taken to its logical conclusion. It was the London of smoke, soot and sulphur, with its belching chimneys, its gasworks and its burning kilns, its enveloping smog and its bursting sewage system; its 'Great Stink', foul river banks, poverty and squalor. Jefferies would have had a bird's-eye view of it all from Eltham, which sits on a hill looking down on London. He would have seen, too, the brickfields marching inexorably towards him. We construct our hell, as we do our heaven, on the basis of our own limited experience.

Jefferies was not a religious man, but he was a spiritual one, as his very personal autobiography, *The Story of My Heart*, makes clear. The full title of his post-apocalyptic novel is *After London; or Wild England* and perhaps Jefferies found his faith in the wildness that went beyond and would outlast humanity; in the 'indefinable aspirations' that he found 'in the grass fields, under the trees, on the hill-tops, at sunrise, and in the night'.

'There was,' he wrote in the autobiography, 'a deeper meaning everywhere,' and it is there in the fish-filled lakes and the forested hills that cover his future England. It is summed up in a poignant entry in *The Nature Diaries and Note-Books of Richard Jefferies*, written in the year he moved to Eltham: '(I) never go for a walk in the fields without seeing one thing that gives me hope.'

Among the first trees to appear in a depeopled Poplar – pushing their way up among the sallows and the elders, the buddleias and the brambles – will be the ash. It is the tree that I have recorded most often as a self-sown sapling across the parish, appearing with a seeming suddenness, often at a considerable distance from any possible parent tree. The goat willow and the grey sallow grow outward as fast as they grow upward, but the ash shoots straight up. It is all about height: as much of it as fast as possible. You may not have noticed it before but there it will suddenly be, already higher than the surrounding hydrangeas, or springing from a pot and dwarfing the rose or the hypericum.

Vitality is surely one of the most notable characteristics of the ash and it has put together a remarkable range of strategies to ensure its reproductive success. There is, to begin with, its liberal approach to sexuality. It is a tree with such gender fluidity that it could be a modern icon. Like the poplars and the willows it is dioecious, having separate male and female, wind-pollinated flowers, but the ash goes considerably further. Some trees are entirely female, whilst others are completely male. Some trees bear both male and female flowers, and some bear hermaphroditic flowers as well. Where they occur on the same tree, the male and female flowers may be mixed together or they may be borne on completely separate branches. And some trees change sex altogether, bearing entirely male flowers one year and changing to female the next. It is a situation described by Alan Mitchell as 'total sexual confusion'. I prefer to see it as an enviable level of flexibility.

The result is a tree that can respond to a range of different and changing circumstances, and one that seeds prolifically, with up to 100,000 on a single tree. They hang in great drooping bunches, remaining on the leafless tree for much of the winter and providing an easy feature for its identification. Each individual seed sits in an elongated pod attached to the top end of a papery wing or blade. The technical name for this type of fruit is an 'amara' but they are commonly known as keys.

With so many of them being produced, it is a pity that there are not more uses to which they can be put. The only one I have come across, and the only edible use of the ash, is the recipe published in 1699 by John Evelyn, one of our earliest silviculturists. The young keys are boiled several times then mixed with sugar, water and white wine vinegar to produce a pickle that was said to have 'the virtue of capers'. I cannot help thinking that with even the youngest keys it would be unpleasantly tough and chewy. Having lost several friends on account of my stringy bean chutney, I have so far refrained from experimenting.

We have a fine ash at the far end of St. Leonard's Road, a mature female tree with beige, shallowly fissured bark, like a lightly sea-rippled sand. Its upright and otherwise open form is darkened by the huge bunches of keys and as they are shed, their massed stems remain on the tree as though it were hung with dozens of shaggy horses' tails. Examining the small shrub beds that line the adjacent flats, I find no less than thirteen well-established ash saplings. They are already a metre or more high, stiff-backed with determination and springing up above the skimmia and sweet box. Their stems are a dull green, darkening to tawny brown, speckled with white spots and holding their distinctive cocoa-brown buds tight against the stem. Effective dispersal is the third element of the tree's success, and it is the amara that makes it happen.

A few years ago, I visited the Sagrada Família, Antoni Gaudí's famous, fantastical and unfinished basilica in Barcelona. Gaudí took his inspiration from the stories, symbolism and liturgy of Christianity but also from his observation of the natural world. He did not so much copy it as analyse it to understand its shapes and their functions, and to formulate from them designs which he could apply to his architecture. Around this amazing, and almost unbelievable, building there are details based on the structure of a flower, on the curving walk of a lizard, on the arrangements of the scales on a pineapple. There are spiral staircases based on the whorls of a snail's shell, whole bunches of fruit on finials, turtles supporting the bases of columns, arches which mirror ribcages and roof structures which mirror leaves. The wonderful nave is held up by pillars that branch at the top like spreading boughs, reflecting his idea that the inside of the temple should be like a wood inviting prayer.

Having seen all this, I went into the basilica's little museum and came across some of Gaudí's early design work. Here amongst the sketches were studies he had made of a falling amara, the single-bladed seed from a Spanish species of tree. The weight of the seed at one end of the wing causes it to auto-rotate as it falls and in doing so it describes a perfect helix. It was this pattern, described by the falling key, that had given Gaudí the idea for his double-twisted, helicoidal columns.

I have seen the ash keys twirling as they fall, and buzzing sometimes, like a large moth, or maybe a doodlebug. If it is not quite flying, it is what *Toy Story*'s Buzz Lightyear would call 'falling with style'. But it is not an aesthetic exercise; it has a function for the tree.

When Edward Salisbury was chronicling the flowering of the London bomb sites, it led him to question the techniques that plants employed to successfully colonise new areas. He conducted an experiment which consisted of standing on top of a step ladder inside a sealed room, dropping the seeds of various plants and timing how long it took them to travel the ten feet to the floor. The buddleia seed took five seconds, the groundsel eight and the coltsfoot twenty-one. The rosebay willowherb, whose spires of flame-red flowers came to be most closely associated with the bomb sites, took nearly a minute. The longer it took the seeds to fall, the faster the plant was spreading. The point of the ash keys' indirect descent must surely be the same: to maximise the time taken by each seed to reach the ground and to thus increase its chances of being caught up by a passing gust of wind and carried further from the parent tree.

Not all of these wafting keys will germinate next spring. Whilst some will sprout in the first year after falling, others will hold back until a second season, providing a sort of insurance policy against possible poor conditions. This final tactic, combined with the variable sexuality, the profuse seed production and the effective dispersal has made the ash one of our commonest trees. Despite a high level of predation of the young seedlings in rural areas – by birds, caterpillars, mice and voles – there are an estimated eighty to ninety million of them across the country, 2.2 million of these being in urban areas. With the possible exception of 'thorn', it is the commonest tree to appear in our place names. It is there in Ashbourne and in Ashford, in Ashby-de-la-Zouche and in Ashton-under-Lyne, and it appears in no less than 217 London street names.

To the foresters the ash was a 'weed tree', though it did the valuable job of filling the gaps left by dying elms after the disease that removed so many of them. It is now widely suggested that the ash itself is doomed. It faces twin threats. Ash dieback disease, or *Chalara*, is a fungal infection that spread from Asia into Eastern Europe in 1992. It now affects more than two million square kilometres stretching from Scandinavia to Italy. In Denmark alone, it is said to have killed two million trees.

By 2012 it had reached England, first appearing in Norfolk in a consignment of imported trees and then occurring independently elsewhere. Its fruiting bodies begin as tiny mushrooms growing on the stems of fallen leaves, but its fungal filaments become established in the tree itself and multiply within it, affecting first the branches then the trunk and eventually the whole tree.

Worse is apparently to come, for scientists now predict the imminent arrival of a second threat that could be even more destructive. The emerald ash borer is a bright green beetle that is also native to Asia. It, too, is spreading across Europe and has so far penetrated as far as Sweden. The adult beetles feed on ash leaves and cause little damage, but the larvae bore under the bark and into the wood, so extensively that they can kill the tree. Some scenarios suggest that the two threats combined could remove as many as 95% of our ash.

Disturbed by these thoughts and by this uncertain future, I looked up all the local ash on which I had taken notes and abandoned my desk to walk around them. I took the dog, not just because it is very hard to get out of the door without him, but also because his name is Ash. It is not a name we gave him. He is a rescue dog, a greyhound that was not so much retired from the track as sacked for a sensible lack of effort. His racing name was Curragh Ash, and Ash is the name he arrived with. Perhaps, with him as a talisman, we could weave some protective magic of our own.

Together we visited the broad-trunked and strangely large-leaved ash in Daniel Bolton Close; the handsomely flowered Manna ash on Cordelia Street; the female ash on St. Leonard's Road still heavily laden with bunches of keys, and with its saplings like surrounding attendants; the row of large ashes, erect and airy, beside a block of flats on Poplar High Street; and the Raywood's ashes on Bright Street, which change colour in the autumn from the top downwards, as if molten copper were being poured over them from a giant vat. Alongside the canal ramp, where it climbs up to join the A12, the saplings I had earlier noted were all still there, twelve of them, from one metre up to four in height, crowded together along the towpath. On the other side of the main road there were now more, jammed between fences or in the corners of school playgrounds or on forgotten spaces on the estate.

I decided to be optimistic about the ash. Some studies have suggested, after all, that British trees are more resistant than those on the continent. More significantly, their reproductive versatility must count for something, continually manufacturing new genetic possibilities and the likelihood of resistant strains.

This is a very different situation from the loss of our lanky, hedgerow elms. The elm rarely, if ever, sets fertile seed in this country and its spread is by suckering, making almost our entire national population a single clone. Despite this absence of genetic diversity, the elm continues to hang on, even in the face of disease. It has enclaves in East Sussex and on the Isle of Man and, across the country, thickets of short-lived suckers survive until, reaching five metres or more, they become reinfected. Nor is this the first episode of Dutch elm disease, for the pollen record shows there is a historic and naturally recurring pattern of decline and recovery, spread across some 6,000 years. The elm may yet be back in our hedgerows, along our lanes and finely fingering our skyline; and if there is hope for the elm, how much more so for the ash, with all the techniques it has at its disposal? For now, at least, it remains part of my picture of a possible later London.

The ash is a powerful plant in English folklore. Like many others, it has both positive and negative attributes. Such mingling of virtues with vices was commonplace before the arrival of the monotheistic religions and their need for an absolute separation of good and evil. The failure of the seed crop was held to foretell dire happenings in the kingdom, and possibly the death of a monarch. It is said to have failed completely the year that Charles I was executed. More wide-spread was the tree's associations with witches, and it was from ash branches that they made their flying broomsticks. M.R. James wrote a ghost story called 'The Ash-Tree', which captures some of these darker associations. I first came across it as a teenager scouring the school library for summer holiday reading and it led me, eventually, to read and collect every one of his spectral stories. At Castringham Hall a large dark ash tree stands uncomfortably close to the house, overshadowing the master bedroom and banging on its windows in the wind. After the owner has testified to seeing a local woman sit in the tree cutting switches at dead of night, she is hung for witchcraft. Life in the Hall will never be the same again.

A number of gruesome deaths of successive proprietors follow and, after a cat falls into the hollowed-out heart of the tree, and is torn to pieces, it is found to contain a number of giant, malevolent and venomous spider-like creatures, together with the mummified body of the 'witch'. James' attitude to witches is, perhaps, as questionable as his frequent use of pseudo-arachnoids, but it was enough to keep me awake those summer nights and I have read his stories to my family ever since.

In fact, the beneficent uses of the ash far outweigh its negative associations. For the most part it was a protective tree and even, in some parts of the country, a barrier against witchcraft itself. Its bark was burnt to banish the Devil; it could remove warts; it was effective against serpents; and Gilbert White famously describes how sealing an unfortunate shrew alive inside an ash was used to cure lameness in cattle. It was a tree whose tips, leaves, bark and roots all had healing uses, not surprising perhaps in a tree whose active ingredients include quinine.

People once lived in much closer association with their trees and the attributes with which they invested them were a reflection of their essential character. Thus the ash, with

its vigour and its reproductive capacity, had particular associations with sex and fertility. It was known amongst older
writers as the 'Venus of the Woods', a reference not so much
to her beauty as to her role as the Goddess of Love. It was
associated with childbirth and with the cure of childhood
ailments; in Scotland, newborn babies were welcomed with
a spoonful of sap from a heated ash twig. In later Christian
stories the newborn Christ is given his first bath by an ash
wood fire. In a classic application of sympathetic magic,
ash keys were recommended as an aphrodisiac, and its bark
used as a cure for impotence. As the tree of the maypole, it
represents the ultimate phallic symbol.

The best-known story of the ash comes from the Nordic
tradition. Yggdrasil was the tree of life, an eternally green
ash tree of vast dimensions. Its three roots grew down into
the subterranean worlds, its trunk encompassed the nine
realms of Norse mythology and its branches rose high into
the heavens. There was a golden cock, a buried horn, a
browsing goat, a squirrel that scampered up and down the
trunk, and much else besides. Beneath one root lay the well
of Urd where the gods of Asgard held their meetings and
where the wise Norns drew water every day to sprinkle on
the ash tree so that it would neither wither nor rot.

The details are contained in two mediaeval Icelandic
collections called the *Eddas*, written in the 13th century but
based on material from older sources. The earlier of the two is
known as the *Poetic Edda* and one of its poems, 'Hávamál', sets
out a story which strangely echoes the Christian account of
Easter. In his search for increased wisdom, and to understand
the meaning of the runes used by the Norns, Odin, the chief
of the Gods, sacrifices himself by suspending himself from

Yggdrasil and piercing his side with a spear. Staring down into the shadowy waters beneath, he forbids any of the other gods to grant him the slightest aid or even a sip of water. He remains there for nine days and nights, teetering on the precipice between life and death. Eventually he penetrates the meaning of the runes and the secrets that lie within them, his self-sacrifice is accepted, he falls from the tree and finds himself rejuvenated. His resurrection is accomplished.

The parallels with the crucifixion story are striking: the sacrifice of a god; the hanging on a 'tree'; the thirst, the suffering and the sense of abandonment; the stabbing with a spear. In this confrontation with darkness, Christ's three days become the three times three of Odin. Christianity was already an influence in Iceland when the *Eddas* were written and this story of Odin could have been shaped by this meeting of faiths. Equally, it could be pre-Christian in its entirety. Or both stories could have been influenced by a shared source from an earlier tradition. Essentially, however, the Odin story is another account of regeneration, of death as a prelude to greater possibilities, of an ending that is also a beginning; and the ash tree is at its very heart. It seems fitting that the scientific name of the tree, *Fraxinus excelsior*, sounds itself like the culminating line of a hymn of praise.

Excelsior is the Latin for 'higher'. So *Fraxinus excelsior* is higher in comparison with other species of ash. *Altissima* is the Latin for 'highest'; and it is half the name of *Ailanthus altissima*, the most exotic of our self-establishing trees. And where the ash is the tree of Asgard, the ailanthus is the Tree of Heaven.

Like Blake with the Peckham mulberries, I have sought for choirs of angels attending its upper branches, but to no avail. Apparently its name is something of a mistake and was wrongly transferred to this Chinese species from a taller variety that grows on the islands of eastern Indonesia. It remains nonetheless a tree with a distinctly different air. It throws out great sprays of frothy white flowers in July and then, through late summer and into the autumn, is hung with panicles of keys that tint the whole tree crimson. But its leaves are perhaps the most impressive feature. Bright red when they first unfold, they are huge in size. Like those of the ash, they are pinnate; divided, that is, into separate leaflets on a central stalk. But unlike the ash they can reach, on young trees, or on sprouting stems, nearly a metre in length, with as many as forty leaflets arranged along them. Flapping on a summer breeze, they are more like strings of green bunting than individual leaves.

A curious feature of the leaflets, especially those near the base of the stalk, is their two or three projecting 'teeth'. Turn these over to examine them and there is, on each, a crinkled circular gland. Several times I have found them being actively investigated by ants. They are a small detail, but one that can help distinguish this tree from other exotic species; for this is a tree we will be meeting with increasing frequency in the future. It is fast becoming the commonest 'escapee' tree of our cities and the Tree of Heaven will certainly be one of the dominant species of the future Poplar forest.

Originally from northern China, the Tree of Heaven is another of the plants introduced to us by the Jesuit missionaries. Combining their mission work with a botanical and zoological zeal, they might well be considered a Catholic equivalent of the parson naturalists. It was the marvellously named Pierre Nicholas le Chéron d'Incarville who first shipped ailanthus seeds into Europe and by 1751 they were being grown in the Chelsea Physic Garden. It might still have remained a tree restricted to a few private collections had not its arrival coincided with the rage for chinoiserie.

The growth of trade with China, Japan and other Asian countries had given the wealthy access to a new range of expensive imported goods, with porcelain, silk and lacquerware becoming particularly fashionable. This enthusiasm was accompanied by a fair amount of imaginative reconstruction and an idealisation of the Oriental. Between 1750 and 1765 the rage was at its height. British designers and craftsmen were imitating Asian designs, overdoing the lacquer, emphasising blue and white and letting their imaginations loose on dragons, pagodas, fantastical landscape and Chinese figures, often in highly imaginary clothing. There was an emphasis on scrolling forms and curving shapes, and on an aesthetic asymmetry.

Chinoiserie was not restricted to the decorative arts. It appeared in architecture, literature, theatre, music and interior design. In country houses, like Claydon and Badminton, whole rooms and sometimes suites were designed in a faux-Chinese style whilst elsewhere it was applied to garden design. In contrast to the previous rather stiff formality, it was held to represent beauty without excessive order and a pleasing irregularity. Among its proponents was William Chambers, who had at least the advantage of having visited China, and who designed for Kew Gardens its fifty-metre-high pagoda, though it is a pagoda with some distinctly English architectural elements. For the adherents of chinoiserie, the Tree of Heaven could hardly have arrived at a more propitious time and it was soon being widely, and fashionably, planted.

The largest and finest ailanthus in Poplar grows on the western edge of the Lansbury estate. One of the oldest members of the All Saints' congregation had told me that when the grand old buildings of the East India Dock Road had been demolished, the new housing blocks had been built on their gardens, and their trees had been incorporated into the estate grounds. The age and quality of the trees here would seem to support this: evergreen oaks, scented Balsam poplars, a fine tree magnolia and this magnificent Tree of Heaven, which almost certainly represents a local landowner's venture into chinoiserie. It is ironic that this area was once part of Poplar's Chinatown and that the street it stands on is now named Nankin Street.

No longer part of a dock master's or a sea captain's garden but set on an estate cul-de-sac surrounded by four-storey blocks, it remains a fine specimen tree. It has a surprising girth for an ailanthus and it takes me nine large paces to walk around it. From this broad trunk it spreads upwards and outwards to form a handsome, domed crown, its strong boughs performing interesting contortions: kinks, curves, abrupt turns and sharp angles. Though it is not as pronounced a feature as in the robinia, or even the common oak, it fits the idea of an 'aesthetically pleasing irregularity'.

This is an old tree now, and it shows the signs of ageing. Areas of bark are cracking and scaling, but its trunk is still marked with the pale, curling streaks characteristic of this tree, as if dozens of small, creamy snakes were swarming up it. Like many of its kind this tree has a misplaced feel, of something vivaciously tropical set on our mean city streets. I have the same feeling about the ring-necked parakeets that visit the winter feeders in my garden. They too seem somehow incongruous, welcome but inappropriate, with their bawdy un-English behaviour and their flashing colours defying our dull and steel-grey skies. The Tree of Heaven is their arboreal equivalent. If the brilliant green and red-billed parakeets of my garden were to visit this ailanthus… that would be a design worthy of chinoiserie.

There was a lapse in the planting of the ailanthus after the fashion for chinoiserie had faded, until, in the late 19th century, it became recognised for a different attribute: its resistance to pollution. It was first planted as a street tree in the cities of Canada and the USA and was soon being recommended for the poorer and smokier districts of London. Its first great stronghold here was just across the river in Bermondsey, mainly thanks to the Salter family.

During my childhood on that opposite bank, the Salters were still revered local figures. The beautiful library with its stained-glass windows, which I used every Saturday, was a part of their legacy, as were the new estates that I walked through daily, and the health clinic which we children knew as 'the solarium' for its large room of sun lamps for the treatment of rickets. The Salters were Quakers who had come to live in this poorest of boroughs and had devoted themselves to its people. Alfred was a brilliant doctor, who had settled for being the local GP here, offering his services free to those who could not afford to pay. His social engagement led to political activism and to his election as a local councillor, a member of the Board of Guardians and, eventually, an Independent Labour Party MP. Ada was also to become a Bermondsey councillor and later the borough's mayor, the first woman mayor in London.

Their dedication came at a high personal cost. Committing themselves to share the lives of the poor around them, they had declined to remove their daughter Joyce from the local school when outbreaks of scarlet fever swept the borough, even though they could have afforded to send her away. She contracted the disease three times and died of it in 1910. She was just eight years old.

One of Ada's great works in Bermondsey was the Beautification Committee. She believed that you could only be truly human by valuing nature and that 'the cultivation of flowers and trees is a civic duty'. She set out to ensure that there were trees in every street and alley in the borough and flowers on every square and churchyard. Aiming to make 'every front garden a flower garden' she provided seeds, bulbs, seedlings and window boxes and encouraged their planting in tenement windows, on balconies, in forecourts and on landings. Such was her success that in May 1931 the *Observer* reported of this previously squalid and desolate place that 'outside the Royal Parks it would be difficult anywhere to find such masses of colour'.

As for the trees, the Tree of Heaven was one of Ada's personal favourites and she pioneered its planting on the borough's previously barren streets. It was a tree well able to cope with the sooty conditions but its name must also have appealed to her devout Christian faith. According to *The Countryman*, there were 383 of them by the late 1920s. They constituted the third most planted tree in the borough, after the Black Italian poplar and the London plane, and ahead of the seventeen other species tried out by the Bermondsey Gardens Department.

Both the idea of the Beautification Committee and the use of the Tree of Heaven for urban street planting were models followed widely across other British and European cities. Ada herself, together with Alfred, Joyce, and even their cat, are remembered today by statues on Bermondsey Wall, and in Bermondsey Spa Gardens a new Tree of Heaven has been planted to celebrate their pioneering work. As the plaque beside it declares, 'Those who plant trees love others beside themselves.' It is a fitting tribute to the woman who worked so tirelessly for 'socialism with flowers'.

Poplar had its own proud tradition of tree planting and the Tree of Heaven was used in some of the most demanding locations. On a wide pavement beside the polluted A12, a grove of eleven of them stands between a factory wall and the underpass, black plastic bags flapping forlornly in their branches. Several metres away, they are throwing up suckers along the fence line of a nearby builder's yard, a 'ready mix and concrete pumping company' whose lorries once bore the logo 'Jim'll Mix It' before the title became a liability. Perhaps this tendency to sucker was not known to the tree's early champions but it produces them profusely and they grow as much as twenty to thirty metres from the parent tree. They are prevalent over much of Poplar and on a neglected strip of land outside our Tesco store they have produced an extended thicket. The dense stand of young trees with their large, divided leaves has taken on the appearance of a small jungle, rather like the one in the well-known painting by Rousseau, in which a bare-fanged and rather terrified tiger slinks through a dense growth of wind-battered tropical foliage.

As long as suckers alone were the issue, the tree could be fairly easily kept in check, unlike in the warmer cities of North America where it sets seed and quickly becomes an invasive nuisance. When Ada Salter was planting her ailanthus, the tree was unable to produce fertile seed in this country, but sometime in the second half of the 20th century the situation began to change. Though Alan Mitchell was still asserting in the 1988 edition of *Trees of Britain and Northern Europe* that the ailanthus does not set seed here, he was already out of date. A warming climate has seen ailanthus seedlings pop up all over Poplar; in gardens, in factory yards, along fence lines, around the Lochnagar edgelands, against the walls of the local Baptist church.

A number of other features have assisted in this colonisation. Though it is relatively short-lived, it can grow very rapidly. In warmer climates it can put on up to four metres a year, and even here it can manage two. It also releases an allelopathic chemical into the soil, suppressing the growth of any surrounding competition. The result, according to the charity Plantlife, it that the ailanthus has increased as a wild plant in Britain by 115% since the turn of the century. It is now our most rapidly spreading species, ahead even of such exotic expanders as the skunk cabbage and the piri-piri bur.

There are ailanthus sprouting on the pavement of Dewberry Street, outside the local community centre with its uncut, weedy lawns. Though occasionally hacked back, they sprout again, throwing up downy, green-brown stems bearing massive leaf scars, the shape of dissected strawberries. Here they are on the same site where, more than 200 years ago, mulberries were grown on a plantation – and like the mulberry, though far less famously, the Tree of Heaven is also the food plant of a silk-producing caterpillar.

The Ailanthus silk moth is nearly thirteen centimetres across, marked with scalloped patterns in beige-browns and cream, and bearing the form of a quarter moon on each of its four wings. Though not as domesticated as the silkworm, it was used in China in the commercial production of a silk that is less fine and glossy but cheaper and more durable than that of the silkworm. In 1860, a supply of these Ailanthus silk moth caterpillars was delivered to the Academy of Natural Sciences in Philadelphia, where some were released onto a large ailanthus growing in the courtyard outside. The next year there were forty cocoons hanging in the tree and from there the moths went on to colonise both Philadelphia and several other industrial cities in the eastern USA.

Today, the Ailanthus silk moth can still be found in Philadelphia, though it is in decline. Perhaps with warming temperatures and milder winters, it could have managed on our own urban ailanthus thickets, and provided an opportunity, where the mulberry had failed, to set up a silk industry in London's East End.

Suckering and seeding are regarded as bad form in a street tree, but the ailanthus has an even greater indiscretion. It smells. An article in the *Toronto Star* in 2010 went so far as to complain that the flowers on the street trees made the city smell of sperm for two months of the year. Many accounts also rail against the leaves, which are said to emit an unpleasant odour when crushed. It is the 'rank' ailanthus to T.S. Eliot in 'The Dry Salvages', and other accounts are even more graphic. They suggest a smell like 'well-used gym socks', 'old tennis shoes', 'cat urine', 'burnt peanut butter', 'rancid peanuts' and, the surprisingly specific, 'rancid cashew nuts'.

Wanting to put this to the personal test, I assembled a jury of family and friends, provided leaves from the local ailanthus, and issued instructions: 'Crush, sniff and describe.' The younger participants displayed a disturbing adjectival deficiency and their descriptive efforts got little further than 'leafy' or even 'green'. Amongst the adults, 'nuts' featured prominently and unprompted, but there were also suggestions of 'green apples', 'corned beef' and also 'a hint of bracken', as though it were some curious new eau de toilette. It is only fair to say that, despite its reputation, none of us found it particularly unpleasant. Certainly it was no competition for the black horehound that grows outside my kitchen door and smells, perpetually, of cat pee.

Despite this brief rehabilitation, the reputation of the Tree of Heaven remains tarnished. Here is a tree once renowned for its interesting appearance and celestial name, its role in a major fashion trend and its connection with the saintly Salters. Now it is better known for its dubiously scented flowers, its allegedly rank leaves, its connection with the poorest parts of the city and its weedy spread. They are attributes that have earned it the nicknames of 'stink tree', 'ghetto palm' and, inevitably, 'Tree of Hell'.

Tree of Heaven or Tree of Hell, it will be there, amongst the goat willow and the grey sallow, the buddleia and the scrambling bramble, the elder and the ash, in a post-human Poplar, forming groves and thickets, spreading by sucker and seed.

There will be other trees and shrubs beside: the pyracanthus with its berry-borne seeds spread in the guts of birds, the thorny acacias and the false locust trees, the sycamores and the Norway maples with their double-bladed helicopter seeds, the cherries, the alders and the birches that grow from the masonry of buildings or colonise the old river wall. As civilisation ceases in the 'After Poplar', there will be new forms of natural organisation and a resurgent burst of life. It will come poking through the choked grates of gutters, heaving up pavement slabs, breaking through tarmac and cracking open sewers. It will penetrate brickwork, dislodge slates, penetrate walls, colonise cellars and conceal houses beneath and between its unstoppably enthusiastic growth.

In Poplar there will be wilderness again. But in some form it has always been there. Though the marshes retreated and the black poplar was lost, it remained in the brownfield site and the building plot, in the disused gasworks on the Aberfeldy estate and the broom forest on the Blackwall Way, in the ash and the sallow unbidden in the shrub bed, in the buddleia concealed behind the hoarding and the ailanthus suckering beside the fence. It has always been biding its time.

As Gary Snyder wrote in *The Practice of the Wild*, 'Wilderness may temporarily dwindle, but wildness won't go away. A ghost wilderness hovers around the entire planet.'

Chapter Eight

The Beating of the Parish Bounds

It is Good Friday and I am planting potatoes. Throughout the winter months they have been chitting in my dark cellar and now the white buds are pushing from them, eager to grow. I place them in the pale soil then rake it across them, forming low stony ranges. It is a chilly day and I reach for the rapidly cooling tin mug of tea that sits on the garden table. It was a present, this mug, from the children and bears the motto, 'I garden, therefore I am.'

As I stand sipping, the noisy chorus of sparrows continues in the pyracanthus. Others fly to and fro to squabble on the feeders. I have always been proud of their presence, justifying, as it seems, my lax horticultural practice and the inordinate amount of money I spend on bird food. They are a particular token of the area. Recent studies in London and Bristol have shown that there is a correlation between deprivation in an area and the size of its house sparrow population. The greater the poverty, the greater the number of sparrows. Officially then, there really is a Cockney sparrow.

Older styles of housing, and housing in poorer repair,

provide more opportunities for nesting and I wonder whether these birds will survive the new wave of blank-faced blocks that are both unfriendly to sparrows and unaffordable to local people. From where I stand, mug in hand, I can see the towers rising, twenty or more storeys in height. They seem to shrink the size of my garden, for everything diminishes in their shadow.

I turn back to my potatoes. They are not a sensible crop, for it would almost certainly be cheaper to buy them in the market than to grow them myself. But my motives are hardly financial. It is the process I want to be part of; to experience the rhythm of planting and harvesting, to put my own food occasionally on my own table, to assist in the act of creation. I am an unlikely angel, with dirty fingernails.

Good Friday is a late date for the planting, but it has the virtue of tradition. It is the appropriate day, says my almanac, for potatoes, peas, beans and parsley, though for full compliance I should be doing it with a wooden spade. It is another example of sympathetic magic; the tubers that are buried alongside the crucified Christ will rise with him in potato glory, though the time scale may be a little longer. The peculiar imprecision of the practice is that Good Friday can vary in the calendar by as much as thirty-three days. Easter is still determined by the phases of the moon, with Easter Day having the complex designation of the first Sunday after the first full moon on or after the vernal equinox. It means that the earliest possible date for Good Friday is March 20th and the latest, April 23rd. In fact, it takes 5,700,000 years for the full Gregorian lunar calendar to repeat itself and for the exact same dates of the Easter cycle to recur. It would hardly do for *Gardeners' Question Time*.

The high end of the Anglican church does mystery well and during the time I have now been an unintentional clergy spouse I have come to enjoy its deep-rootedness in the calendar, its ritual celebration of the natural year and the flow of times and seasons. I have travelled with it through the solstice celebration of Christmas, the coming of the light at Candlemas, the wilderness weeks of Lent, the welcoming of new life at Easter, the wind and flame of Whitsun, the darkening of the year and the celebration of mortality at All Saints and All Souls, and the anticipation of Advent. It is a great and theatrical annual cycle of life and death and life again. It reflects a religion that arose from the land and the people that worked it, a religion that absorbed a multitude of influences from its precursors and whose festivals mark cycles in the natural world, in the life of society and in the individual psyche. To experience this and its liturgical expression had been one of the pleasures of my otherwise tentative ecclesiastical experience.

This rootedness of religion in nature is further evidenced in the popular traditions that once linked almost every part of the liturgical year to a specific wayside or woodland plant. The 'Candlemas bell' was the snowdrop, the 'Lenten lily' was the daffodil. St. John's wort was picked on his saint day at the height of midsummer, and Michaelmas had its daisy. There were pussy willows for Palm Sunday, a Pasque flower for Easter and almost every event in the story of Passion Week could be told through an associated plant. The Bible stories repeated week upon week from the pulpits had ceased to be the sole possession of the churches. They had been read into the landscape by the working people and were retold through the everyday plants that they met on their walks and in their work.

This annual cycle of church festivals was one of the important ways in which communities located themselves in time, in space and in relation to the natural world, and there was one festival which particularly interested me. In 465 AD, a series of violent storms and earthquakes destroyed the crops across much of Western Europe. Mamertus, the Bishop of Vienna, responded by ordaining that prayers and litanies be said in solemn procession around the shattered fields. They were called Rogations, from the Latin *rogare*, 'to ask'; in this case for a blessing. The practice was formally approved by the First Council of Orleans in 511 and the first three days of the week preceding Ascension Day became 'Rogation-tide'. Though this was now a Christian festival it had pagan antecedents, in particular the Roman feast of Ambarvalia. Celebrated each year on May 29th, it involved crowds processing around the cornfields, singing and dancing, sacrificing animals and driving away the winter with sticks.

Rogation arrived officially in England in 747 when it was sanctioned by a great gathering of the Anglo-Saxon church at the Council of Clovesho. It soon began to take on a particular national character. Though there were many variants, a typical Rogation procession might see the local people, led by priest and cross-bearer, setting out to trace the parish boundaries. Latterly, choirboys or schoolchildren would accompany them, led by their master and bearing slender wands of willow, stripped white and sometimes crowned with a knot of flowers. At well-known landmarks – perhaps a pond, a bridge or a stile, but most often an ancient or prominent tree – they would pause and gather around the priest to hear a gospel reading or to recite a psalm. Here, too, they would say a 'rogation', imploring God to send seasonable weather, to keep the crops in good health and provide an ample harvest.

The echoes of an older magic are clear in a description of the proceedings provided by Richard Taverner, an associate of Thomas Cromwell, in 1540. 'For this cause,' he says, 'be certain gospels read in the wide field amongst the corns and grass, that by the virtue and operation of God's word, the power of the wicked spirits which keep in the air may be laid down, and the air made pure and clean, to the intent the corn may remain unharmed and not infected of the said hurtful spirits, but serve for our use and bodily sustenance.'

The English Rogation processions gradually morphed into the 'Beating of the Bounds' as a strange new ritual developed. When the company halted for psalms or prayers beside the boundary markers and beneath the 'Gospel oaks', it became the custom to beat or bump or duck one of the boys, perhaps even to hold him upside down and strike him with the rods of willow. An account by Laurence Whistler in *The English Festivals* is perhaps slightly romanticised but describes how the 'wand-bearers' would begin by beating the landmark then suddenly transfer their attack to one of the boys 'who offered himself, half-willing and half-reluctant. They rolled him in a briar bush, flung him in a pond, or, seizing him by shoulders and heels, bumped him several times against the boundary stone ... The sacrificial victim did not show any great reluctance, for a new shilling was likely to be his reward.'

With the passage of time, and with changing sensibili-ties, it became more customary to beat the landmarks than to beat the boy but, even in this more civilised mode, it remains easy to see in these proceedings the re-enactment of the ancient theology of the scapegoat and the relics of animal sacrifice.

Inevitably, the Rogation customs, just like the Palm Sunday processions, were seen by many as remnants of paganism and of Popery, which amounted, in the popular mind, to much the same thing. They were the last survivors of the many mediaeval ceremonies that had been conducted in the open air to secure fertility and good weather: the blessing of trees on Twelfth Night; the reading of gospels to springs to make their water pure; the blessing of the corn by young men and women on Palm Sunday. All these lost the sanction of the Protestant Church and the Puritans set their sights on Rogations too, particularly as they became more disorderly. 'Uplandish processions and gangings about,' the 18th-century Quaker minister John Banks described them, 'which be spent in rioting and beastly belly-cheer.' In the name of keeping them properly Protestant, many compromises had to be made over the years and, while the festival survived, it was hemmed about with ordinances determining what was, and what was not, acceptable. The wearing of surplices, the carrying of banners, the cutting of wayside crosses were all prohibited and the outings carefully described as 'perambulations' rather than the more popish 'processions'.

The fact that they continued at all is almost certainly due to the fact that they simultaneously fulfilled several different functions. George Herbert, the wonderful 17th-century poet and parson, ascribed four virtues to the Rogation procession: blessing of God for the fruits of the field; justice in the preservation of bounds; 'charity' in 'loving, walking and neighbourly accompanying one another'; and mercy 'in relieving the poor by the distribution of largesse'. What might be called the magical dimension, the seeking of a blessing for the land, was at the very heart of the Rogation festival and is manifest still in the words of the modern liturgy:

> *Upon the rich earth send a blessing O Lord*
> *Let the earth be fruitful*
> *and its resources be hallowed.*

But 'neighbourly accompanying one another' was also an essential element. The reinforcement of community, the enjoyment of a convivial shared occasion, the settlement of disputes in the levelling process of walking together – all served to strengthen the identity of the parish. As part of this, proceedings were usually followed by a meal, sometimes elaborate, sometimes the simple sharing of beer and cheese. Such meals would be paid for from parish funds or by small endowments made specifically, though not always willingly, for the purpose.

For the parish to be strengthened it had also to be properly identified and the Rogation perambulations acted as a form of map-making before printed maps were easily available. They defined, and defended, the parish perimeters, checking the boundary markers and restoring them where necessary. And they impressed upon young people, sometimes quite literally, where the parish borders lay. A boy who had been struck with staves whilst suspended upside down over a boundary marker would no doubt remember where it was located.

Ignoring these more physical expressions, it was the combination of magic and mapping, of landscape and community that had convinced me that the Beating of the Bounds should be once more celebrated in Poplar. I had walked every street in the parish, watched a single tree for a year, dowsed the Black Ditch and now, as a sort of culmination, I wanted to be part of a collective circumnavigation, something that would be a celebration of the parish, its history, its natural history and its people, and that would, however briefly, undo our disconnects in 'time and space and meaning'.

So it was that a good proportion of our joint congregations gathered in the St. Nicholas church hall on Ascension Day for a shared lunch of soup and cheese. We had, regretfully, foregone the beer. In another departure from tradition, we moved our perambulation to the nearest available Sunday. Such was the fate of many English festivals, moved from the working week to weekends or the nearest convenient Monday, separating productivity from celebration in a triumph of the Calvinist ethic.

Since the parish had two churches, we would start at one and end at the other. Completing our route at All Saints' would also give me the chance to fulfil another ambition: we had arranged to plant a native black poplar in the churchyard, thus bringing about the return of the species that had given the parish its name. Working with the local authority I had managed to source one from the Hackney Community Tree Nursery. A couple of metres in height and set with its root ball in a large builder's bag, I had transported it to All Saints' Church in the back of my car. I had obtained permission from the Archdeacon, agreed a site with the churchwardens and prepared a hole in the appropriate spot. The tree now sat in a side room awaiting its ceremonial investiture.

More than fifty of us set out to attempt the route; the youngest four, the oldest eighty-two. Another group, less able or less willing, walked straight across to All Saints' to await our arrival there, whilst the church Prayer Group, which had the ability to extemporise to the point of exhaustion, gathered in a side room to seek a heavenly support for our endeavour. Some forty days earlier we had set out from St. Nick's on our Palm Sunday pilgrimage. Now we were here again, heading across the Millennium Green towards the old gasworks.

We were by no means the first party to have beaten the Poplar parish bounds. I had, in my researches, come across a photograph of the proceedings which, although undated, seemed to belong to the late 19th century. It shows the old Poplar Town Hall before it was demolished as a result of damage sustained during the Blitz. Here it was again, in all its former glory, a grand entrance of three columned arches, reached up a flight of ceremonial steps. To one side of the picture stands a group of schoolboys with their gowned master, wearing caps and carrying willow wands that are some two or three times their own height. The rest of the scene is packed with well-bearded men bearing shorter staves and almost universally dressed in frock coats and top hats. I cannot claim that our straggling column beside the gasworks was anywhere nearly so neatly attired.

The gasworks closed in the 1970s but until then its sickly-sweet smell had permeated the parish. Since 1878 the Commercial Gas Company had been a significant local employer, and a good one too. Workers were taken on as 'co-partners' and shared in a small portion of the profits.

In the 1930s, when the Mission to Seamen left its beautiful mock-Jacobean buildings on the East India Dock Road, the gas company bought them and opened them as a 'Co-Partnership Institute'. The chapel was converted to a gymnasium, and there was a restaurant, two halls for meetings, a stage for concerts and plays and events including an annual children's party. Next to the Institute the company had built rows of workers' cottages where at least one member of the congregation had been born.

On Oban Street, beyond the gasworks but still in its shadow, raised brick planters had been built on the estate lawns, often with the addition of home-made pergolas. They had been planted by the tenants with giant tomatoes, nasturtiums and large trailing marrows. A meadow brown butterfly flew among them as we passed. They were like trace memories of our landed past. Here, just as the Huguenots had brought their vines and figs and mulberries, the new wave of Bengali immigrants were planting the vegetables with which they were familiar.

The far end of the Aberfeldy estate tapers away to a point where the A13, on the one side, meets and crosses the River Lea on the other. It was here, where London had once tipped over into Essex, that we made our first stop. This part of the estate had already been rebuilt as the new Aberfeldy Village, and in Catkin Place, a small square where squat fountains gushed like burst water mains, we gathered about our priest. She blessed the people of the estate, and of 'the village', those moving in and those moving out and all those undergoing change and disruption. Then came the sprinkling of holy water; liberally, on our surroundings, on us and on any passer-by who wandered close enough. But we refrained from beating anything.

This area had once been the Bromley marshlands, and even now it is hardly above sea level. In an unconscious echo of the dykes that would once have criss-crossed the wet fields, the developers had included a 'swale' on the new site. Along one side of a long central space lined with alders and liquidambar trees, a grassed ditch provided the opportunity for water runoff and rainwater infiltration. It had been sown and planted with native wild flowers and was now lined with wild carrot and cowslip, tufted vetch and tares, ragged robin and ox-eye daisy, massed in the centre of the housing. It was an encouraging sign.

As the urbanisation of the globe continues, with two thirds of us expected to live in cities by 2050, we are increasingly removed from the natural rhythms of the growth cycle, from the sight of clear night skies, from the seasonal sequence of plants and the passage of birds. As the cities come to occupy more of our lives and more of our land, it is essential that we find a radically different approach to designing the townscape, one that sees it as a shared space, a place where humans can flourish alongside other species.

We have the tools and knowledge enough already for this integrated city: for green roofs and living walls and rooftop gardens; for parks which permeate estates; for wild areas in our open spaces; for dykes and ponds and sustainable urban drainage; for natural corridors that allow for the flow and spread of species; for mature trees and new hedgerows; for bat-friendly lighting; for community orchards and pocket parks; for homes that are willingly shared with house martins, starlings and swifts. Cities which are understood as shared ecosystems are cities in which we would be safer from flash flooding, air pollution and extremes of temperature, and from noise and stress. They are cities in which humans would be happier and healthier. As Gary Snyder put it, 'Civilisation is permeable and could be as inhabited as the world is.'

Back in the world as it is, we crossed and followed the A13, with its mechanised torrent of traffic, between the roaring main road and a council waste vehicle depot where, along its untended edges, goat's-beard bloomed beneath buddleia and an unexpected song thrush sang. Before the river crossing we turned off along a footpath next to our first open stretch of the River Lea, one my favourite local places for wildlife. There were grey poplars here and osiers, and a small reed bed on the river mud where, in summer, reed warblers conduct those long and tuneless but amiable chatterings that pass for song. I had even once heard a Cetti's warbler here, with the distinctive and explosive burst of notes that sound as if the bird has been trying to keep a secret but can hold it in no longer. In winter there are teal and gadwall and even the occasional shelduck, venturing up river from their regular haunts on the estuarine Thames. At low tide, herons stand on the exposed mud and a redshank might come fluting by. Further up, beyond Bow Locks, the Lea has been dammed to promote marinas and riverside development, with the mud banks eliminated as unsightly. Here, they are the very source of life.

On the landward side of the path, a strip of thin soil supports clumps of feathery fennel, campanulas and teasels, and a national rarity with the name of Jersey cudweed.

Although only a few inches high it is a distinctive plant, rather ragged in appearance with cottony hairs on its greyish leaves and stems, and clusters of rusty-yellow flowers. It likes bare, sandy ground where there is little competition, and it survived in just two locations in the country until its recent appearance in the docklands.

The riverside led us onto the Orchard Place peninsula, with the multi-coloured blocks of City Island on the one side and brownfield land of buddleia, butterfly and bramble on the other. Pellitory-of-the-wall grew in clumps from the walls and a sapling of grey willow was doing well on a pavement corner beside blocked drains.

At the very tip of the peninsula is Trinity Buoy Wharf, where Trinity House had once repaired its buoys and light-ships and where the 19th-century scientist and inventor Michael Faraday had a workshop. Here, where the muddy waters of the River Lea meet and mingle with those of the Thames, we made our second stop, blessing all those whose lives were bound up with the river and sea.

The East India Dock once handled up to 250 ships at a time, traders of up to a thousand tons, bearing spices, tea, indigo, silk and Persian carpets. All this came into the dock through the East India Dock Basin and whilst the dock itself has been infilled, the entry basin has been preserved and allowed to silt up as a nature reserve. We came through it at low tide with coots tracking across the deep mud leaving long, looping trails behind them and making their calls, like a squeaky toy being gnawed by a dog. Teal and gadwall gathered on the stretches of open water and a heron sat hunch-shouldered on a little island.

There was a small copse of birch along one side of the reserve by which I was glad to pause, for the birch has a particular connection with these parish peregrinations. It is one of our most beautiful trees, the wispiest and the most wistful. It has a delicacy matched only by its flexibility, and its mass of thin pendulous twigs trail like a fine summer shower. It is only when their leaves are shed in the autumn that you become aware of their distinctive pinkish-purple colouration which stands out particularly well against a wintry sky. With its bright, white bark this was my mother's favourite tree and, because of that, the first tree I ever learned to name. She would not have known, good Puritan that she was, that this was a magical tree, protective against lightning, witchcraft and the evil eye.

Although many accounts of the Beating of the Bounds mention the carrying of staves or wands of birch, they steer clear of these deeper connections. The birch has supple twigs that do not easily snap and which made a useful besom or broom, bound together, perhaps, around a rod of ash. As Geoffrey Grigson points out, a house that was being swept with a besom of birch was not just being cleaned of its dirt, it was simultaneously being swept free of evil. The same tough pliability made birch twigs the equipment of choice for punitive beatings. The practice of 'birching', once widespread, remained a legal punishment on the Isle of Man as late as 1996, although its last actual use was in 1973. Beating a recalcitrant child with a switch of birch was not just about inflicting pain; it was also a way of literally beating the evil out of them. In this light, the carrying of birch rods around the

Rogation procession and their use in the beating of boundary markers, was clearly about expelling evil from the parish, ridding it of those 'wicked and hurtful spirits' described by Richard Taverner.

Further along the Thames shore we made our third stop, this time at Virginia Quay, on the site from which John Smith had sailed. The platform-planted aspens I had noted on my earlier walks were now all dead or dying and being replaced with less resonant but more resolute cherries. A few yards further on, a line on the pavement marks a significant, if conceptual, boundary between the eastern and western hemispheres. The Prime Meridian, or Greenwich Meridian as I was brought up to call it, is the line determined for zero degrees longitude. It was a vital navigational aid and is marked out here along Prime Meridian Walk on a strip that eventually meets and climbs the twenty-two storeys of Elektron Tower. This has been its line since 1884 when the International Meridian Conference determined that Earth's prime meridian 'be employed as a common zero of longitude and standard time-reckoning throughout the globe' and that it 'pass through the centre of the transit instrument at the Observatory of Greenwich'. The only problem is that it no longer does. The original method for its determination was by telescopic measurement of star positions. Today, the satellite measurement of GPS is far more accurate, with the result that the actual meridian is now 102 metres further east.

Beyond Virginia Quay, the Blackwall stretch of the riverside is privatised. We followed it as close as we could, inland along the Blackwall Way, and beside one of our few remaining 'urban commons'. The still undeveloped site was thick with Spanish broom, its fragrant pea-like yellow flowers already beginning to open. Beneath it was goat's rue and wall rocket, lucerne and melilot and the young stems of common toadflax. In a gateway, with its flowers almost finished, was some London rocket, the plant that had colonised London so suddenly after the Great Fire. Bindweed scrambled up the chain-link fences, making a fine effort at concealing them completely. Later in the summer it will form its long white trumpets held in the calyx like a chalice. As children we used to squeeze them at the base shouting, 'Granny, jump out of bed!' as the entire flower shot out of the calyx like a pilot activating an ejector seat. The species here is actually a hybrid between our native form and a newer American arrival, and one that is becoming increasingly common. It is one of the many things they have sent back to us in return for John Smith.

Beyond this brief eruption of the unruly, we were back in the well-ordered world of the Radisson Hotel and of gated roads with security guards leading through luxury development. We made our way, unexpectedly unchallenged, through horse-shoe shaped apartment blocks with flowing water features, feeling like trespassers on our own territory. It was almost a relief to reach Yabsley Street, the waste transfer station and the council's recycling centre. It was on this site that the demolition of a pub and excavations for new buildings had uncovered evidence of ancient occupation. Amongst the shards of pots, the flint flakes, the knives and arrowheads, was a single grave with a female skeleton laid in the foetal position. An oak plank in the grave, perhaps used to retain the soft riverside sand, enabled it to be dated to around 4000 BC and the beginning of the British Neolithic, making it one of the earliest burial sites in Britain and the first known settlement in the London area. These were a people in transition from hunter-gathering to a permanently settled agriculture, for an analysis of plant remains in the immediate surrounds showed that they were both growing their own early emmer wheat and still gathering wild foods, such as hawthorn berries and mallow seeds. Among the remains was an abundant supply of hazelnut shells.

Separated by just a few hundred yards, and 6,000 years, huge cranes topped with red lights are hauling up the very latest settlement and the largest of the many developments in the parish. Wood Wharf will cover twenty-three acres with 3,610 new apartments and two million square feet of office space, in towers rising up to fifty-seven storeys. In a hubristic height-race they will become some of the highest skyscrapers in the country, dwarfing the buildings of Canary Wharf, which briefly held that title for themselves. At the centre of this whole new district will run a 'high street' which, according to the 2007 master plan, will have a glass, 'snake-skin' roof. It will, according to the publicity, be 'vibrant', 'urbane' and, of course, 'iconic'.

You can, in the different styles and stages of housing across the parish, trace something of the journey that has led from our life on the land to this enclosed existence that attempts to turns its back on the natural world and the weather. It is a relatively recent separation. It was for several hundred thousand years that we roamed as hunter-gatherers. It was for many generations after that, that we dug and sowed, tended, tilled and harvested. From the time of those early Yabsley Street people through to the mid-19th century it was a direct and daily dependency. It is, in comparison, just a few short generations since we left the land in our masses, seeking work and survival, and crammed ourselves into the cities. Arriving to work in the factories of Canning Town and Poplar, or to excavate the local docks, the people brought a memory of the land with them, with their allotments and their little backyards.

The Second World War, and the slum clearance that accompanied it, brought about a new generation of housing on estates surrounded by a collectivised open space. It was space that was owned on behalf of everyone, and therefore by no one. There were lawns and trees and shrub beds, and perhaps some children's play equipment, but they were impersonal, tended by council staff or, worse, by roving gangs of contract mowers with little horticultural training and no long-standing relationship with the site. Idealistic, and often ill-designed, they degraded into dull, flat and poorly used expanses. Even at their worst, however, they remained as breathing spaces, as pores in the city's skin.

Now a new wave is arriving, higher again and with greater density. The new blocks cast their smaller, tightly landscaped, open spaces into shade for much of the day and whip up a wind that blows around and between them. They are places for looking at but not for using, and definitely not for any form of communal assembly. The high-rise flats represent a very physical separation from the earth, above which we now live suspended in unrooted space. A last gasp at the outdoors is their balconies. These small projecting spaces are the new reduction of the garden. Attending a planning consultation in my local library, I had been told that they were part of the local plan and a condition required in new developments. They represent, perhaps, a close-to-final stage of the transition: from fields to allotments and backyards, from backyards to the collectivised open space, from the outside space to the balcony; a waning echo of our long relationship with the land.

I once watched a neighbour walk past my house with a flowerpot in her hands. She told me that she wanted to grow some plants on the landing of her tenement and had been to the park to 'steal' some soil. She had spoken of it guiltily but I had felt, as she bore this small portion of our common heritage carefully in her hands, that she was bearing a sacrament. There is a counter movement and she was a small part of it. Here and there across the parish, tenants have got together and turned dull green estate squares into community gardens or built raised beds on their small fenced lawns. They have built chicken coops on a disused tennis court at Balfron Tower, dug vegetable plots in the grounds of Robin Hood Gardens, put planter boxes outside their windows on the Will Crooks estate, and planted an orchard and keep bantams at the local primary school. Here, despite the massive surrounding land-grab and all the other forces ranged against it, the instinct to sow and grow, to tend and prune, to be in touch with the world and its weather, survives.

Beyond Wood Wharf the main road crosses the entrance channel to the docks. With its single massive bascule it looks like the drawbridge from a giant's castle. Known locally as the Blue Bridge it is held by most people to be the real portal to the Isle of Dogs. Beneath it, the river runs into the West India South Dock, which extends for the whole width of the island, and exits back into the Thames on its western side. This western exit is now infilled but, in the heyday of the docks, when the Blue Bridge and the western bridge both were raised, the island was isolated and long queues of traffic would form to get on or off it. From the days of the marshes to the days of the docks, the island was always a separate and rather secret place, isolated and independent, and with its own strong identity. Apart from those who lived or worked there, it was an area that few would enter.

The island makes an appropriately mystical appearance in the work of William Blake. He sees it as home to the dogs of Leutha, which 'lap the waters of the trembling Thames'. They represent the 'baser passions', an association which may well be based on the large number of prostitutes that then thronged the area. In his long poem 'Jerusalem; The Emanation of the Giant Albion', the island is crossed by Los, as he walks his circuitous route into the city. He is the 'eternal prophet', representing creation, inspiration and the divine aspect of the imagination; a messianic figure who will bring about a world based on the creative imagination rather than the tyrannous rule of reason.

> *He came down from Highgate through Hackney and Holloway*
> *   towards London*
> *Till he came to Old Stratford, and thence to Stepney and the Isle*
> *Of Leutha's Dogs, thence through the narrows on the river's side,*
> *And saw every minute particular, the jewels of Albion, running*
> *   down*
> *The kennels of the streets and lanes as if they were abhorred.*

'Los' is generally accepted to be an anagram of 'sol', the sun, and it has been suggested that his route, coming into the city from the east, tracks the rising sun. The 'kennels' have nothing to do with dogs; they were the open drains that bore their unpleasant cargo down the centre of the city streets. Perhaps, however, this really is a place of the imagination. Wes Anderson's 2018 film, *The Isle of Dogs*, came out while I was writing this book and I took my son to see it. Its narrative has nothing to do with the island, but he was inspired to write it after seeing a sign bearing the island's name.

It is not just a film that bears its name; there is also a missing play. *The Isle of Dogs* was written by Ben Jonson and Thomas Nashe in 1597 and its first performance was held at the new Swan theatre in Bankside. For reasons that remain unclear, it caused an uproar and was a matter of serious offence to the authorities. Possibly it contained satirical references to members of the Court circle, and even to Queen Elizabeth herself, whose Palace of Placentia faced the Isle of Dogs from across the river in Greenwich. Whatever the cause, the consequences were dire. The Privy Council ordered that the play be immediately suppressed for sedition and several actors, including Jonson, were arrested and jailed. A warrant was also issued for the arrest of Nashe and when he fled London, his papers were seized and destroyed. A general closure of theatres was ordered, extending to the whole of London. But the affair seems to have subsided as suddenly and as mysteriously as it had begun. After a few months, Jonson and the other actors were released and a few days after that the theatres were re-opened. But a manuscript of the play has never since been found.

The islanders themselves can be impatient with authority and their sense of a separate identity reached its fullest, and most symbolic, expression when the island declared its 'independence' in 1970. At that time the Isle of Dogs had few shops, poor healthcare facilities and no secondary school, and its public transport infrastructure consisted of a single bus route. These already limited amenities were being put under further strain by the arrival of families moved out from war-damaged homes in the rest of the borough.

On March 1st, several hundred protesters occupied both the Blue Bridge and the western bridge for a period of two hours, thus effectively blockading the island. The protestors called for better services and a cut in rates, announcing to the press their decision to declare independence. Just a few years earlier Rhodesia, under Ian Smith, had made its Unilateral Declaration of Independence (UDI) and its consequences had been dominating the news. Consciously and ironically mimicking this the protesters announced, 'We have declared UDI and intend to set up our own council. We can govern ourselves much better than they seem to be doing. They have let the island go to the dogs.'

It was intended as a one-off protest but it captured both press attention and the public imagination. Warming to their theme, the protestors set up a thirty-strong Citizen Council of the Isle of Dogs, threatening to withhold payment of rates and devote the money instead to the island. Lighterman John Westfallen became their 'Prime Minister' and began to issue entry permits to the island. Ted Johns, who did most of the media appearances, was appointed 'President'. He was a Poplar man who had worked on the barges before being injured on National Service in Korea and his was one of the families that had been moved onto the island following bomb damage to their homes. His fourth-floor flat in Skeggs House became the Presidential Palace and his wife Sylvia, the 'First Lady'. Despite this elevation, she declared of her husband that 'he'll always be Ted to me'.

The story made the national media and secured Ted and John a meeting with Harold Wilson, the other Prime Minister. When Ted was interviewed by Walter Cronkite from CBS via satellite link, coverage can truly be said to have gone international. The 'rebellion' lasted a few weeks. By that time its point had been made and Tower Hamlets Council was promising more investment.

It was, then, by the historic Blue Bridge that we made our fourth stop. Between the Neolithic burial site, the cranes of Wood Wharf and the island of Leutha's dogs, we blessed this portion of the parish. And then we crossed the portal. Our route was now along Marsh Wall, a straight and busy road lined with blank-faced steel and glass blocks, and with plane trees that seemed to be going through another period of heavy shedding.

But this border had once been indeterminate, a place where the relationship between earth and water was uncertain and continually on the move. River, marsh and flood meadow faded into each other, channels changed course and shorelines shifted. Until at least 50 AD most of the island south of here lay, at least some of the time, below the waters of a much broader river. It was the Romans, those fixers of things, the builders of aqueducts and central heating, of straight roads and sanitation, who first erected a sea wall here. But there were still breaches and inundations and, for a time, a tidal lake known as 'the Poplar Gut'. Even today Poplar lies only fifteen feet above sea level, reducing to ten feet in this southern portion. Yet few going about their business here now are aware of what a transient place it is.

Two thirds of the way along Marsh Wall we turned northward crossing the South Dock to enter Canary Wharf over a curving modern footbridge held up by wires from a leaning spar, so that it looks like a thinly stringed harp. It brought us to the heart of the Canary Wharf estate.

This was once the busiest port in the world but after years of decline the last of the docks closed in 1981. As an uneasy quiet descended over the acres of water, the warehouses, the jetties and the cranes, the future of the site became a subject of public debate until Margaret Thatcher and Michael Heseltine came up with the idea of the Urban Enterprise Zone. The London Docklands Development Corporation was established and by 1988 the Canadian company Olympia and York had begun work on delivering a master plan that would transform the site. It was supposed to be a model of the free market economy at work. In reality it was nothing of the sort. Canary Wharf was developed on the back of massive public investment. As well as huge tax waivers, billions of pounds were spent on the infrastructure and on new transport links that included the most expensive road in Europe as well as a light rail link direct to the City. They were, in fact, some of the most heavily subsidised office blocks on Earth.

Despite all this assistance, Olympia and York were filing

for bankruptcy by 1992. Control of the estate was taken over by a consortium calling itself the Canary Wharf Group. This, too, was hit by financial difficulties and was taken over in 2004 by a Morgan Stanley-led consortium using the improbably named Songbird Estates as their acquisition vehicle. But the story of wheeling and dealing continued and in 2014 the Qatari Investment Authority (Qatar's sovereign wealth fund) made a bid of £2.6 billion to seize control of Canary Wharf, including the Wood Wharf scheme. The sum was considered surprisingly small and was initially rejected by Songbird, but by early 2015 they had capitulated. Like the Shard, Chelsea Barracks, Harrods and the Olympic Village at Stratford, Canary Wharf is now owned by an arm of the Qatari state.

In an article in the *Evening Standard* in November 2014, Simon Jenkins made a case as to why the valuation had been so low. His contention was that Canary Wharf is already 'yesterday's infrastructure' and that what office workers and the new industries increasingly require is not these 'over-developed and personality lite' mega-projects but an 'experience environment; informal, diverse, preferably historic corners of the city in which to relax'. Whilst the 'boss of Canary Wharf' is belatedly and rather desperately announcing his eagerness to build new infrastructure, schools, parks and playgrounds, what he actually needs is 'what his greed has destroyed, at least some of West India Dock's warren of warehouses, quays and lanes he wiped out; the reason why high-tech entrepreneurs are now in Shoreditch, not the Isle of Dogs'. Canary Wharf, he complains, 'has no funky hinterland. It is a stylistic asylum with no tangential personality. Canary Wharf has Poplar, as Croydon has Thornton Heath.'

Despite these challenges Canary Wharf still rivals the City as the country's financial centre and houses the national, and international, headquarters of numerous banks and finance houses and the auditors that legitimise them. These high towers house a roll call of the companies that fuel our finance-led economy: HSBC, Ernst and Young, Morgan Stanley, Citibank, Barclays, Clifford Chance, Deutsche Bank, Credit Suisse, Merrill Lynch and many more, often with their names emblazoned across the summit of their towers. The average salary of those working here is £100,000. In Tower Hamlets as a whole it is £29,500, with one fifth of the working population earning less than £15,000. It is here on the Wharf that Leutha's dogs are really on the loose.

We walked on, we people of the unfunky hinterland. And it is true that this far through the walk we were becoming a little dog-eared. This being Sunday, the Wharf was desultory and almost deserted. We made our way through the conceptual squares and canyoned streets or detoured down long corridors in the underground malls in search of toilets. At one stage a peregrine drifted overhead but hardly another bird stirred. The advertising for luxury flats on the estate describes this as 'one of London's greenest areas'. It is a startling claim for what must be one of London's most sterile; the place where the wild things aren't. You could spend all day here and not see a sparrow – a very precise illustration of the finding that quantities of wealth and numbers of sparrows exist in inverse proportion. The sheer faces of the buildings are inaccessible for nesting, the open spaces over-designed and free of invertebrates. Even the large water bodies of the remaining dock basins seem bleak and bottle-green, lifeless save for the occasional grebe or the ubiquitous gulls. This is a zone of total control and you feel that even an ant might need some sort of permit. Nonetheless, we sprinkled the holy water and blessed the high blocks and all who worked in them; the caretakers and the cleaners, the fund managers and the investment bankers alike.

It was our fifth stop. Uncertain of the exact boundary we had held it next to the trees of Jubilee Park, one of the few significant groupings of trees on the Wharf. More than 200 trees of a single species have been planted here in sunken, irrigated containers. They make up a small glade of dawn redwoods. It is a tree that was known as a widespread fossil from the Mesozoic era but that was believed to have been extinct for at least sixty million years. Then, in 1941, a Chinese forestry official found a single, large specimen growing in Sichuan province. Subsequent investigations located several small groves and eventually a forest of roughly 5,000 trees. Nonetheless, it remains critically endangered in the wild. Known also as the water fir, it is a tree of damp, mountain valleys, a habitat that has been extensively cleared to make way for rice paddies. Both its attractiveness and its rarity ensured that it very soon entered cultivation and seeds were brought to Britain as early as 1948. Here it remains primarily a specimen tree of parks and gardens, but in one place in China it has been put to use to form the longest tree-lined avenue in the world. The Picang Highway, at Pizhou, lost some thirteen kilometres to urban expansion, but still it runs for forty-seven kilometres between more than a million closely planted trees.

The dawn redwood is one of the very few conifers that are deciduous. There is something almost insubstantial in its winter appearance, and when its leaves are open it is still delicate and airy with a shade that is dappled rather than dark. The trees are slender and straight like parallel lines on a ruled page. They hold their branches diagonally upwards but towards the tip they droop, in a fashion that is slightly effete. Their bark is reddish brown and stringy, with ribbon-like strips curling off. Now, in early May, the newly opened leaves were soft and surprisingly fern-like, still a fresh, bright green as we gathered beneath them with an air of untested innocence. By November they will take on a darker coloration, somewhere between rust and fox-red, starting at the trailing tips and spreading until it encompasses the whole tree.

It was another footbridge that led us off the Wharf, a futuristic tube suspended from a giant, white pylon, like a rope bridge strung across a canyon. It transported us high over the Aspen Way, the traffic roaring like a torrent beneath us, over the tracks of the Docklands Light Railway and over Poplar Station. When we eventually descended it was into a different country; the streets and estates and people of the other Poplar. We were almost immediately in the High Street, a rather sad shadow of its former self, affected by both the national decline of the high street and the particular circumstances of Poplar's post-war history. It houses the public mortuary, the one-time Town Hall extension and a bowling green which I have never seen in use. There are a few shops – small corner stores, a betting shop, a barber's – but for most of its length it is ungraciously backed onto by estates. The heart of Poplar, if it is defined by shopping, has long since shifted to the Chrisp Street Market.

The street has been planted with Norway maples. In the early part of the year we have the cherry blossom in Poplar but when the first flush of that begins to fade the maple blossom has its much less feted turn. Now their acid yellow-green flowers were also fading and turning to a pale green, but their new leaves shone with a glossy and expectant exuberance. Their seeds are amaras, this time with double-bladed wings. They hold them more upright than those on a sycamore seed; the sycamore has the wings of a hawk moth, the Norway maple those of a gliding bird. They spread so freely that the tree will undoubtedly be a component of the post-human forest, but perhaps this will be just the completion of an earlier thwarted colonisation. Like the sycamore, the Norway maple was naturally spreading this way and would almost certainly have made it, had not, in an earlier geo-physical Brexit, the land-bridge to the continent flooded around 8,000 years ago.

The trunks on this line of trees divide quite low and where they split into two or three main branches there are damp cushions of moss in a dark Lincoln green, as though we were deep in a forest. The bark is surprisingly rich in lichens, with species in brick-orange, in gold and grey-green. There is a contrasting area at the base of each tree which is free of this growth. This is the 'splash zone', or what Oliver Gilbert calls the 'canine zone', where the prevalence of dog urine favours the growth of a completely different flora primarily composed of nitrogen-tolerant algae. Looking down at the base of each tree as we passed, they were of a different, paler colour with the transition from one zone to the other demarcated with surprising clarity. Dogs, and even their defecation, cats and their predation, feral pigeons squabbling over crusts of bread, and, of course, people too, are elements of the shared ecology of the city.

We crossed the clear dip that marks the channel cut by the Black Ditch and, at the end of the High Street, turned to follow the western boundary of the parish. Crossing the East India Dock Road and zig-zagging northward, we were walking the area that was once Chinatown. We made our sixth stop beside the large Tree of Heaven, remembering those of different communities and different faiths. It made an appropriate boundary marker but, though Chinese in origin, it has no direct connection with the people of the local Chinatown. I am intrigued, however, with the idea that there might be a relationship between the people who once lived here and elements of the local flora. Here and there on my parish walks I have found patches of Chinese mugwort. In one neglected front garden on Zetland Street it has completely taken over. It is one of the artemisias, a family which includes the Biblical wormwood, the absinthe of Foreign Legion fame, the fragrant southernwood and the common moth-deterring mugwort.

Chinese mugwort is a tall, rangy plant with spreading underground rhizomes enabling it, at times, to form dense patches that can persist for as much as fifty years. Its leaves are the dark green of cooked cabbage, heavily veined, divided to the point of being almost spiky, and strongly aromatic. They have a smell that is half medicinal and half reminiscent of the hot Mediterranean garrigue. Its flowers, opening as late as October, are clustered along a leafy stem, small and dusty grey with projecting orange anthers. Individually they are insignificant but together they form a mealy, silver haze.

The Chinese mugwort was first recognised as a naturalised plant in this country in 1908, although it had almost certainly been around for longer and was perhaps overlooked as our native species. London is its stronghold, especially close to the Thames, and its presence here could well have arisen from our Chinese communities and their extensive medical use of the plant. According to the Chinese pharmacopoeia, the mugwort contains 106 bioactive compounds. Its properties are described as 'bitter, warm and acrid' and its numerous uses are as diverse as asthma, malaria, hepatitis, inflammation, menstrual problems and eczema. It was said to be particularly useful to help turn a breech baby but, equally, its leaves could be chewed to relieve a cough. For over 3,000 years it has also been used in conjunction with acupuncture.

The Chinese may well have brought their mugwort with them. A more easily established botanical connection exists between the brown mustard plant and the Bengali community that established itself in the East End from the late 1960s onwards. With them they brought their distinctive style of cooking, one of its common ingredients being brown mustard, also known as Indian mustard, a plant with sulphur-yellow flowers that set into compressed and upward-curving pods, each with a little beak at the end. Extracted from these, the fried seeds are said to have a taste that is nutty rather than fiery. I have seen the plant grown in the gardens of Bengali neighbours and even in old cooking oil cans on balconies. From places such as these they have spread to become an East End street weed. When a botanist friend first taught me to identify the plant, I realised that

I had been passing it every day as I walked the boys to school. Later, in Mile End Park I saw a party of Bengali women gathering the pods from brown mustard plants that were growing as weeds in flower beds.

Our flora, it seems, is part of our communal history. The London rocket grows from the ashes of the Great Fire, the Tree of Heaven spreads with the rage for chinoiserie, the arrival of new plants reflects our imperial past or the growth of global trade, and pavement weeds are influenced by the ethnic make-up of the area. Our story is recorded in our street plants.

As for the future, it 'is just like now, except a little later'. So says the graffiti scrawled in red paint on the walls of an old factory along the Limehouse Cut. We have reached the canal now and are following it along the northern edge of the parish. A little further and there is another piece of graffiti sprayed onto the side of a bridge: 'They should give huskies to blind people so that they can go faster.'

These pseudo-philosophic musings remind me of an earlier one that, for a time, Poplar was very proud of. High up on a blank wall on a corner of the East India Dock Road, not scrawled but in perfectly formed print, were the words 'Sorry! The lifestyle you ordered is currently out of stock'. It was generally held to be a Banksy, and perhaps that was true. A year or so after it had appeared I was walking up the High Street in Haworth, West Yorkshire, some 200 miles north of here. There, in the window of a gift shop, was a coaster bearing a picture of this corner of the East India Dock Road and 'our' graffiti. Even Banksy can be capitalised. And it was a good job I bought one, as the original was later obliterated.

The Limehouse Cut was the first canal in London, opened in 1770 to connect Bow Creek with the Thames at Limehouse, thus cutting out the long haul around the Isle of Dogs. On the opposite bank is the parish that was once known as Bromley St. Leonard's. I have a photograph of its people, conducting their own Beating of the Bounds. It is dated 1882 and the officiating vicar is named as the Rev. George Howe. Once again the men are sporting top hats and bearing staves, though there is no sign of the accompanying boys. Whilst some of the men are standing on the towpath, many more are gathered onto a large flat barge. Others stand on a low and rather unsteady-looking skiff. Clearly, health and safety was yet to become a major preoccupation.

I have also found an account of a dinner held as part of the Bromley St. Leonard's Rogation celebrations as early as 1660. Seventeen shillings and ten pence had been 'layed out for the procession dinner'. It included 'fish, lobsters, anchovies, butter, capers, turnips, carrots, sweet sauces, pyes, cheese, fruit, punch, wine, brandy, tobacco, cakes for the boys etc. etc.' It certainly put our soup and cheese in the shade.

When the canal was first dug this had been open country. Soon it was to be lined with factories, wharves and warehouses. Sydney Mattock, a local man, wrote wistfully about it in 1934: 'The waterway, that appears today as an ugly slit, dirty and depressing to view, was pleasant to behold when it went through land unbuilt upon, and then seemed to other eyes than ours, a silver slash across a waste.' Depressing to view it may have been, but for us it has become a favourite walk.

It is, moreover, a link to that lost countryside. Each stage in the evolution of our transport has created a different sort of corridor for the spread of species: foxes and ragwort following the railway lines, kestrels hovering over motorway verges, scurvy grass growing on their central reservations. Along canal towpaths, plants that we might otherwise expect to find only in the further countryside have spread into the inner city. On the Poplar canal there is gypsywort and lesser skullcap, water figwort, hemlock water dropwort and angelica, which bears the peculiarly transcendent scientific name of *Angelica archangelica*. The names of these plants alone are like an incantation conjuring images of some slow-flowing, clear-watered rural stream where dappled trout dart beneath the leaning boughs of, perhaps, a poplar.

Our canal runs between harsher banks. It is dense with duckweed in high summer and bears a cargo of bottles, beer cans and plastic bags, which the enterprising coots collect and include in their nest-building efforts. But the waterside plants establish themselves nonetheless, in cracks in the concrete retaining wall, between buddleias and sweet Betsy, watered by the wash of passing boats. They do not flower until June or July, but I can see their young growth and distinctive leaves, and the strange, winged stems of the figwort, as we pass.

We have some more surprising visitors, too. A friend of a friend once saw an otter in the Cut. He had been overseeing work to the roof of a nearby building and, from some six storeys up, he and the workmen had watched it swimming and diving for ten minutes or more. He had spent much of the rest of the summer on that roof, awaiting a return of its magic as he worked, but he never saw it again.

Just as unlikely was the story, reported in the local paper, of a muntjac found swimming in the Cut. Unable to climb out anywhere along its steep, high bank, it was in danger of dying with exhaustion. The fire brigade had been called and, with the help of an inflatable dinghy, effected a rescue.

I have seen neither otter nor muntjac here, but there is a visitor to our canal that I await every year with both excitement and a degree of nervousness, lest this season it should not make it. The sand martin is one of our earliest spring arrivals, flying in from its southern Saharan wintering grounds as early as March, though it is normally not till mid-April that it reaches Poplar. 'Tends to avoid built-up areas,' it says in my *RSPB Handbook of British Birds*, yet here they are each year, over our houses and warehouses, our parking lots and factory yards. The normal nest site is a hole in a gravelly cliff or sandy bank which the bird must laboriously excavate with beak and feet, progressing some three to four inches a day. John Clare describes the process in his poem 'The Sand Martin', again with the inference that this is a bird that shuns human habitation:

> *Thou hermit haunter of the lonely glen*
> *And common wild and heath – the desolate face*
> *Of rude waste landscapes far away from men*
> *Where frequent quarrys give thee dwelling place*
> *With strangest taste and labour undeterred*
> *Drilling small holes along the quarrys side*
> *More like the haunts of vermin than of bird*

Here we have no soft banks where martins might drill. Instead they have taken to nesting in the small round drainpipes which open from the stone walls or concrete banks of the canalside. It takes patience but on a summer's day you can detect the ones they have chosen, watching until a martin suddenly drops out of the end of a pipe and rises up into flight.

We find them as we approach the eastern end of the Cut, flying up and down above the water and feeding in the air. Like swifts and swallows, sand martins catch their food on the wing but I have seen them unexpectedly land on the towpath in front of me, just feet from my feet, picking insects from amongst the gravel. On this occasion they are entirely aerial. They are smaller than swallows, and slimmer than house martins. Neither are they quite as graceful as the one, nor as agile as the other, their flight being more hurried and a little more fluttery. There are at least five of them, and maybe as many as eight. An exact count should be easy but they contrive to make it impossible. They duck and swerve, descend on the curve, rise and loop, and interweave until it is impossible to determine which is coming and which is going and which you have already counted. They are fast, dark silhouettes, until the sun catches them and lights up their warm brown backs and their white undersides. They are threads of joy and we are honoured that they have come to be with us.

From the Cut we take a short cut. To complete a full tour of the parish boundary we should continue along the canal as far as Bow Locks and then head down through the post-industrial edgelands squeezed between the A12 and the river. But we have done enough, we decide, and instead we turn off early and followed St. Leonard's Road southward. We have made one stop along the canal and we make a final one here, between the trees with which I am now so familiar; the pale-patched roadside planes, the dark limes of the Teviot estate, the prolific ashes of the Brownfield. And then we continue down the route that once linked Poplar with Bromley St. Leonard's, beneath the shadow of the Balfron Tower and passing our own St. Michael's Vicarage, where we can hear the chickens clucking from the other side of the slatted wooden fence.

Recrossing the East India Dock Road, we pass through the dark brown iron gates of All Saints' to enter its cool, green churchyard. Soon there will be tea and home-made cakes in the crypt, but our efforts are not yet over. Tired, and just a little triumphant, we straggle across the grass, sprinkled with spring daisies, and pass the secretive hollies to reach the spot, between an Indian bean tree and a flowering horse chestnut, where our black poplar will be planted.

Now the prayer group, and all those who went direct to the church, come streaming out of its doors and down the steps to meet us. It is a considerable crowd that gathers and together we read the traditional psalm for Rogation. They are an expression of awe at the extent of creation and the power of its maker:

> *You stretch out the heavens like a tent,*
> *you set the beams of your chambers on the waters,*
> *you make the clouds your chariot*
> *you make the winds your messengers*
> *fire and flame your ministers*

The tree is lowered carefully into the hole, and we take it in turns to shovel earth over its roots, including especially the oldest and the youngest. There are thirty-five verses to Psalm 104 but we read them all.

> *You make the springs gush forth in the valleys;*
> *they flow between the hills,*
> *giving drink to every wild animal*
> *...You have made the moon to mark the seasons;*
> *the sun knows its time for setting.*

We welcome the tree, which is blessed by the priest and, once again, the holy water is sprinkled. A tree played a central role in the recently celebrated Easter story and once again it is central here. The psalm comes to its conclusion:

> *The trees of the Lord are watered abundantly,*
> *the cedars of Lebanon that he planted.*
> *In them the birds build their nests;*
> *the stork has its home in the fir tree.*
> *...O Lord how manifold are your works!*
> *In wisdom you have made them all.*

We pat down the earth, pick up the spade and depart. There is a black poplar again in Poplar.

For the purposes of 'watering abundantly', I continue to visit the young tree every week or so. And then, one day in June, I notice that a colony of black ants has built a nest in its roots. Columns of them are processing up and down the trunk and spreading out along its branches to reach small groups of green aphids beneath the leaves. Others are travelling further to prospect higher branches and inspect beneath leaves that, as yet, are aphid-free. The tree is filling with life. It is part of the local ecology. A line comes to me that is spoken by Badger in *Toad of Toad Hall*:

> *We may move out for a time but we wait. We are patient. And then we return. So it will ever be.*

Bibliography

Ackroyd, Peter, *Albion* (Chatto, 2002)

Allen, David Elliston, *The Naturalist in Britain: A Social History* (Allen Lane, 1976)

Baillie, Eileen, *The Shabby Paradise* (Hutchinson, 1958)

Barton, Nicholas, *The Lost Rivers of London* (Historical Publications Ltd., 1982)

Brockway, Fenner, *Bermondsey Story: The Life of Alfred Salter* (Blackfriars Press, 1949)

Clout, Hugh (ed.), *The Times History of London* (Times Books, 1991)

Cooper, Fiona, *The Black Poplar: Ecology, History and Conservation* (Windgather Press, 2006)

Deakin, Roger, *Notes from Walnut Tree Farm* (Hamish Hamilton, 2008)

Deakin, Roger, *Wildwood: A Journey Through Trees* (Hamish Hamilton, 2007)

Edlin, Herbert Leeson, *Trees, Woods and Man* (Collins, 1956)

Fitter, Richard, *London's Natural History* (Collins, 1945)

Gilbert, Oliver, *The Ecology of Urban Habitats* (Chapman and Hall, 1989)

Gilbert, Oliver, *The Flowering of Cities* (English Nature, 1992)

Glinert, Ed, *East End Chronicles* (Allen Lane, 2005)

Graves, Robert, *The White Goddess* (Faber and Faber, 1948)

Grieve, Maud, *A Modern Herbal* (Jonathan Cape, 1931)

Grigson, Geoffrey, *The Englishman's Flora* (Phoenix House, 1955)

Grigson, Geoffrey (ed.), *The English Year* (Oxford University Press, 1967)

Hutton, Ronald, *The Stations of the Sun* (Oxford University Press, 1996)

Irving, Henry, *How to Know the Trees* (Cassell and Co., 1910)

James, Montague Rhodes, *The Ghost Stories of M.R. James* (Edward Arnold, 1931)

Jefferies, Richard, *After London; or Wild England* (Cassell and Co., 1885)

Jefferies, Richard, *The Nature Diaries and Note-Books of Richard Jefferies* (Grey Walls Press, 1948)

Kafka, Franz, *The Great Wall of China* (Martin Secker, 1931)

Kightly, Charles, *The Perpetual Almanack of Folklore* (Thames and Hudson, 1987)

Lopez, Barry, *Arctic Dreams* (Scribner, 1986)

Mabey, Richard, *Flora Britannica* (Sinclair Stevenson, 1996)

Mabey, Richard, *Weeds* (Profile Books, 2010)

McCarthy, Michael, *The Moth Snowstorm* (John Murray, 2016)

Maitland, Sara, *Gossip From the Forest* (Granta Publications, 2012)

Martin, W. Keble, *A Concise British Flora* (George Rainbird Ltd., 1965)

Mee, Arthur, *The King's England: London* (Hodder and Stoughton, 1937)

Milner, Edward, *Trees of Britain and Ireland* (Natural History Museum, 2011)

Mitchell, Alan, *A Field Guide to the Trees of Britain and Northern Europe* (Collins, 1978)

Mitchell, Alan, *Trees of Britain and Northern Europe* (Collins, 1988)

Ó Tuama, Pádraig, *In the Shelter* (Hodder and Stoughton, 2015)

Phillips, Roger, *Wild Food* (Pan Books, 1983)

Plath, Sylvia, *Winter Trees* (Collins, 1972)

Rackham, Oliver, *Woodlands* (Collins, 2006)

Raine, Kathleen, *The Lion's Mouth* (George Brazilier, 1978)

Richman, Geoff, *Fly a Flag for Poplar* (Liberation Films, 1974)

Salisbury, Edward, *Weeds and Aliens* (Collins, 1961)

Skene, Keith, *Escape from Bubbleworld* (Ard Macha Press, 2011)

Snyder, Gary, *The Practice of the Wild* (Farrar, Straus and Giroux, 1990)

Talling, Paul, *London's Lost Rivers* (Random House, 2011)

Vickery, Roy, *A Dictionary of Plant Lore* (Oxford University Press, 1995)

Webster, Angus Duncan, *London Trees* (Swarthmore Press, 1920)

Whistler, Lawrence, *The English Festivals* (Heinemann, 1947)

White, Gilbert, *The Natural History of Selborne* (Thames and Hudson, 2004)

White, Robert, *Creation in Crisis* (SPCK, 2009)

Williams, Raymond, *The Country and the City* (Chatto and Windus, 1973)

Wood, Paul, *London's Street Trees* (Safe Haven Books, 2017)

Acknowledgements

Writing is a solitary occupation and not one, therefore, for which I am entirely suited. Without the constant encouragement, and sometimes the more vigorous pushing, of my friends and family, this book might never have reached completion. I am grateful to Jim Nicholson for special help on 'A Year Observed' and to all those who read chapters at different times, or who helped me with their comments: Joel Gilbert, Gill Cross, Chris Smith, Al Dix, Joe Shute, Ken Worpole, Lynn Knight and Graham Scrivener. Graham also walked part of the Black Ditch with me, as did Amy Sharrocks, and I am grateful to them both for accompanying me on that rather eccentric expedition. Two friends in particular, Gordon Willis and Rod Harper, became my permanent 'panel' and their constant enthusiasm, and flow of supportive emails, was invaluable. I would like to thank Margaret Keep, Edna Howard and Joan Lewis for supplying me with innumerable stories about Poplar, and I owe a particular debt of gratitude to Rosie Bailey for permission to use extracts from the U.A. Fanthorpe poem 'Rising Damp'. On those occasions when I could get away for a while, my parents-in-law, David and Christine Hodges, provided me with somewhere to escape to. Thank you, Christine, for all the wonderful food, and David for the whisky and beer.

Writing a book is one thing; getting it published is another. My friend Claire Grove was a wonderful source of advice in the early stages and she is sadly missed. Sara

Fielden, too, gently but firmly pushed me in the right direction. I owe a special debt of gratitude to Louise Doughty who was not only enthusiastic about the book but introduced me to my agent. From the moment he read the Introduction, James MacDonald Lockhart has been a constant source of support and a pleasure to work with. Thanks, too, to everybody at Saraband; to Sara for believing in the book, to Madeleine and Katharine for their proofreading and indexing, to Craig for his sympathetic editing, and to Don Shewan for the map.

And, finally, a huge thank you to Jane, for balancing the demanding roles of priest, parent and part-time literary critic, for putting up with my bad moods, and for sustaining me throughout the whole prolonged process.

About the Author

Bob Gilbert is an author, broadcaster and environmentalist. A long-standing campaigner for inner city conservation and chair of 'The Garden Classroom', a charity that promotes environmental education in London, his first book was *The Green London Way* (Lawrence & Wishart, 2012). He has also been a columnist for *Ham & High,* writing on urban wildlife, for the last twenty years. He has written, presented and contributed to television and radio programmes including BBC Two's *Natural World* and BBC Radio 4's *The Susurrations of Trees* and *The Food Programme*.

Index